C000046835

Financial Models and Society

Financial Models and Society

Villains or Scapegoats?

Ekaterina Svetlova

University of Leicester, UK

Edward Elgar
PUBLISHING

Cheltenham, UK • Northampton, MA, USA

Published by
Edward Elgar Publishing Limited
The Lypiatts
15 Lansdown Road
Cheltenham
Glos GL50 2JA
UK

Edward Elgar Publishing, Inc.
William Pratt House
9 Dewey Court
Northampton
Massachusetts 01060
USA

A catalogue record for this book
is available from the British Library

Library of Congress Control Number: 2017953154

This book is available electronically in the **Elgar**online
Economics subject collection
DOI 10.4337/9781784710026

ISBN 978 1 78471 001 9 (cased)
ISBN 978 1 78471 002 6 (eBook)

Typeset by Servis Filmsetting Ltd, Stockport, Cheshire
Printed and bound by CPI Group (UK) Ltd, Croydon, CR0 4YY

Contents

Figures

Acknowledgements

This book is the result of ten years of research on the use of financial models in market practice. I wish to thank all of those who supported me in writing it.

The interviews that constitute the main data source for the empirical case studies used in the book were completed within the framework of the Deutsche Forschungsgemeinschaft (DFG) project "Economic calculations: Creation of the calculative realities in the financial markets" in 2007–08. I would also like to acknowledge the research fellowship awarded by the Centre of Excellence "Cultural foundations of integration" at the Institute for Advanced Study at the University of Constance, where I spent a sabbatical in 2013–14 and started to develop some chapters of this book. I would also like to thank the interview respondents and those who helped me to organize the field work for their support, effort and time.

I am also grateful to all colleagues and friends who discussed my ideas with me at numerous conferences and workshops or commented on earlier versions of the book. The comments from Dirk Baecker, Ivan Boldyrev, Maria Puig De La Bellacasa, Iain Hardie, Donald MacKenzie, Yuval Millo, Nikiforos Panourgias, Birger Priddat, Marcel Tyrell and Zsuzsanna Vargha were especially valuable. Furthermore, very special thanks are due to a particularly loyal and thorough reader – my husband, Karl-Heinz Thielmann.

As this book sums up my research on financial modelling conducted over many years, parts of it incorporate revised and reworked versions of material that was previously published. I would like to thank the editors and publishers involved for permission to use that material here. The following articles were used in this book:

Value without valuation? An example of the cocos market (2016), *Critical Perspectives on Accounting* (online first), special issue on Critical Finance.
Performativity and emergence of institutions (2016). In: Ivan Boldyrev and Ekaterina Svetlova (eds), *Enacting Dismal Science: New Perspectives on the Performativity of Economics*, New York: Palgrave Macmillan, 183–200.

Models at work: Models in decision-making (2014), *Science in Context* **27** (4), 561–577 (with Vanessa Dirksen).

Modelling beyond application: Epistemic and non-epistemic values in modern science (2014), *International Studies in the Philosophy of Science* **28** (1), 79–98.

De-idealization by commentary: The case of financial valuation models (2013), *Synthese* **190** (2), 321–337.

On the performative power of financial models (2012), *Economy and Society* **41** (3), 418–434.

Talking about the crisis: Performance of forecasting in financial markets (2012), *Culture and Organization* **18** (2), 155–169.

Plausibility check of consensus: Expectation building in financial markets (2010), *Journal of Financial and Economic Practice* **10** (1), 101–113.

Full references will be found at the end of the book.

Finally, I would like to thank Amanda Habbershaw for her excellent help with my English.

1. Introduction

Today's financial market participants seem to be madly in love with models and algorithms. The recent McKinsey report (Crespo et al. 2017) suggests that the number of models used by banks to make various decisions is rising by 10 to 25 per cent annually. Quantitative model-based investing is growing fast: quantitative hedge funds are prospering; exchange-traded fund (ETFs) and other forms of passive, index-based investing are booming. JP Morgan estimates that only about 10 per cent of recent trading volume in stocks is generated by old-fashioned fundamental investors (Cheng 2017). The jobs of active fund managers, security analysts and financial advisors seem to be threatened by machines. Recently, BlackRock, one of the biggest fund companies in the world, announced that it will merge some of its expensive stock pickers into the quant department and lay the rest of them off. The newspaper headlines on the day of this announcement read: "Robots Are Replacing Humans" (Shen 2017). There are also reports on security analysis becoming increasingly computer-based and "virtual" in order to conquer the subjectivity and emotionality of human analysts (Wigglesworth 2017a). Robo-advising – when algorithms instead of humans provide investment advice – is on the rise. Finally, algorithmic trading is on everyone's lips because, according to various estimates, 50–70 per cent of the equity trading in the world is computer-based today. It seems that modern financial markets are all about models, algorithms, big data and artificial intelligence.

At the same time, this "love affair" with formal technologies is often discussed with scepticism, and gives rise to worry and anxiety. Models can be dangerous because they might not sufficiently help people make sound investment decisions. This was the gist of the sweeping criticism of financial models in the aftermath of the 2008 crisis. Models were accused of causing the turmoil or, at least, of failing to give advance warning.

The arguments behind these accusations are familiar: financial models are abstract and unworldly constructs, so their users are predestined to be misguided. Thus, the argument goes, as insufficient models became widespread tools for decision-making in financial markets, the vast majority of market participants were seduced by their mathematical sophistication and followed them towards alleged safety. Love is blind (and stupid), which is why model users in financial markets are frequently described as "F9 model monkeys" (Tett and Thal Larsen 2005) who confuse "illusion with reality" (as the title of the 2011 book about financial models written by the famous quant turned publicist and educator Emanuel Derman suggests).

The general problem related to this blindness is so-called "model-based herding": widespread use of similar models can lead market participants to behave similarly. Indeed, if investors were to use formal models in the same way, they would make similar decisions. This means that all of them would favour the same side of the market; in other words, they would want only to buy or only to sell at the same time. Markets would start to move in resonance (Beunza and Stark 2012) and such a development could threaten the markets' stability, causing bubbles and crashes. One recalls discussions about the so-called "quant crisis" in August 2007 which was explained by the similarity of quantitative strategies used across hedge funds (Tett and Gangahar 2007). In this debate, financial models were portrayed as a time bomb, as highly explosive, dangerous stuff that possesses the power to severely damage economic and financial systems.

For example, if every risk manager were to use the Value at Risk model (VaR), then he or she would inevitably underestimate risks in unusual (extraordinary) situations (when liquidity is scarce, interbank funding is hardly available and the correlations between assets are high). This underestimation would encourage users to take more risks; thus, too many risks would be taken in the entire financial system, leading to catastrophe (Nocera 2009; Croft 2009). This critique of VaR in the context of the 2008 crisis was aptly summarized in a book with the telling title *The Number That Killed Us* by veteran derivative trader Pablo Triana (2011). Famously, Nassim Taleb also blames risk models for increasing "risk exposure instead of limiting it"; these models, he says, "can be worse than nothing, the equivalent of a dangerous operation on a patient who would stand a better chance if left untreated" (Economist 2010). The Gaussian copula formula – which was used to assess the probability distribution of possible losses for structured products such as collateralized debt obligations (CDOs) that were at the core of the 2008 crisis – was discussed in the press with similarly strong wording as "The formula that killed Wall Street" (Salmon 2009). This discussion frequently boils down to the idea that we should "kill the quants and their technology before they kill us" (Brodie 2012).

While following this "sanguinary" debate, a serene observer might wonder how financial markets manage to survive at all. The question arises as to why we still experience "normal", boring days without wild volatility and turmoil. In other words, why do markets continue to function and prosper *even though* they are dominated by models? Maybe financial models are not as dangerous as some of their critics believe. On the contrary, it seems that markets manage to generate enough diversity to stay alive precisely due to the widespread use of models. This book deals with the question of how this diversity in model-driven markets is produced.

Generally, I claim that the discussion about dangers induced by financial models is based on the principal misunderstanding of models' roles in markets. The aforementioned accusations are rooted in a conceptualization of models as "calculative tools" which directly guide investment decisions. In other words, there is an implied assumption that models tell people what to do and that the latter blindly follow models' advice. However, this book suggests – and demonstrates using various empirical examples – that financial models do not ultimately determine investors' decisions and actions. The role of models is more subtle: they do not dictate financial decisions but *make them possible*. Models help bridge genuine non-knowledge and uncertainty, which are characteristic of financial decision-making, and, thus, help solve the central problem of financial markets – the problem of investability. In other words, models assist investment professionals in "overlooking" uncertainties and in generating willingness to invest. To do this, models do not have to be perfect representations of reality; in fact, the inevitably insufficient models are used as *one of many* resources in the multifaceted decision-making practices of financial markets. Let me explain what I mean by this.

Financial decision-making is characterized by radical uncertainty which is not calculable. Thus, calculations provided by models are unable to grasp the ever-changing, uncertain reality of markets. In other words, there is always a gap between models and (market) reality. This gap is characteristic of all models used in science or elsewhere. All models are "wrong" in the sense that they do not perfectly represent reality and are merely imperfect idealizations. However, while scientists generally can live with this gap – and this is a crucial difference – financial market participants cannot allow themselves to be detached from the markets. They are a part of the markets themselves and, thus, their decisions cannot be based on model calculations only: that is, on calculations that leave out expectations, emotions, stories, judgments and – importantly – the modelling efforts of other market participants.

In this book, I suggest understanding financial decision-making as *action-like decision-making* which implies that *more than calculation* is required in the always incomplete situation of markets. Action-like decision-making overcomes the traditional dichotomy between action and decision, and involves engaging with the world by simultaneously observing, deciding and taking actions that have severe consequences (are fateful).

Models constantly matter for this kind of decision-making *in situ* in markets: calculations are "effected" (Derrida 1994) and "done and undone" (Kalthoff 2011); they are combined with judgment, market observations, news, stories, rumours and so on. This book will show that this "qualculation" (Cochoy 2008) happens in various ways and styles. There are manifold *cultures of model use*, that is, specific practices of integrating models into financial decision-making and combining them with emotions, views and stories of their users. The social studies of finance (SSF), an emerging interdisciplinary field that applies the findings and the methodological apparatus of various social sciences to the analysis of financial markets, has pioneered the investigation of financial models' applications in the practice of markets. It has provided numerous empirical descriptions of *cultures of model use* which I will use and further develop in this book. Nevertheless, there is a lot more to be done.

Careful analysis of the styles of applying financial models helps us realize that the general claim that financial markets have become a purely analytical and quantitative place might be exaggerated. Human influence has not disappeared; rather, it unfolds in the multifaceted interplay between users and models in the practice of markets. Investors might use their formal tools but ignore the tools' recommendations in the very process of decision-making; they might not use models at all or "overlay" the decisions models prescribe. Thus, the book demonstrates that, in many cases, financial models do not provide direct prescriptions for decisions; and, therefore, the link between models, decision-making and market events is not as straightforward as the ongoing critique of financial models indicates. We find large "pockets" where human judgment and stories are as important as the complicated formulas and algorithms.

This is an experience that many novices encounter when they first arrive in financial markets. It also happened to me. After graduation, I started working as a portfolio manager in a big investment bank in Frankfurt. On my first day, I was very nervous but kept telling myself that I would be okay. At university, I had spent most of my time calculating models and shifting very complicated formulas, so, I reassured myself, I should be very well equipped for the job. But from the beginning it seemed that my mathematical skills were less in demand than I expected. "Forget those models. Now you should learn how to invest," one of my colleagues told me, and gave me a book by the famous stock-picker Peter Lynch to read. Another colleague said, "You should understand how markets work", and recommended reading the novel *Money* by Zola. I was perplexed: Had I joined a literature club? Is investing not about maths? I wanted to do "the real stuff". It was only a while later that I realized that doing "the real stuff" in markets involves far more than calculation.

Of course, things have changed since I went through the revolving door of the investment bank in Frankfurt for the first time. However, also today, we are far from a situation of "financial singularity" in which powerful computers and sophisticated algorithms have fully replaced human intelligence. "Human judgment, good and bad, will drive investment decisions and financial-market outcomes for the rest of our lives and beyond," said the Nobel Prize winner Robert Shiller (2015). Although the role of stories in investment decisions has been prominently highlighted recently (Beckert 2016; Tuckett 2012; Chong and Tuckett 2015) and I tune into that debate with this book, my goal is not to claim that models are unimportant and that judgment dominates the markets. The book strives to provide a subtler picture, and argues that we should pay more attention to how models are used in – not always purely calculative – decision-making; how human judgment and stories are formed *with* models; and how models *and* judgment together matter for what happens in financial markets. Again, the picture I present in the book does not boil down to a bunch of wild stories and rumours that circulate in the markets and render models unimportant.

What we find in financial markets today is not an "either judgment or model" dilemma; there are various regimes of combining models with judgment, regimes that ensure a diversity of views and decisions in markets. In some situations, models determine the actions; sometimes, however, judgment and stories dominate the decision-making process. This book is the first step towards better understanding this interplay and demonstrating its non-uniformity. There is no general way of talking about model use in markets, and thus no general way of voicing (blanket) critique of financial models.

Indeed, markets are characterized by a huge diversity of financial models, goals and styles of model use – depending on who uses them and how they are used. In order to paint a picture of this non-uniform landscape, one could conceptualize markets as an investment chain, as "the sets of intermediaries that 'sit between' savers and companies/governments, along with the links among those intermediaries" (Arjaliès et al. 2017: 4). Indeed, money, information and decision-making today "flow" through such a chain (from savers to money managers to brokers and traders) and are distributed among its intermediaries. Nowadays, all market participants in the investment chain use models to make decisions; however, those models vary and are used for diverse purposes (for example asset allocation, stock-picking, risk management, trading and so on) and a varying amount of importance is attached to them. Figure 1.1 maps the major groups of market participants and the models they use which will be discussed in this book.

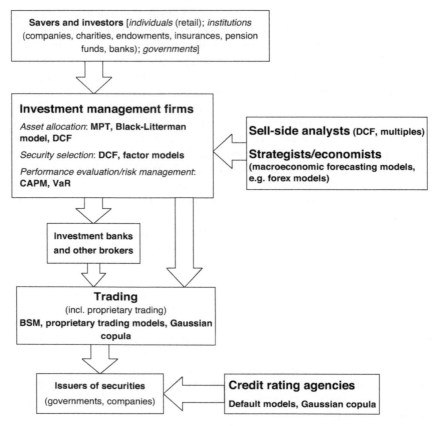

Note: MPT = Modern Portfolio Theory; DCF = Discounted Cash Flow model; CAPM = Capital Asset Pricing model; VaR = Value at Risk model; BSM = Black-Scholes model.

Source: Based on Arjaliès et al. (2017: 5); reused with permission from Oxford University Press.

Figure 1.1   Investment chain: financial models and their users

The differences in the purposes of model use within the chain should be particularly highlighted. Some professionals (for example investment managers and traders) are focused on financial *decision-making* (selling or buying), while others (for example security analysts and economists) are primarily involved in gathering and interpreting information, giving advice and making clients invest; in other words, their domain is rather *decision-selling*. In Chapter 4, I will particularly focus on several styles of model use for decision-making; that is, I will focus on how models are applied to overcome uncertainty and to make investment decisions possible for model users, whereas in Chapter 5 I will analyse model use for decision-selling, exploring how models are utilized to justify decisions and convince others to invest. Hence, I will demonstrate that financial models are applied not only to make decisions but also to provide legitimacy for decisions, perform impression management, reach a consensus and so on. These secondary functions can overlay the primary goals of model use (that is, calculation) and render models less important for immediate decision-making.

The variety and mediating nature of *cultures of model use* presented in this study has consequences for the question of whether models are villains or scapegoats; in other words, the question of whether they are truly dangerous and have the power to destroy markets or whether they are just harmless camouflage which is frequently used to hide risks emerging somewhere else.

My argument is that it is exactly because the styles of model use vary that there is no way that different users derive the same results from their models and make the same decisions. As empirical studies in the book will demonstrate, financial models are used by market participants to disagree with the market or, at least, to question the market's views. Thus, the various strategies of model use do not automatically promote a particular behaviour in financial markets, but enforce disagreement and support "dissonant" tendencies. In other words, models as time bombs are defused through the various practices of their use.

The analysis of cultures of model use also suggests that model users are by no means "model dopes", people who "unthinkingly accept the outputs of a model"; there is not enough "empirical evidence of them" (MacKenzie and Spears 2014b: 419). Noticeably, of all people, practitioners demonstrate a particular awareness of models' deficiencies and limitations (Triana 2009; Derman 2011). Recently, model insufficiencies were prominently acknowledged by one of the highest financial authorities, the Bank of England. Monetary policy committee member Gertjan Vlieghe told MPs "that central banks' financial models 'are just not that good' for predicting even a recession" (Guardian 2017). Extensive empirical analyses presented in this book demonstrate that the users of financial models are aware of model limitations and account for them in the process of model use. They do not "blind out" model deficiencies, but rather consciously make "insufficient" models work. The central goal of the book is to show that practitioners in financial markets use their models very tentatively. It seems that the ostensible "love affair" with models is in fact "a marriage of convenience". Hence, the general designation of financial models as the ultimate villains is questionable because their influence on markets is clearly mediated by the practices of their use.

CONTRIBUTIONS TO THE LITERATURE

This book aims to advance research on modelling within the social studies of finance. The social studies of finance emerged as an independent discipline from science and technology studies (STS) as well as from sociology of knowledge at the turn of the millennium and, as already mentioned, has made first important steps in investigating practices of model use in financial decision-making. Still, those practices widely remain a "black box". Remarkably, there are plenty of books and articles on financial mathematics and finance that discuss models as theoretical constructs; that is, they discuss models' assumptions, mathematical structures and largely theoretical potential applications. However, the literature on why and how models are used in the practice of markets, particularly in financial decision-making, remains limited. This book aims to close that gap.

At the same time, there has been extensive research on model use in science. Indeed, until recently models have predominantly been analysed as instruments of scientific inquiry in the philosophy of science and in STS. Undeniably, this research has provided important insights into how models are used in various scientific disciplines (I will outline the most important accounts in Chapter 3). However, as models have increasingly been incorporated into practical decision-making (for instance, in financial markets), the need to understand how they structure decisions and actions in the actual practice of investing and trading has become very pressing. Financial models are applied in the context of markets which are not purely epistemic. Here, the goal is not knowledge production (explanation, understanding or representation) but successful decision-making (which ultimately leads to making money). Thus, although I do not deny that there is an epistemic dimension in the work of investment professionals, it is not my focus. Rather, I claim that the goals and ways of model use in science and in financial markets are fundamentally different, and address those differences in detail.

Moreover, pointing to the origins of the social studies of finance in science studies, this book suggests going beyond the traditional understanding of modelling practices in financial markets as "calculative practices" and "epistemic cultures". In the book, financial models are conceptualized not as "knowledge devices" but as practical decision-making instruments. Re-focusing on the practices of model use in decision-making and on non-epistemic aspects of model applications helps overcome the overemphasis on knowledge in the social studies of finance. This step allows us to conceptualize financial markets as markets of *nobody knows* and decision-making as *action-like decision-making*. I consider these concepts to be important contributions to the field.

Furthermore, using various empirical accounts, the book fills concepts of non-analytical decision-making such as "qualculation" (Cochoy 2008), heuristics (Gigerenzer 2007) and "acting sensibly" (Smith 2011) with life. While opening the black box of model use in financial markets, I stress that there is no separation between models, markets and users. Models are not "outside" market reality; they are involved in the decision-making situation, are part of it, and are analysed as such in this book.

The idea of the book is to show what happens within some boxes of the investment chain in more empirical detail; that is, to show how models, users and markets are interrelated in the processes of decision-making and decision-selling. Notably, until now, the social studies of finance has provided some insightful, yet isolated, investigations of how models are used by various intermediaries such as security analysts, traders and fund managers. This book represents the first attempt to place these accounts alongside each other in order to identify regularities and common paths of model use. Thus, it provides a *classification* and *systematization* of distinctive styles of model applications observed in modern markets. Particularly, I identify three major patterns of model use in financial decision-making – "qualitative overlay", "backing out/implied modelling" and models as "opinion proclaimers" – and highlight the major commonalities and differences between them. This systematization is an important novelty of the book.

Finally, the book furthers our understanding of financial models' influence on markets and society more broadly. This issue is related to the question of *societal* model risks. The insights set out in the book suggest that the image of financial models as brutal "killers" of markets should be relativized. They are rather scapegoats that are made responsible for what goes wrong in the complex, empirically "messy" decision-making processes in financial markets. The book demonstrates that models very often do not even get a chance to shape market events because various other factors play into decisions and "overlay" models. Model influence is mediated by the practices of model use and their elements (e.g. the institutional environment, selling considerations, political interests and the power of the involved actors, etc.). Understanding the interplay of models and various auxiliary factors is crucial for producing a valid account of the financial crisis and, more generally, for understanding what happens in markets today. It seems that excessive trust in models and their extensive use were not the cause of the last financial crisis, but rather the opaque interplay between models and human judgment within financial organizations.

This book supports the view expressed by Engelen et al. (2012: 373) that the fundamental problem is not the extinction of practical tacit knowledge due to increased formalization of financial markets but, on the contrary, overreliance on the informal, interpersonal knowledge that often accompanies the application of models. For example, when rating agencies use their models to get the results they "want" to get (e.g. higher ratings for particular clients) or when executives in risk management departments decide to simply ignore the warnings of models that have been specifically installed to warn them, models can hardly be blamed. What happens *around the models* or how models are actually involved in decision-making is crucial. Thus, the book contributes towards understanding how this "around the models" functions, and shows that the radical, general accusations directed at models are not justified.

METHODOLOGY AND DATA

A concept that facilitates the investigation of cultures of model use is "the notion of practical action" (Stark 2009: 165), which is central to the social studies of finance. Consequently, adopting the social studies of finance perspective for this book implies the application of a particular methodology – that is, decision-making in incomplete and problematic "situations must be investigated in situ" (Stark 2011: 336). This is the only way of overcoming the traditional economists' dichotomy between actions and decisions with respect to choice – as represented by the Savage matrix (1954) – and of efficiently analysing alternative concepts of decision-making, such as action-like decision-making or acting sensibly, for example. It is why Stark (2011: 336) pleads for "methodological situationalism":

> Situations occur in practical settings. They can be a fleeting event or they can have longer duration. But we know what is meant when someone says, "We have a situation here." It suggests that something is problematic. Indeed, it is almost redundant to say that a situation is perplexing or troubling. Situations are methodologically privileged because they are moments when the open-ended character of the world is revealed.

If one aims to investigate action-like decision-making in markets *in situ*, a methodological shift towards analysing the practical situation in detail becomes necessary, and the ethnographical apparatus becomes indispensable. Recently, in-depth semi-structured interviews have been successfully applied to investigate financial decision-making (Tuckett 2011, 2012). Following this example, this book utilizes ethnographical methodology to investigate patterns of model use in decision-making under uncertainty among various groups of market participants.

My original research, however, focused on one particular group of investment professionals, namely fund managers. The data were collected using primarily the ethnographical apparatus of interviews and participant observations. More precisely, the research drew on three sets of interviews. The first set was conducted in the context of the DFG project "Economic Calculations: Creation of the Calculative Realities in the Financial Markets" in 2007–08. The overall aim of the project was to understand how formal financial models are created and used, and how these processes of model creation and application influence economic reality. Hence, one part of the project was dedicated to the development of financial mathematical formulas in science, and the other was concerned with the application of models in the practice of markets.

Thus, the data pool for the analysis initially encompassed eight semi-structured, in-depth interviews with financial mathematicians at universities in Munich, Frankfurt/Main, Kaiserslautern and Zurich. Seven of the mathematicians held the title of professor and were established figures in the field; one interviewee was a junior professor. With one of the interviewees (in Kaiserslautern), a follow-up interview was conducted in 2014.

The second set of interviews (with financial market practitioners) encompassed 28 semi-structured interviews in several German and Swiss asset management companies and banks. The respondents were employed as fund managers in Frankfurt and Zurich, and generally pursued an active investment strategy. Six of the respondents were responsible for European blue-chip portfolios; two for European small- and mid-caps; four for emerging markets; two for tactical asset allocation; two for bond investments; and three for structured products. Three fund managers were responsible for quantitative investments. One informant was a financial advisor who owned an independent investment company. Follow-up interviews were performed with several informants.

Within the same project, the interviews were complemented by a three-month participant observation, conducted in the portfolio management department of a private Swiss investment bank in Zurich (henceforth referred to as a Swiss bank). I performed certain portfolio management tasks to gain first-hand experience of the department's daily practices. Participation in verbal discussions – such as internal and external investment meetings, morning meetings, informal talks on the floor, and the creation of spreadsheets and presentations – provided additional insights into the investors' practices. Furthermore, I observed how fund managers use models while making forecasts and decisions, and thus investigated the roles that models play in the investment process.

The third set of interviews was conducted later, in 2014, in the initial explorative phase of the EU project "Evaluation Practices in Financial Markets" (EPIFM). Twelve semi-structured, in-depth interviews were conducted with financial market professionals in Germany. Nine respondents managed equity and bond funds as well as balanced portfolios in leading German asset-management companies; they were responsible for both mutual funds and clients' money. One respondent was the head of credits in a big investment company; another was responsible for a rather small equity fund in an investment boutique. Another important interview partner was Ralf Frank, the Chief Executive of the German Association for Financial Analysis and Asset Management (DVFA).

Most interviews were performed in person, and only one was conducted by telephone. The interviews lasted between 45 minutes and two hours. The interview guidelines, which were established in advance, focused on the processes of individual and organizational decision-making and the use of financial models in those processes. All the interviews were digitally recorded and transcribed.

The evaluation of the interview transcripts, the observation protocols and field journals included manual coding and categorization and subsequent qualitative interpretation according to Corbin and Strauss (2008). These empirical materials served as a basis for several studies that I had previously authored and used in this book.

However, in order to go beyond the field of fund management, I drew extensively on empirical studies on other participants of the investment chain performed within the social studies of finance, as well as on practitioners' literature. The utilization of this research allowed me to compare and classify cultures of model use in the fields of security analysis, merger arbitrage, option trading and others.

READERSHIP

This book addresses multiple audiences: academics, students and practitioners. By highlighting the alternative functions of models in decision-making as well as providing practical examples and case studies of model use, this book opens up novel perspectives and delivers useful materials for academics in social studies of finance as well as economic sociologists; scholars in studies of science and technology; philosophers of science (especially philosophy of economics); economists; and, in particular, financial mathematicians and finance scientists. Particularly by analysing the use of models in financial decision-making, I hope to support the still nearly non-existent conversations of economists and economic sociologists/social studies of finance scholars: Decision-making might indeed provide a common platform for fruitful exchange across disciplines.

As the book provides a thorough overview of the basic concepts of SSF, it can be considered as an introduction to the field, and might be of interest not only to academic specialists but also to advanced undergraduate and graduate students. The book can be used in graduate courses not only in STS, economic sociology and the philosophy of science, but also in basic finance courses and courses on financial modelling. I personally consider the latter to be particularly important because consideration of how financial models are used in investment practices is usually not part of standard finance modules, but is essential for future investment professionals. The book might prevent finance students from becoming "model dopes" already at university and, not much later, in their jobs. Also, it needs to be stressed that the social studies of finance is currently being established as a scientific discipline – dedicated modules are already taught, for example, at the London School of Economics (LSE) and the University of Leicester; for students on these programmes, this research could serve as a textbook.

Furthermore, the book might be of interest to the large group of practitioners who design and apply models in various fields of financial markets. Particularly, it addresses open-minded professional investors who are interested in the latest developments in scientific debates on modelling and who welcome thoughtful reflection on their own everyday work. The book will provide them with insights into the benefits and limitations of models, as well as opening up the black box of model use in decision-making. Consideration of the risks models pose to society at large, particularly to herding, might be considered helpful by regulators and policy-makers.

ORGANIZATION OF THE BOOK

The structure of the book is very straightforward: In Chapters 2 and 3, the theoretical basis is provided for the empirical discussion that follows in Chapters 4 and 5. In Chapter 2, in particular, financial decision-making is conceptualized as action-like decision-making in markets of *nobody knows* – that is, as a practice of decision-making under conditions of radical uncertainty and *symmetrical ignorance*. This concept suggests that the existing accounts of model use are insufficient as they particularly focus on scientific practices and ignore the specific, not solely epistemic, nature of financial markets.

To further this critique, in Chapter 3 I provide an overview of the existing accounts of model use in the philosophy of science (with a focus on economic modelling) and STS. I particularly highlight the pragmatic turn in modelling research that has taken place in these disciplines since the mid-1990s. Models are no longer considered by philosophers and STS scholars to be purely theoretical and abstract entities; rather, they are considered "dirty" and insecure tools that must be manipulated and "made to count" *in situ* in order to produce knowledge. The pragmatic accounts argue that the gap between models and reality can be closed in the process of model construction and model use by means of pre-formulating the anticipated results, narratives, interpretations, power relations and the audience. In other words, it has become clear that the social contexts of model use are crucial for the very understanding of the models' nature. In the chapter, I show how the social studies of finance have pursued research in this field, focusing on the pragmatic practices of modelling and model use in financial markets. The performativity account is also discussed here, and a plea made for the "emancipation" of the social studies of finance from its heritage – that is, from science studies and, particularly, from understanding models as purely "epistemic tools". I argue that further steps are necessary to properly understand the specifics of model use in action-like decision-making in financial markets.

Following this theoretical discussion, I present numerous empirical accounts of financial model use in decision-making (Chapter 4) and decision-selling (Chapter 5). Here, I classify and compare various patterns of model use in financial markets, and discuss in detail the different latent functions of models. I show that, as models are combined with, overlaid and influenced by judgment, stories, emotions and the institutional environment in which they are applied, they are far less omnipotent than one might expect. The related *model risks* are also discussed in detail.

The concluding chapter considers implications of the book's findings for further research in decision-making theory, economics, valuation studies, ignorance studies and the ethics of financial markets.

2. Models in finance: general considerations

THE NATURE OF FINANCIAL DECISION-MAKING

In every "box" and link of the investment chain, financial market partici-pants have to cope with future uncertainty and the problem of incomplete information. The price development of all financial instruments is related to the future, and thus *knowledge about the future* is crucial. One might expect that financial models help translate the uncertain future into a certain future, non-knowledge into knowledge, by means of exact calcula-tions. The probability calculus on which many financial models are based is one example of how such a translation can be performed. Think of Savage's "axiomatization" (1954), according to which the future is fanned out as a matrix of possible states of the world, including the related probabilities, actions and their outcomes; with this matrix, the uncertain situation is so well structured that the expected utility can be calculated. Notably, probability theory and the expected utility concept have given rise to modern, model-based finance (Bernstein 1992; Jovanovic 2012): the uncertain future movements of asset returns can be formalized as fluctua-tions around mean returns and, thus, be mathematically represented by a probability distribution. This modelling is performed with the concept of risk instead of with uncertainty. This approach is based on the differ-ence between *risk* and *uncertainty* (as introduced by Knight 1921) which is now widely accepted in economics and finance (for example Frydman and Goldberg 2007; Akerlof and Shiller 2009): in a situation of risk, all relevant states, probabilities, alternative actions and their consequences are known, while in a situation of uncertainty they are not known. Thus, one possible view on models is that they reduce uncertainty, translate it into risk (a situation with known probabilities) and produce knowledge for various groups of investor.

This so-called *over-calculative position* (Beunza and Garud 2007) is related to the "modern worldview" as formulated by Max Weber (1948: 139). Weber pictured a deterministic and, thus, rationally explainable and predictable world that can, in principle, be controlled through knowledge and calculations. Porter (1995) shows how the modern worldview came to be accepted and, as a result, formal models and algorithms were used more intensively in all areas of science and human life, including finance (Bernstein 1992). Production of exact, objective knowledge is usually considered to be the *manifest function* of modelling (Shackley 1998; Tayler 1998).

In this book, however, I take a subtler view on models and their role in financial markets. I argue that coping with uncertainty by means of calculation is part of a broader problem which financial market participants encounter and solve, namely the *problem of investability*. Financial markets are characterized by *radical uncertainty* which is not reducible to risk. But, if uncertainty cannot be eliminated, we have to understand why investors are not paralysed by it, why they continue to bring their money to the market – that is, how they solve the problem of investability under circumstances in which no rational person would have any good reason to invest (Keynes 1936).

Let us discuss the issue of uncertainty and investability in more detail as it is crucial for understanding models' roles as well as the ways in which they are used in financial markets. Investors confront genuine uncertainty because the situation in which they find themselves is *emerging* (not given). Here, we refer to real contingencies: an economic decision-making situation involves many independent heterogeneous actors who interact with one another and orient their expectations and decisions towards the expectations and decisions of others. This often produces unpredictable effects. Decision-makers are a part of the system which they observe and decide about: they influence and change the system and, in turn, those changes influence their decisions and expectations. We are talking about a two-way feedback process. Von Foerster (2003, 2008) and Soros (1998) refer to this interconnectedness as "reflexivity". Arthur (1994, 1995) investigated the related phenomenon of *self-referentiality*. The major idea is that expectations and decisions in economic life and financial markets have a *recursive character*. For example, economic agents make decisions based on their expectations regarding future prices; at the same time, these decisions, when aggregated, influence prices. Thus, to correctly predict an economic event or phenomenon, one must anticipate the expectations of other agents that affect the event or phenomenon about which one is forming expectations. The recursive character of such events causes *systemic* or *endogenous* risks, the risks created within the financial system (Danielsson and Shin 2002; Danielsson et al. 2009). In such a situation, the future will never be identical to past or pre-formed expectations because it is yet to be created by recent expectations and actions; that is, the future is emerging.

Serious consideration of reflexivity and self-referentiality requires acceptance of the idea that time is not linear but circular in financial markets (Esposito 2011): the present depends on the future, which in turn is determined by present expectations and decisions. As Oskar Morgenstern (1928) explained, this is why forecasts and expectations in economics often fail (cf. Betz 2006). Every forecast must take into account all factors that influence future events. However, some relevant factors are unknown in the evolving situation; or, as Taleb (2007: 172) formulates: "to understand the future to the point of being able to predict it, you need to incorporate elements from this future itself." Soros (2013: 310) refers to "fallibility": "the participants' views of the world never perfectly correspond to the actual state of affairs"; *only partial knowledge of the situation is possible*, and thus the only matter that can be expected with certainty is *a surprise* (Esposito 2011; Taleb 2007; cf. "potential surprise" in Shackle 1949). The list of possible events and alternatives for action is genuinely unknown because this list is partly created when economic agents act and decide.

This understanding of the basic situation in financial markets implies that economic agents confront a "big world" (in contrast to the "small world" in Savage's axiomatization). It is a world that is characterized by an indefinite number of possible unknown events that are interrelated. These events are often *endogenous*; they are evolving within financial markets and *socially contingent* – that is, contingent on the thoughts, decisions and actions of all interconnected actors. If one subscribes to this view, calculations – as a basis for choice decisions – generally performed with Savage's matrix and probabilistic instruments do not seem to be of much help: the probabilities and future events to which the probabilities should be assigned in order to maximize the expected utility or the optimally diversified portfolio might be unknown (Svetlova and van Elst 2015).

FINANCIAL MARKETS AS MARKETS OF "NOBODY KNOWS"

More generally, the basic situation in which financial market participants find themselves can be characterized by the principle of non-knowledge which cannot be reduced to the problem of asymmetric information (Akerlof 1970). In the event of information asymmetry, one market participant (in this case a used-car seller) possesses the relevant knowledge and is perfectly aware of the car's qualities and condition, whereas the other party (the buyer) is in the dark. However, the buyer *principally could know* the hidden details about the car: for example, the information about a defective motor is available. In this case, access to the omniscient party's knowledge is crucial; it is about *imperfect knowledge* that is meant to be "completed" – the principle knowability is the "flipside" of ignorance.

In financial markets, in contrast, we deal with distributed non-knowledge, a situation that principally differs from the situation with asymmetric information. Financial markets as *markets of nobody knows* are characterized by "symmetrical ignorance" (Caves 2003: 75; Skidelsky 2009: 45). Here, non-knowledge cannot be conceptualized as principally knowable and, therefore, cannot be eliminated through knowledge production and knowledge work. This is so because, as argued above, the information that is relevant for decisions, negotiations and so on is often non-existent in the present, at the moment of decision-making. As Esposito (2011, 2013) stresses, this information is created in the very interactions of market participants, particularly in the process of observing each other and expecting each other's expectations. In other words, expectations and forecasts in financial markets inevitably have a blind spot that relates both to the future and to real-time (current) market processes and phenomena (prices, expectations of others, news and so on) which "happen" at the same time when various market participants make their decisions. This blind spot is necessary for the very existence of markets: "One doesn't step into the market because one knows something, but because one *does not know* something and *cannot predict* something. (Why would one exchange if one did know?)" (Ayache 2010: 62, original emphasis).

Indeed, financial markets can exist only as markets of "nobody knows". Importantly, investment professionals cannot simply ignore market blind spots – being a part of the market themselves, they have to factor in what is happening while they decide.

DOUBTS ABOUT FINANCIAL MODELS: FIRST APPROXIMATION

How can financial models help in this situation? Can they grasp the emerging (becoming) reality? Can they nevertheless reduce *genuine* uncertainty? In the aftermath of the 2008 crisis, sharp critics of financial models suggested that models cannot do much in this respect. This gave rise to doubts as to whether the complex, contingent and endogenous nature of markets could ever be grasped by means of analytical calculations. *Probabilistic models* such as Value at Risk (VaR) and the Black-Scholes model (BSM) were broadly criticized in academic publications and the media (Taleb 2010; Triana 2011; Esposito 2013; Lockwood 2015). Based on the ideas of Hume, Knight, Keynes and Shackle, such critique highlighted the fact that probabilistic models rely on a unique probability measure associated with a presupposed *complete* list of consequence-relevant possible future states of the world. Thus, probability calculus translates uncertainties into risk (Svetlova and Fiedler 2011) and clearly precludes the consideration of surprises, "unknown unknowns" (for example Li 2009: 977) or "black swans" (Taleb 2007) which emerge at the very moment of decisions. Probabilities aim to formalize the non-knowledge of *which* event is most likely to occur from a given list of possibilities. However, in a situation of radical uncertainty, the list of possible events is never complete. The incorporation of *surprises* into a theoretical framework necessitates the formalization of *incomplete sets of possible future events*; but surprising events – by definition – cannot be known at the moment of choice and, thus, cannot be part of the set of possible events (see Svetlova and van Elst 2013, 2015 for a detailed discussion). Thus, the critique highlights the fact that financial models that are built upon the probabilistic framework are inherently insufficient and thus useless and dangerous if blindly applied – this is the quintessence of the post-crisis debate on modelling (see, for example, Triana 2011 on VaR for a detailed discussion). This critique that financial models can be based only on partial knowledge was widespread.

Furthermore, another important critical observation was made. Financial models – as they became widely used – contributed towards producing uncertainty rather than to reducing it (Esposito 2013). Financial models produce their own blind spots because they insufficiently take into account the reflexivity of markets, that is, the beliefs and actions of other actors. Particularly, they disregard the fact that models make assumptions about actors who also use models to observe the markets and make decisions. Esposito's example relates to risk models such as VaR:

> Risk calculation models calculated all possible futures, except the one resulting from the fact that markets use models. This future could not be foreseen, because it results performatively from the very diffusion of (performative) models. *The models correctly predicted the evolution of markets with no use of models*, but were not able to take into account the possibility that the future would react negatively to the prediction itself (to the model). (Esposito 2013: 119, my emphasis)

Similarly, Lockwood (2015: 735ff.) explains that VaR became an endogenous factor of market instability after banks had widely adapted the model and, as a result, started to rely on similar, highly correlated investment strategies:

> When the widespread use of VaR changes the behaviour it purports to model objectively – when its use becomes endogenous to the system it claims to model – it fuels the unpredictability of the financial system as a whole.

Models have difficulties in accounting for this unpredictability stemming from how market participants use models and act upon them. Thus, financial models are inaccurate not just because the world outside is too complex and incalculable, but also because they do not take into account the social aspects of their own application, co-producing herewith their *own blindness and fallibility*.

PROBLEMS WITH FINANCIAL MODELS: AN EXAMPLE BASED ON THE DCF

Let me illustrate these rather theoretical considerations by means of an example, namely the discounted cash flow model (DCF), as it is used by active portfolio managers. Portfolio managers invest their clients' money in different assets – such as equities, bonds, derivatives and other financial instruments – in order to earn a desired (absolute or relative) return for a given risk profile. If the money is provided by an individual client, an asset manager assesses that client's individual needs and allocates the funds among assets and securities. The money is usually not invested in a single asset but in a group of financial instruments, which is called a portfolio. A portfolio is a diversified mix of securities. For this reason, asset managers in big investment firms are frequently called portfolio managers. If the money of many investors is pooled in a portfolio, such a portfolio is called a mutual fund. In all cases, the primary task of a portfolio manager is to *decide* which and how many securities to buy, as well as to observe and adjust the portfolio over the course of time.

Uncertainty and expectations are at the core of their decisions: "the investor is trading a *known* dollar amount today for some *expected* future stream of payments" (Reilly and Brown 1997: 5, original emphasis). The future stream of payments consists of the yield – such as dividends, coupons or interest rate payments – as well as the earnings or losses due to price changes of the security. These prospective flows of payment and the future movements of the asset price are uncertain; at the same time, an active investor must choose assets that will bring the best return for a given risk profile. Thus they must be able to compare investment alternatives and choose the best – that is, those that will outperform the market or bring the maximum absolute return. In other words, asset managers have to be able to *value* assets and to form *expectations* about their returns; or, rather, they have to *believe* that they can do it, otherwise they would not be active in the market. They need a rationale for making decisions under uncertainty to solve the problem of investability.

One would expect financial models to be able to provide this service. For example, the DCF supposedly helps identify the "fair" value of an asset, and thus choose the undervalued investments. The general idea behind this model is that an investor should not pay more for an asset than it is worth. If there is a discrepancy between the fair value and the current price, it is a case of market inefficiency and mispricing. Active portfolio managers are generally convinced that such inefficiencies disappear with time and that the market price moves towards the fair value. There is a belief that if you know the fair value of an asset, you also know how its market price will develop; this knowledge should enable the portfolio manager to make informed investment decisions.

Investors who use the DCF aim to identify the fair value of a company or an asset class by means of a fundamental analysis: the fair value is anchored in future cash flows. In other words, they believe that "perceptions of value have to be backed up by reality, which implies that the price paid for any financial asset should reflect the cash flows that it is expected to generate" (Larsen 2012: 15).

The DCF model represents the valuation methodology that presumes that the fair value of a company or an asset class can be derived from the present value of its projected cash flows. These projections are based on a variety of assumptions about the key financial characteristics of a company or a market, such as growth rates, profit margins, capital expenditure and others. One crucial variable in the model is the discount rate, which is the sum of the time premium (the riskless rate) and the risk premium (the extra return that would compensate investors for taking the risk of investing in the particular asset class or company). The risk premium is particularly tricky to determine.

It is quite obvious that the DCF model requires inputs that are future values and cannot be specified with certainty. The *future* cash flows and the discount rate which determine the outcome of the model cannot be simply calculated or empirically determined. To calculate future cash flows, model users have to make various assumptions about factors that influence the cash flows and quantify them. They have to *estimate* growth rates, profit margins, capital expenditure and other elements of the cash flow statement to make cash flow projections. Equally, estimating the discount rate requires them to forecast the risk premium. However, there are also factors behind these obvious inputs, such as macroeconomic conditions (for example GDP growth, inflation and currency developments), political expectations (for example tax policies, state subsidies and political stability) and some company-specific issues (management quality, brand value, corporate governance and so on), as well as the psychology of market players (for instance risk preferences or the already-mentioned collective perception of the asset). A flawed assessment can lead to an inaccurate calculation of the fair value, and thus to incorrect investment decisions.

A particularly severe problem related to the DCF input factors is that they often cannot be quantified. They are soft factors, which are very important for the future development of an asset class or a company, but cannot be put into an Excel spreadsheet. Furthermore, the model's input factors are often not directly observable because they are estimates. *Projected* cash flows are needed, not current cash flows. As the prominent quantitative analyst and practitioner Derman (1996: 3, original emphasis) wrote:

> [We are] dealing with variables that clearly represent human expectations [. . .] These are hidden variables: they cannot be directly observed except perhaps by surveying market participants or by implying their values insofar as they impact other measurable quantities *by way of* a theory or model.

The input variables in valuation models are self-referential and reflexive because they are expectations. In the case of the DCF model, this self-referentiality manifests itself, for example, in the fact that future cash flows are not solely determined by a company's fundamentals but also by the expectations of others related to the company's business model. When the majority of market participants anticipate that a company will be a success in the future and buy its shares, the share price appreciates. Because of this favourable valuation, the company can re-finance itself under attractive conditions; its risk premium goes down, and its "fair" value increases. This increase induces further buying, and so on. The original expectation is undermined due to the self-referentiality and "emerging" character of financial markets.

Furthermore, although only future cash flows are relevant for the DCF model, investors often have to rely on historical data. In my ethnographic interviews with portfolio managers, this problem was given as the reason for not entirely trusting models: as the inputs are supposed to be projections, feeding the model with past data is unsatisfactory. Historical data provide only partial knowledge.

This brief initial discussion of the DCF model suggests – in accordance with existing criticisms – that models in financial markets might be insufficient *as a formal tool for forming expectations and decision-making*. When relying on models, financial decision-makers might lose sight of the markets. This argument echoes the leitmotiv of Ayache's book *The Blank Swan* (2010): financial products (e.g. derivatives) are *modelled* and, simultaneously, effectively *bought and sold* in the real markets (see Taleb and Haug 2011 for a similar argument). In order to understand the formation of derivative prices, observing market activities is as important as modelling. However, trading (actual buying and selling) is not part of the model (for example of the Black-Scholes model for option pricing), although it is crucial for price formation. Again, models inevitably observe market reality only partially.

These are the reasons why financial models – as calculative tools – became considered as doomed to hardly ever do justice to their complex surroundings. This message became a mantra in academic journals, practitioners' books and the professional media after the 2008 crisis. It seems that, after being imprisoned for years in the "modern worldview", people "freed" themselves from the concept by reinventing the wheel: the importance of the uncertainty, complexity and sociality of markets was (re-)discovered, and financial models were openly criticized as inevitably being inaccurate, abstract and unworldly. It was broadly claimed that, in genuinely complex social settings such as financial markets, models cannot account for the unpredictability and incomputability of the social. They can be compared to a torch that lights up only some corners of the room, so that its user stumbles around in the half-darkness.

As a result, models have become official villains that constantly have to atone for their imperfection. Critique of models has also been frequently combined with statements about the naivety of financial market participants who are depicted as being completely blind to the inability of their models to grasp reality with their probabilistic or any other formal framework – financial model users supposedly ignore their models' insufficiencies and stubbornly continue to apply these "useless" and dangerous calculative instruments. Demands to reduce the application of models in the practice of markets, or even to ban them completely, have become loud.

WHEREFORE MODELS THEN?

I would argue, however, that one can draw different conclusions from the above analysis of radical uncertainty, social contingencies and the insufficiencies of the related models. If we indeed conceptualize financial markets as markets of "nobody knows" and agree that models do not produce reliable knowledge about financial product valuations, future prices and so on by means of calculations, we might want to understand why models are so widely used in financial markets. Thus, we should turn to the practice of model use in markets and find out how and for which purposes market participants use models. The case studies in this book, which are based on empirical materials, illustrate that we are not merely dealing with people who make blind calculations. We are rather dealing with various professional groups (securities analysts, portfolio managers, traders and so on) who realize (like Keynes already did) that radical uncertainty implies that it is impossible to approach financial problems in a strictly mathematical way; or, rather, that different problems require different degrees of calculation. Our discussion will not be about what academics think people do with models, but about what people effectively do with models in their everyday practice.

Generally, financial market participants use their models to achieve various goals that are "overarched" by the general problem of investability. Market participants strive to bridge their genuine non-knowledge in such a way that *investments become possible*; they seek to "overlook the awkward fact" (Keynes 1937: 213f.) of their inevitable ignorance and *make indecidable situations manageable and decidable*. To do so, financial market participants mobilize various tools, such as models, which do not necessarily produce precise calculations, but more generally *enable actions*. To stay liquid, markets do not need knowledgeable people who do perfect maths, but people who are willing and able to act – that is, to invest.

On the one hand, the ability and willingness to act are produced in every *individual* decision; on the other hand, investability is also *socially* established and supported in the markets every time anew. Indeed, investors who are directly involved in decision-making, for instance in making choices about buying and selling securities, should find convincing arguments *for themselves* to "overlook" uncertainty and invest in a particular quantity of an asset at a particular price at this very moment. At the same time, market participants who *sell* decisions to others – for example, enhance or enable the decisions of clients – must find and convincingly present reasons as to why others should trust them and the market with their money.

My point is that formal models play a crucial but *not leading role* in those processes. Having said that, I would like to stress straightaway that I do not support *the under-calculative view*, which renders calculations and modelling useless or unimportant. The under-calculative view suggests that, when facing uncertainty, agents do not rely on calculations, and might even avoid them; instead, they rely on *conventions* (Keynes 1937), *traditions, customs* and *institutional routines* (Beckert 1996). Thus, decisions might be framed by norms, institutions, social networks and culture to such an extent that modelling becomes obsolete, and decision-makers rely on social structures rather than on models. Moreover, based on findings in behavioural finance, one might suggest that investors compensate for the imperfectness of their models and calculations by mimicking each other. Market participants communicate with each other intensively, observe each other's movements, adopt each other's views and mutually copy each other's investment decisions. Thus, at the crucial moment of decision-making, they may abandon their own models "for the reassurance of following others" (Beunza and

Stark 2010: 3). In addition to mimesis, behavioural finance also suggests judgment and heuristics (Gigerenzer 2007; Gigerenzer and Todd 1999) as efficient substitutes for rigorous calculations.

Blind acceptance of the under-calculative view and related over-emphasis of the cultural and institutional framings, mimesis and heuristics are, however, as dissatisfactory as the unquestioned belief in the superiority of calculations and algorithms. Indeed, how can we claim that financial agents completely ignore or neglect models when the latter have become important and ubiquitous tools in all fields of financial markets? Again, it might be more productive to understand *how* and *why* models are used in the practice of markets. In this book, I claim that financial models are important because they provide the markets with a great service by making them investable in various ways; however, their role is often not a leading role but a secondary one.

CREATING FAITH IN MARKETS

Models create faith in markets and produce reasons to invest when there are none. The problem of investability can be compared to the central issue of trust in sociology. Famously, there are no "good reasons" for trusting – that is for participating in a social interaction – because reliable knowledge about the true intentions of the counterpart is never available (deception is always an option); or, in other words, rational calculations of the probability of deception lack a firm grounding (Wenzel 2001; Möllering 2001; Beckert 2005). The possibility of social action can be explained by a leap of faith, as *suspension* "of the unknown, unknowable and unresolved" (Möllering 2001: 414). To be able to trust, one needs "quasi-religious faith", "some additional affective, even mystical, 'faith' of man in man" (Simmel 1908: 318). Without such faith, any future-related decisions would be impossible. For this reason, Mouritsen and Kreiner (2016: 22) recently suggested that decisions in a situation of radical uncertainty should be understood as *promises*. Referring to Nietzsche and Arendt, they define the decision as "a commitment to *engage* with a world that is not yet seen" (but emerging).

Financial products also imply promises in the ever-evolving world of financial markets (Knorr Cetina 2015). Thus, radical uncertainty, the unknown, must be suspended by procedures and tools that produce and support quasi-religious faith in markets. As John Bogle, founder of the Vanguard Group, formulated in the very first paragraph of his famous book *Common Sense on Mutual Funds* (1999), "Investing is an act of faith." I will take this statement as a point of departure for my discussion of financial models in this book, and focus on the question of *how models help to make markets work*; that is, how they help their users make situations in which decisions are seemingly impossible (undecidable situations) decidable, and how they co-produce faith in markets.

"Faith in markets" does not mean just "closing your eyes and hoping for the best". Rather, as Keynes (1937: 213f.) famously stated, it is about "doing our best" in "overlooking the awkward fact" of genuine uncertainty. This "overlooking" cannot be based only on models and calculations (Zaloom 2009; Akerlof and Shiller 2009; Chong and Tuckett 2015); but, at the same time, it does not imply reliance solely on "animal spirits" and "convincing narratives". It is rather about the combination of both. This issue is crucial for our understanding of the role of models in financial markets, and is clearly related to how we conceptualize financial decision-making. I will develop this point in the next section.

FINANCIAL DECISION AS "INCISION" AND "ACTING SENSIBLY"

To be able to act in the "emerging" world, financial market participants have to find approaches to decision-making that are not purely analytical, or to non-routine decision-making. They should be able to close a genuinely incomplete situation in a non-trivial way. This closure means *making an uncertain situation manageable and decidable* and involves "the choice of the framework in which [questions] are asked and [. . .] the choice of the rules used to connect what we label 'the question' with what we take for an 'answer'"(von Foerster 2003: 293).

Beunza and Stark (2004: 369) formulate this challenge in the form of the question: "What counts?" In the words of Kay (2011: 98), "closure means deciding what to bring in and what to leave out." In the process of situation closure in financial markets, models get connected to market events and become instruments that allow their users to ask the right questions and to pay attention to the essential issues around. At the same time, their presupposed dominance in financial decision-making becomes relativized.

In order to better understand the role of models in financial markets, the idea of abstaining from understanding decisions as mechanical choices between some pre-known alternatives (à la Savage) should be highlighted. Decision is not a fluctuation between alternatives; it is an "incision" (note the same word root). Decision is a cut in the process of situation closure (Chia 1994), the cut that is inevitably made "too early" because there are never unequivocal, justifiable rules and there is never enough information.

Hence, decisions are never utterly wise (completely informed or precisely calculated). Famously, Derrida (1994: 967, original emphasis) formulates this idea as follows:

> the moment of *decision, as such*, always remains a finite moment of urgency and precipitation, since it must not be the consequence or the effect of this theoretical or historical knowledge, of this reflection or this deliberation [. . .] The instant of decision is a madness, says Kierkegaard. [. . .] Even if time and prudence, the patience of knowledge and the mastery of conditions were hypothetically unlimited, the decision would be structurally finite, however late it came, decision of urgency and precipitation, acting in the night of non-knowledge and non-rule.

True decisions cannot "simply consist of applying a rule, of enhancing a program or effecting a calculation" (Derrida 1994: 961); they are "regulated and without regulation":

> [They] must conserve the law [a rule, a formal calculation] and also destroy it or suspend it enough to have to reinvent it in each case, re-justify it, at least reinvent it in the reaffirmation and the new and free confirmation of its principle. Each case is other, each decision is different and requires an absolute unique interpretation, which no existing, coded rule can or ought to guarantee absolutely. (p. 961)

This is an apt description of decision-making in financial markets. Financial models – as laws, as rules – are more rigid and fixed than a fluid decision-making situation, and thus are inevitably incomplete and imperfect by nature. This is also the Wittgensteinian theme that MacKenzie (2009) highlighted while providing ten characteristics of the social studies of finance; he generally referred to "meaning finitism" (Bloor 1997) as the "in-principle flexibility" of rule-following that is typical for financial markets. From this perspective, the role of models and calculations is necessarily relativized. To understand and to analyse this role, we should be able to grasp the process of *simultaneous calculation* and *its suspension*, the unique moments of reinventing, confirming and interpreting what has been calculated.

This understanding of decision-making, which implies *more than calculation* in a given situation, has been addressed in the literature in various forms: "practical judgement" (Dewey 1915), "estimates" (Knight 1921), the "successive limited comparison" or "muddling-through" (Lindblom 1959), the process of "calculating where we can" (Keynes 1936), "framing" (Goffman 1974), "heuristics" (Gigerenzer and Todd 1999; Gigerenzer 2007), "bricolage" (de Certeau 1984) and "overflow" (Callon 1998), as well as "mindfulness" and "sense-making" (Weick 1995, 2001; Weick and Sutcliffe 2001). All of these concepts share the doubt that decisions can be reduced to choice, and abandon clear-cut, one-step calculation as a way of deciding.

A useful classification of approaches to non-analytical decision-making was suggested by Smith (2011: 277ff.). He differentiated between:

- An engagement "in one or another familiar 'routine or performance'" as a way of imposing "some sort of behavioral order". Such engagements might be habits or "rules of thumb", heuristics and other types of unthinking response.
- "Making sense" as "the form of finding, creating, and imposing some sort of ordering narrative account on events initially experienced as chaotic", as "imposing some sort of cognitive order".
- "Acting sensibly" is "a method for handling the disorder", which is accepted as "ontologically real". This coping method is characterized by acting towards many objectives simultaneously, monitoring the constantly changing (manifest and potential) markers, identifying and juggling rules of thumb, which are constantly adjusted, discovering the way *en route* and constantly maintaining an escape path. Decisions occur in small sequential, iterative and recursive steps.

Although Smith (2011: 278) states that "all three methods work in different situations where different objectives are desired", I would suggest that in financial markets, where the basic situation is incomplete and fateful, "acting sensibly" is the central method for coping. This more general method includes the first two: routines (heuristics) and sense-making (framing and interpretations). It involves "preparatory work and the work of seeing and attention that readies [market participants] for unthinking responses" (Knorr Cetina 2009: 76). While acting sensibly, agents develop routines or explanatory narratives. However, they are ready to *adjust* these routines and narratives in response to changes in the situation (markets). The agents are aware that the situation is never completely closed and that no rules and interpretations can be taken for granted. In this case, the iterative and recursive steps of decision-making are not the results of purely mental activity. They are true actions. That is, individuals act, stay alert in order to adjust their goals, rules and methods, and discover a posteriori what has occurred, how they can explain the events and what to do next (see Ortmann 2003, 2004; Weick 1995; Heath et al. 2002). While determining the route, so to speak, in the process of deciding and acting, individuals may rely on the wrong map – but they successfully find their way *while moving (acting)*. Recall Weick's discussion of the mountaineers lost in the Alps who rescued themselves after one member of the group found a map of the Pyrenees. This wrong map helped the group become active and alert and, thus, to save itself. Exactly in this sense, in financial markets, a formal model can be considered a map that may not be true (although truthfulness is the central issue in science); a model should enable its users to take actions in the ever-changing world and to "overlook" the awkward fact of radical uncertainty and non-knowledge.

Importantly, decisions in financial markets are not abstract choices and pure calculations, but imply *true actions* (for example, buying or selling securities, that is, stepping into the market, becoming a part of it). I refer here to *action-like decision-making* (Goffman 1969), which enables an individual to cope with genuine uncertainty and undecidability in an incomplete situation by *engaging with the world*. This concept can also be considered akin to Weick's enactment: in undecidable situations, people do not decide in the common sense of the word; that is, they do not choose between the alternatives because the alternatives, preferences, decision rules and so on are unknown. Decision-makers often act first and, in doing so, determine, frame and close the situation – and only later do they interpret or "sell" their actions as decisions. In action-like decision-making, people simultaneously create and perceive their environment (Weick 1995), for instance, the market.

The necessity of active intervention to prevent an individual from not being paralysed by uncertainty makes the required decisions and actions *fateful* (Goffman 1969; Knorr Cetina 2009). When actors take actions, they know that there is a lot at stake (Dewey 1915: 507) or, as Taleb (2012) formulates it, financial market participants have their "skin in the game". As opposed to killing time (for example thumbing through a magazine) or following an everyday routine, a fateful activity (for example gambling) is consequential in that the activity has "the capacity [. . .] to flow beyond the bounds of the occasion in which it is delivered and to influence objectively the later life [of the gambler]" (Goffman 1969: 116).

Importantly, the consequences of financial decisions are not abstract; they are real, have monetary expressions and are able to change the situation. But exactly because financial decisions are fateful and their consequences are severe and co-determine market events, financial market participants cannot allow themselves to ignore markets when making decisions; that is, they cannot rely only on calculations (models) that inevitably ignore what is going on in real time. Otherwise, investors would be navigating a ship in the ocean using instruments that ignore the weather around the ship.

As we will see in the later empirically based discussion, financial market participants are perfectly aware of this and structure their practices of model use accordingly. They understand their decision-making as *a constant process of discovery*, as fateful. And, *acting sensibly*, they search for productive methods to simultaneously calculate and suspend calculations. But how exactly can we account for "effecting calculation"? In other words, what is "more" than "just calculation" in decision-making? How does action-like decision-making work?

EFFECTING CALCULATION AND "QUALCULATION"

The inappropriateness of formal models as a sole basis for decision-making under uncertainty has not been ignored by researchers in economics and sociology. The latter have developed various non-analytical decision-making concepts (such as "practical judgment", "tacit knowledge" and "situated rationality") and compared them to calculation. One might even argue that it is old hat: we have long been debating about calculation versus non-formal, situation-related decision-making – for example, "techne versus episteme" and "know-what versus know-how". Indeed, it has been recognized that technical rationality (episteme) – perceived as objective knowledge based on disembedded abstract rules – does not work perfectly in situations under uncertainty. Thus, decision-makers often rely, for example, on heuristics (frugal and robust simplifying rules; e.g. Neth and Gigerenzer 2015), sense-making (Weick 1995; also Smith 2011, discussed above) or judgment (Karpik 2010). For instance, Gigerenzer (2007) has been propagating the use of heuristics as an effective tool in situations under radical uncertainty for decades, whereas, as he puts it, formal decisions à la Savage are appropriate only in the "small" world of risk.

In all of these concepts, there seems to be an implied controversy between "calculation" and judgment or heuristics, between formal and informal methods of decision-making. In his study of choices in consumer markets, Karpik (2010: 41), for example, clearly juxtaposes judgment and decision: "Judgment is [. . .] primarily a qualitative choice, whereas decision is based on logic and calculation." Thus, for him, "decision and judgment are two different modalities of choice and two different frames of action".

This controversy is highly relevant for financial markets: the battle between quantitative and qualitative approaches to decision-making seems to be ubiquitous and essential. Bernstein (1996: 6) formulates it very pointedly in his book on the history of (financial) risk:

> The story that I have to tell is marked all the way through by a persistent tension between those who assert that the best decisions are based on quantification

and numbers, determined by the patterns of the past, and those who base their decisions on more subjective degrees of belief about the uncertain future. This is a controversy that has never been resolved.

Thus, with respect to financial models, we should ask: do they represent the purely quantitative "pole"? Are they merely the means of performing mathematical operations, and thereby principally opposed to judgment? And, more generally, are we really confronting the existential "to model or not to model" question here?

As already discussed, in the practice of markets, the juxtaposition of "under-calculative" and "over-calculative" views is not satisfactory. As models have become important and ubiquitous tools, the not-to-model option is rather out of the question. The social studies of finance have striven to develop a third – integrative – view of financial markets in which mental and social determinants are combined with technology and formal models. In other words, they conceive of financial markets as a place where "equipment matters" (MacKenzie 2009) but does not dominate. Power (2003: 14) refers to "calculative pragmatism", the "logic of practice" according to which adherents use numbers but do not expect them "to represent reality". Analysing the use of models by merger arbitrageurs, Beunza and Stark provide an empirical example of model use as "the interdependence between the social and the calculative". The authors claim that no aspect – neither social (mimesis, networks, institutions) nor calculative (models) – should be neglected when explaining decision-making in financial markets:

> the notion that a trader would give up his or her own model for the sake of conforming to the dictates of the majority is unrealistic. [. . .] it overlooks the fact that the positions adopted by traders are not based on the latest piece of gossip but on databases, equations, and routines developed over years. (Beunza and Stark 2010: 4)

The calculative, social and technical aspects of financial markets should be simultaneously taken into consideration. The analysis of this "collectively constructed calculative technology" (Beunza and Garud 2007) has become the key programmatic issue of the social studies of finance and is followed in this book.

But how can we overcome the juxtaposition between calculation and judgment? In order to do this, Callon and Muniesa (2005: 1231) suggest understanding calculation more broadly:

> Calculating does not necessarily mean performing mathematical or even numerical operations [. . .] Calculation starts by establishing distinctions between

things or states of the world, and by imagining and estimating courses of action associated with those things or with those states as well as their consequences.

Thus, Callon and Muniesa (2005: 1232) continue: "calculation can either meet the requirements of algorithmic formulation or be closer to intuition or judgment"; in other words, calculation may include both formal operations and qualitative judgment. Drawing on Heidegger's work, Kalthoff (2005: 73) similarly argues that:

> calculation is not limited to operations with numbers: 'Computing in a broader more essential sense means: to calculate with something. That means to take into consideration, to count on something, i.e. to set into expectation' (Heidegger 1954: 54). It also means to form a judgment with something upon something – activities, in which images, categories and distinctions are involved.

Also, Cochoy (2008: 15) suggests moving the analysis "from mere calculation (price-based computing) to 'qualculation' (i.e. quality-based rational judgements)", and offers examples of shopping carts and shopping lists as "qualculation devices". He explains:

> Even if the shopping list occasionally displays information about prices and quantities, it is a very poor "pure calculation" instrument. In fact, the shopping list rather poses the problem of "qualculation", that is, *the very delicate evaluation of the best choice when calculation is not possible* [. . .], when the lack of explicitly quantified points of reference hinders the use of strict "consumer arithmetic". (Cochoy 2008: 26, my emphasis)

Karpik's "judgment", Callon's "calculation" and Cochoy's "qualculation" all address ways of coping in situations under radical uncertainty in which calculation as a strictly numerical procedure is not possible or is useless – that is, exactly the decision-making situations that are characteristic of financial markets. Now, where do we find financial models here?

The integrative view of the social studies of finance implies that financial models are frequently not used as tools of pure calculation, but fulfil various *non-calculative (latent) functions* and that their use is complemented by a whole set of non-numerical competences and skills that are necessary to make financial decisions. Models *matter* for non-analytical, *action-like decision-making* in various ways.

For example, in her programmatic study on derivatives trading, Zaloom (2003: 261) highlights that "[t]he first thing traders learn is that numbers tell very little". Numbers "tell little" because they "stand on their own without reference to events outside". However, Zaloom shows how calculations are constantly *put in relation* to what happens in the markets – to market rumours, changing economic data, moods of investors, activities of other traders and so on. Based on these empirical insights, Zaloom suggests conceiving of traders' practices as "flexible interpretation rather than formal calculation", and thus reiterates the juxtaposition between calculation and judgment; she clearly points to "the tensions between rationalization and situated action" (p. 269). At the same time, she highlights the interdependence of numbers, actors and the incalculable social contents of markets: "In contemporary trading rooms, sentiments, actors, and market numbers are always in flux. Traders know that market numbers carry social content that cannot be computed" (p. 269).

Here, Zaloom's text rather suggests that – in the flux of trading – numbers and interpretations are constantly combined with each other in order to overcome the "quantitative vs qualitative" controversy. In the practice of markets, it is not an either/or issue (techne vs episteme, know-what vs know-how, the Savage matrix vs heuristics, etc.) but a question of how models and judgment supplement each other, how models are set in relation to the market so that their inevitably insufficient formal structure is "made to count". This happens in the practice of model use.

MAKING MODELS COUNT: AN EXAMPLE OF THE BLACK-SCHOLES MODEL

To illustrate how financial models could be connected to the markets, and thus made to count, we will look at the use of the Black-Scholes model (BSM). Haug and Taleb stress that option traders are engineers who have their "skin in the game", and thus never blindly rely on models (episteme). Rather, traders develop their know-how (techne) in the very practice of markets:

> For us practitioners, theories about practice should arise from practice or at least avoid conflict with it. This explains our concern with the "scientific" notion that practice should fit theory. Option hedging, pricing, and trading are neither philosophy nor mathematics, but an extremely rich craft rich with heuristics with traders learning from traders (or traders copying other traders) and tricks developing under evolution pressures, in a bottom-up manner. It is technë, not ëpistemë. (Haug and Taleb 2011: 97)

Here we are again confronted with the juxtaposition between calculation and tacit knowledge. However, it does not seem to be an either/or debate. Haug and Taleb (as well as Ayache 2010 and Roffe 2015) do not describe option trading as a practice *without* the BSM. Rather, they depict the model as having only a limited capability to price options, particularly due to its reliance on the probability calculus. In the idealized probabilistic world of the BSM, "demand and supply for options simply should not affect the price for options" (Haug and Taleb 2011: 105). Thus, as Roffe (2015: 22) argues, the probabilistic theory "liquidates what is specific about the market as a part of the process of pricing". The formula – in the very process of pricing – should be connected to the market. Importantly, Haug and Taleb describe how this problem is solved, and thus how the controversy between techne and episteme is overcome in the very practice of model use – that is, in the process of model calibration and trading:

> Probability is always defined relative to a given context or collection of states of the world. By replicating the derivative in all possible states of the world, the derivative pricing model exhausts probability and saturates the context. However, this is not trading. Trading the derivative is precisely what *happens next*. (Ayache 2010: 5, original emphasis)

This "what happens next" is crucial for our understanding of model use. The BSM is applied in the process of calibration to determine implied volatilities which are "unsettled", questioned and judged by traders. In other words, the model might be imperfect as a theoretical edifice but can be *made useful* in the process of its application. In the case of the BSM, this "manipulation into rightfulness" (Triana 2009) happens in the process of *calibration*. Traders calculate the model parameters "backwards" from the observed market prices of the derivative instrument. The central parameter that results from calibration is the *implied volatility*. The implied volatility tells the traders which volatility – if inserted into the Black-Scholes formula – will allow them to obtain (or reproduce) the recent market price. Being aware of the flaws of the formula, the traders understand that straightforward application of the model – as an "unworldly" tool to calculate the theoretical (fair) value of a derivative – does not make much sense. Instead, they take the market price as given and calculate the implied volatility, *bringing markets back* into the pricing process. This "inversion" of the BSM makes the formula useful for market participants:

> [T]he derivative valuation algorithm, pioneered by Black, Scholes and Merton has been a perfect trading tool and traders have consistently used it, not in order to compute a theoretical value for the derivatives but *to price them in the market*, that is to say, to trade them and exchange them and *unsettle any computed results*. (Ayache 2010: 55, my emphases)

Thus, the process of calibration as a flexible procedure for connecting the model to markets transforms the BSM into an essential template behind "embedded", situated trading:

You need the model *to insert the trader on the floor*, and you need the trader, of course, to go and address the contingency of the contingent claim [a derivative in Ayache's parlance] and *take it outside the frame of possibility and probability and redundancy*. (Ayache 2007: 48, my emphases)

Indeed, models "insert" financial market participants into the market; they allow users to open up their decision-making to incorporate market contingencies, to observe and to expect others' expectations, and thus to go beyond the model calculation. By constantly calibrating and recalibrating the Black-Scholes model, traders "*contradict* the model that brings [them] here in the first place because by recalibrating [they] are making volatility stochastic, [they] are killing the very assumptions of Black-Scholes" (Ayache 2007: 48, my emphasis).

This "killing" is necessary to "make the model count". Let me explain this. The process of calibration helps traders express their judgment. Effectively, every trader in the market has his or her own opinion about the price, and is convinced that he or she can retain profits only by referring to his or her own, subjectively correct, prices. The implied volatility parameter is *estimated* by model users. The purpose of traders is to "price" (not to "value") options (Haug and Taleb 2011: 103). Traders want *to express their subjective truth*, their judgment about the market; thus, *they use the model as a device for this particular – latent – purpose*. Option pricing by means of the BSM takes into account only some of the factors that influence price. Some relevant factors cannot be captured by the model, but still affect prices – for example discrete dividends or what other market participants do and expect (i.e. demand and supply in the market). These factors can be incorporated into the price calculation through a *judgmental* choice of the volatility number. This flexible procedure – at least partly – closes the gap between the model and the world.

An estimation of the implied volatility is not a strict mathematical calculation, but rather a kind of cheating called "volatility fudging" (Triana 2008: 2). Traders simply use the model to obtain "the price they want"; and the price they want comes from the judgment traders "outside the model" while observing the market and interacting with it.

Due to this specific use of implied volatility, one can claim that the pure version of the Black-Scholes formula has never been used. Pablo Triana (2007: 6) explains:

[Option traders manipulate] the volatility number that goes into the model, by definition the only input that is manipulable. Volatility will be changed so as to arrive at the price deemed more appropriate by market players. For instance, deep-out-of-the-money options are assigned a higher volatility parameter to compensate for the fact that pure Black-Scholes results yield too low a price for such an option, on account of the normal distribution assumption that undervalues the possibility of extreme market movements, such as a crash. Since traders know full well that in real life extreme movements take place quite often they push up the price of the option accordingly by manipulating the volatility parameter.

In other words, traders, while using the formula in their practice, effectively reject some of the model's assumptions – for instance that the volatility parameter is independent of its strike level and that stock prices are log-normally distributed. The horizontal line of implied volatility in the pure version of the Black-Scholes model is transformed into the famous "volatility smile" (MacKenzie and Millo 2003: 127; Triana 2008: 2).

The volatility smile destroys the mathematics of the original Black-Scholes formula but *makes it possible to apply the model in a useful manner*. In fact, this specific way of connecting judgment and model seems to be the reason for the successful usage of the model:

> Black-Scholes became so immensely popular precisely because professionals know that the markets can't really be modelled and look sceptically at mathematical trickeries [. . .] Traders know that the markets are not ruled by precise laws, but by maverick economic agents who refuse to bow down to the authority of the mathematical sheriff. Thus, option players would only embrace a model that allows them to impose their own law, free from any theoretical straitjacket. Black-Scholes has become the consensus pricing model because it easily makes mathematics irrelevant. The secret to Black-Scholes is that it comes with its own built-in self-correcting mechanism that allows traders to conveniently obtain the price that they (and not some unrealistic theoretical construct) consider to be optimal given real-world realities [. . .] Traders don't look for mathematical truth, they look for a way to express their truth easily and comfortably. Black-Scholes provides such service. (Triana 2007: 6)

In other words, exactly due to this mechanism of correcting the model's unrealistic assumptions about volatility and stock price distribution, the model became a widely used instrument for determining option prices in the markets. Option traders could escape the mathematical restraints of the formula and develop their "silent production" (de Certeau 1984: xxi) with a new calculative instrument that is still called "the Black-Scholes formula", albeit possibly not entirely correctly. The formula that is used by option traders in their practice is the manipulated or adjusted version of the original Black-Scholes formula. As an adjusted tool, the formula is able to serve the goals of practitioners: namely, in the practice of markets, the BSM is used to identify and communicate the subjective views of traders that deviate from the model calculation. It connects traders to the markets so that "the model and the market do not stand in opposition to one another nor is there a directional sequencing from model to market"

(LiPuma 2017: 11). In doing so, the model enables trading transactions and makes option markets investable.

CULTURES OF MODEL USE

Thus, the BSM can be considered as a heuristic tool that is quantitative and social at the same time; it is part of a very sophisticated decision-making process that is performed *with* and *around* the model. There is no juxtaposition of the model (a rational calculative tool) and a heuristic method (a non-analytical, simplistic rule). It is not about the model *or* a heuristic method; rather, it is about the *heuristics of model use*, or various styles of using models in the practice of markets. Throughout this book, I will refer to them as *cultures of model use* (Svetlova and Dirksen 2014; Wansleben 2013), as specific styles of the interplay between formal and non-formal elements of decision-making in the practice of markets. The empirical work within the social studies of finance has already pointed out their importance, but more research is needed in this field.

Cultures of model use can be understood as the ways of *doing/undoing calculations*:

> The notion (of undoing calculations) describes the phenomenon of neutralization or bracketing of calculative practices in economic life-worlds. Undoing something means that actors interrupt the continuous flow of their attentiveness; they (actively) shift the focus of their concentration to another object – and they might do this even for a very short time period. This modification of attentiveness goes along with a shift of the social relevance attributed to an observed object. Applied to calculative practices, the phenomenon of undoing calculation shows that economic calculation is not only realized in the media of its representation and within the context of actors' interactions, but that it is a completely *temporal phenomenon*. What is important in my view is that downsizing the calculation in this sense takes place in the *temporality of the representation and its performance*. The question of how the actors temporally defer economic calculation in their area and update other practices and arguments while at the same time bearing in mind what has been calculated is a part of the [outlined] empirical research program. (Kalthoff 2011: 15, original emphases)

The concept of "undoing calculations" clearly points to the temporal, situational shifts of market participants' attention *to* and *away* from models. Models are not equally relevant and important at all times when market activities are developing; they might be in focus for some time and then move to the periphery of users' minds, and back again. As I will demonstrate empirically in Chapter 4, such shifts are at the core of cultures of model use in various segments of financial markets.

The central claim of this book is that the controversy between calculation and judgment is *resolved in the very practice of model use in financial markets*. Cultures of model use are elements of "acting sensibly", and represent very broad methods for deciding and closing "incomplete situations". Many *heterogeneous methods* are conceivable for achieving closure; they differ depending on the role that models play in them. As we will see in Chapter 4, there are different "styles" according to which models help to ask the "right" questions, draw attention to "what counts" and choose "what to bring in and what to leave out" in the process of action-like decision-making. The discussion about the Black-Scholes model delivered just one example.

Cultures of model use also shed light on one of the central questions of this book: why and how are inadequate financial models used in the practice of markets? Exactly because they are not omnipotent instruments, but elements of the temporal patterns of doing and undoing calculations, models can be simultaneously central and secondary for financial decision-making; they can be *not trusted but used* or *used but not trusted* while the attention of model users shifts from the models to the market and back.

DECISION-MAKING AT LARGE

Moreover, it should be explicitly stressed that cultures of model use are not only related to the short time for preparing and making decisions ("incisions"). They are clearly part of action-like decision-making which is, first, ongoing and, second, circular. Indeed, numerous alternative actions are created in the process of "enactment" and are then reduced through an incision (a cut) to attain a preliminary ending, just one alternative. Decision-making does not end here, however; every decision is a commitment, a promise that "lives" into the future, and is exposed to future contingencies and opens new, unknown possibilities to which it also has to react. As Mouritsen and Kreiner (2016: 21) highlight, "decisions are endings which stop a process of decision making, but they are also promises which create new beginnings."

These new beginnings are related to the formulation of a retrospective story about a decision that has just been made, and to the creation of strategies for negotiating and justifying decisions. As Graaf (2016: 14) states, "decision-makers must continuously negotiate their decisions to support their claim." Thus, decisions are ongoing, and our goal is to understand how models play into this decision-making at large (Svetlova and Dirksen

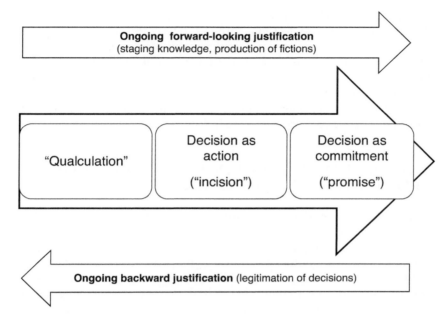

Figure 2.1   Models in decision-making at large

2014) – that is, how models contribute to *what happens before the decision* (as incision) and to what "happen[s] to the decision" (Mouritsen and Kreiner 2016: 29). Thus, models' roles in the decision-making process are not restricted to calculation and its suspension (qualculation) prior to the decision. As Figure 2.1 illustrates, models enable promises as they are involved in the ongoing forward and backward negotiation, legitimization and justification of decisions. These are practices through which models are made relevant.

Action-like decision-making produces a promise, a commitment (e.g. when portfolio managers buy equities or when security analysts publish their forecast). This production of promises must be made possible in the ongoing process of self-motivation (*decision-making*) and motivation of others (*decision-selling*) to overlook radical uncertainty and to act (to invest, trade, etc.). In this book, I suggest that, in order to provoke financial activities, reasons for investing are *feigned* while mutual *non-knowledge is staged as knowledge*. Contributing to this forward-looking *production of fictions* is one of the major functions of models in financial markets; for example, they might stage uncertainty as risk and provoke feelings of security and necessary faith in the future. At the same time, decisions as promises make decision-makers accountable for future contingencies. As the future develops and decisions turn out to be correct or false, backward justification often becomes necessary (why this security and not the other one was bought; why the recommendation was "sell" and not "hold", etc.). Indeed, sound reasons should be constantly provided as to why exactly this particular decision was made and not the other one. Models help to stage decisions as *meaningful, accountable and legitimate*, and thus are important for the backward-looking legitimization of decisions.

STAGING NON-KNOWLEDGE AS KNOWLEDGE: FRONT-STAGE AND BACKSTAGE

Justification processes can constantly be observed in various links of the investment chain. The necessity to justify decisions is ubiquitous when one professional group presents (stages) its own decisions or supports the decision-making of another professional group. In the first case, it could be fund managers justifying their past decisions to consultants or to investors who entrusted them with their money; in the second case, you might think of security analysts or economists who present their "views" (forecasts and recommendations) to portfolio managers in face-to-face meetings, or of the interactions between financial advisors and clients.

Here, Goffman's (1959) concept of "front-stage" and "backstage" comes to mind. In this book, I argue and show that the role of formal models in the representational mode at the front-stage (where individuals present their organizations, teams and themselves to an external audience) is different from the role of models at the backstage – where market participants discuss relevant events and issues internally and make decisions without spectators and, hence, without any direct pressure to justify their decisions. Obviously, one would never find a professional group that acts solely backstage all the time; however, some investors are less exposed to the influence of different audiences than others. Think about portfolio managers who make investment decisions for mutual funds; although they might have to explain their investments to their superiors or to consultants from time to time, they seldom or never have direct contact with their clients, resulting in much less external pressure than on the so-called "sell side".

At the backstage, investors are concerned with developing their idiosyncratic ways of seeing the market and using the models for decision-making in various ways (discussed in Chapter 4). However, as soon as investment professionals go front-stage, they rely on models in a different sense. In the process of justification and legitimization of decisions, models exercise significant *symbolic power*. This power is famously emphasized in Porter's

(1995) book *Trust in Numbers*: the "modern-world view" ascribes to models *the capability to guarantee scientific objectivity* and to emotionally defuse decisions. In this sense, models are endowed with symbolic authority that is referred to in presentations front-stage (see Chapter 5).

This symbolic authority, however, is not absolute; it has gradations. Shackley (1998) observed that the more complex and more politically laden a decision-making situation is, the more important models are as justification tools. In other words, in situations in which the role of the audience is strong and the autonomy of model users rather restricted (as typical at the organizational front-stage), models are strongly inclined to fulfil their "latent" functions of providing legitimacy and accountability.

In this sense, financial markets can be considered as highly uncertain and politicized fields where various audiences tend to disagree on forecasts and the course of action. Thus, in financial markets, the manifest role of models (calculation) is relativized. It is often unimportant what models recommend doing – it is by far more important how the numbers produced by the models are used to *sell*, that is *justify*, decisions to various audiences front-stage. But how exactly do models exercise their symbolic power and justify decisions?

PRODUCTION OF ILLUSIONS AND FICTIONS AS REASONS FOR DECISIONS

A successful justification front-stage usually relies on *an illusion* of objectivity, scientificity and robustness that models and numbers produce. This production is based on the fictional "as-if game" (Ortmann 2004: 12, based on Giddens and Searle), on *signalling the quality of decisions*, on "illusion tricks" (Alvesson 2013). Such illusion tricks are particularly important in situations of *symmetrical ignorance* which (as discussed) are characterized on the one hand, by genuine uncertainty and complexity and, on the other, by a high level of disagreement among experts about what is going on:

> Purely calculative, machine-like solutions to technical problems only work well in situations where there is a very high level of agreement about knowledge and a high degree of organizational and political consent about the issue [. . .]. It is also well known that even expert assessments can exhibit considerable variance (experts disagree), that in some areas extrapolation is highly judgmental and that there is often an impression of "false precision." (Power 2007: 14, referring to Jasanoff 1991: 31)

In financial markets as markets of "nobody knows", the staging of "false precision" is the basis for "overlooking" uncertainty, and thus the precondition for action-like decision-making. Beckert (2013, 2016) suggests that, in order to successfully cope with the unknown future, investors form *not rational* but *fictional expectations*; that is, they strongly anchor their expectations in fictions (false precisions). Fictional expectations can be compared to literary fictions. The point is that literary narratives are read because they are convincing, not because they are true (Beckert 2013: 222), because they create *a plausible world*. Fictions are based on stories *and* numbers that are plausible enough to produce an illusion of certainty, and motivate and force action. Numbers (or models) "provide" for scientificity and objectivity, whereas the related stories are communicated and discussed *as if* the numbers were true. In due course, "disbelief" can be suspended and "*seemingly* good reasons for specific decisions" (Beckert 2013: 222) are provided so that "quasi-religious faith" in markets is established. It is about producing a common ground for shared beliefs. As I will show later in the book, models actively participate in the production of *fictional, as-if realities* that can, however, become part of the *real realities*. This is one of the central functions of models in financial markets.

For example, a financial advisor motivates a retail client to buy a particular financial product in a sales talk while he or she is presenting and explaining the product to the client. This presentation might include calculations, although the latter are not decisive; rather, they are important as part of the more general staging of the financial product in such a way that the client *has a feeling* he or she is making a good decision. The product is usually presented as safe enough for investment but also as promising high returns, as "sexy" (i.e. as a product with an interesting growth or innovation story). In the process of staging products and motivating decisions, clients are given the feeling of knowing, of understanding the products; in other words, *knowledge is staged* for them in a situation where there is no reliable knowledge at all; indeed, knowledge is feigned.

AN EXAMPLE OF CONTINGENT CONVERTIBLE BONDS (COCOS)

Think about contingent convertible bonds, or cocos (based on Svetlova 2016). As a new financial asset, they appeared on the radar screen of investors in the aftermath of the financial crisis of 2007–09. In an effort to create a more stable banking system, regulators allowed banks to issue hybrid capital securities which can absorb bank losses and create fresh equity capital in situations of financial distress. If particular negative events (so-called trigger events) happen – for example if the capital ratio of a bank falls below a specified minimal level or if the share price breaches a pre-set requirement – the cocos can be converted into equities or written down partly or completely. As compensation for these risks, buyers of cocos receive a very attractive coupon (usually between 7 and 9 per cent).

A mathematically stringent valuation of these products is difficult (or impossible) due to their contingent nature. For example, it remains unclear as to whether they should be valued as bonds, equities or derivatives. Furthermore, the valuation of cocos is based on too many future uncertainties which cannot be easily resolved. Nevertheless, there are investors who are willing to buy cocos. This willingness to invest in cocos depends primarily on if and how clients are "educated" about the prospective returns and risks in concrete situations of interaction with their advisors or asset managers who use the uncertainties related to cocos as *an opportunity for selling*.

Particularly the fact that cocos cannot be clearly classified as bonds, equities or derivatives opens the opportunity of presenting and selling them as bonds. They can be submitted to clients as bonds that offer a lucrative yield. The marketing idea (the narrative) behind cocos is that – in normal times – they behave like bonds, and that normal times are the most likely scenario. As a result, the probability of converting cocos is undervalued or neglected in sales talks; supposedly, there has been no history that proves the opposite.

While selling cocos as bonds, investment advisors construct them as "high-yield/low-risk" products and induce clients to overlook or underestimate the complexity and risks related to the product. In fact, roughly 70 per cent of participants in the Royal Bank of Scotland (RBS) survey on the cocos market named yield as the major stimulus for investing in them, and around 40 per cent indicated that they invest in cocos because they consider conversion to be unlikely (Gallo 2014: 2).

The brand of the cocos' issuer, the degree of familiarity to investors, also plays a significant role in presentations to clients. Banks with established brands like UBS or Deutsche Bank are presented in such a way that difficulties are not expected with their capital ratio or share price (although the financial crisis of 2008 teaches quite the opposite). Famous big banks are associated with financial solidity and solvency. Harrington (2007: 22) already recognized the role of brands in dictating investment choices, particularly pointing to amateur investors who buy or avoid stocks on the basis of brand associations: "People buy stocks in much the same way they buy consumer products like jeans and cars," she reported. Thus, similar to iPhones and washing powder, financial products are presented to clients in marketing shows and sales talks.

Particularly the selling strategies for cocos make the radical uncertainties about unfavourable events that influence their value sound impossible and render investments attractive. Here, efforts to strictly calculate the probabilities of a trigger event are replaced or complemented by narratives about why the conversion of cocos will not happen, why the regulator is not interested in pulling the trigger, why coupon cancellation is rather unlikely, why big banks will fulfil their capital ratio requirements and so on. This marketing-driven presentation of cocos enables sellers to "jump" across the gap of the unknown and provoke investing. The (presumably) good decisions are successfully staged for potential clients. This staging is part of the valuation process of financial assets that implies that "new products, styles and practices come to be selected and *positioned as valuable* in communities, organizations and markets" (Hutter and Stark 2015: 5). We are talking about a *consumptive regime of valuation* in which formal mathematical valuation is deferred or plays a secondary – supportive, for example, legitimizing – role in the determination of value and investing.

In Chapter 5 of this book, I use another example of staging. In the case study on economic forecasting in a Swiss bank at the beginning of the 2008 financial crisis, I demonstrate how models and numbers support performances at the front-stage. The pressure imposed by the audience results in economists' forecasts that are rigid, formal, number-oriented and artificially precise. As "trusted" scientific tools, models play a major role in producing these forecasts, and are obligatorily and routinely applied in organizational communication. Thus, at first sight, models seem to fulfil their manifest function (calculation). However, as the study will demonstrate, forecasts by themselves appear not to be important to listeners, as the latter are sceptical about exact numerical predictions and consider them to be impossible or meaningless. It is crucial, however, that the model's results signal the scientific respectability and status of the presenters; they are an important part of *impression management* in markets. Models' numbers are compulsory components of presentations (stories) given by today's economists who are obliged to comply with the requirements of the "market show". To support those presentations is an important latent function of modelling in financial markets.

SUMMARY AND CONCLUSION: DO WE HAVE AN ADEQUATE ACCOUNT OF MODEL USE IN FINANCIAL MARKETS?

In this chapter, we set the framework for further discussion of model use in the practice of financial markets. We have worked out the major points of criticism of formal models as calculative devices in finance. In situations of radical uncertainty, in which models can provide only a partial view of what is happening in markets at the very moment of decision, models' manifest function, namely calculation, becomes less relevant for decision-making. Reliance on formal rules in *action-like decision-making* cannot be the only story.

However, this criticism has led us not to deny models, but rather to realize that it is necessary to understand why and how "inadequate" models are so widely used in market practice. We have said that answering this question requires us to pay attention to practices, or cultures, of model use. If models are not the whole story, what else should we take into account? The issues of judgment, stories, fictions and users' goals have come up, but their interplay with models needs to be specified. We have also suggested that cultures of model use vary significantly – depending on how models are combined with judgment, stories and so on – and should be analysed empirically.

Furthermore, there are differences between how models are used to make markets investable in "decision-making" and "decision-selling". On the one hand, models are used by investment managers or traders to bridge radical uncertainty and participate in markets. On the other hand, past or future decisions are staged (performed) to others (e.g. clients, stakeholders) as "good" decisions. They are justified, explained and interpreted by various market intermediaries, and thus allow further decisions to follow, primarily because well-presented decisions generate trust today and invoke action tomorrow. Models matter in *decision-making at large*.

Thus, to investigate the nature of financial models, we clearly should go beyond the concept of the model as a "calculative tool". As the discussion in this chapter demonstrates, financial models are not blindly trusted or thoughtlessly applied as calculation devices: they are combined with judgments, stories and social observations; there is no "over-calculation". At the same time, financial decision-making cannot be reduced to intuition, power games, storytelling and institutional routines in which models play no role ("under-calculation"). The calculative, social and technological aspects of financial markets should be simultaneously analysed as joint elements of practice of model use. While playing various roles in these practices – for example providing the possibility to express investors' views, to justify decisions, to stage non-knowledge as knowledge and so on (these and other roles will be investigated in detail in Chapters 4 and 5) – models enable decisions and create faith in markets, solving the problem of invest-ability. Thus, the focus of our attention should shift to the practices of model use where the controversy between calculation and judgment is resolved *in situ*.

However, the question is: do we have an adequate account of model use? Coping with the nature of formal models has long been the domain of philosophy of science and science and technology studies (STS). After presenting their major concepts in the next chapter, I will claim that they are not entirely adequate for understanding models' roles and use in the practice of financial markets. Whereas science studies focus on models as "epistemic tools" and instruments of knowledge production, models in finance should be understood as *instruments of action-like decision-making*. It is only by analysing them as such and relativizing the overemphasis on knowledge production that we can solve the puzzle of model use (Why are genuinely insufficient models widely applied in markets?). Maybe we should take Ayache's (2010) idea of the *an-epistemological character of financial markets* seriously. Valuation and pricing are not grounded primarily in knowledge. For example, implied volatility is an important parameter for BSM users, not because it gives them true knowledge about market fluctuations but because the users *can do something* with this parameter: they can make decisions, communicate and act upon it. This seems to be the generic position from which practitioners consider the usefulness of models: *what one can do with a model* is crucial, and not how the model provides abstract knowledge or delivers purely calculative results.

Generally, in my view, the social studies of finance – although clearly originated in science studies – should emancipate themselves more strongly from the influences of the latter and make an effort to overcome their "historical" focus on models as *knowledge-production devices*. In the next chapter, I will provide a brief overview of the accounts of modelling in philosophy of science and in STS in order to show where the social studies of finance come from and how far they have advanced in the modelling discussion. Particularly, I will stress that there is a difference between models' nature in science and in the practice of markets: the modelling accounts developed in philosophy and STS are science-centred and not directly applicable to financial modelling. This analysis will form a basis for the next step of this book, namely the presentation and discussion of concrete empirical accounts of model use in financial markets.

3. From representation to performativity and beyond

The phenomenon of modelling the world and its parts has been fascinating thinkers for centuries. However, as models were primarily used by *scientists* for a long time, systematic thinking about what models are and what they can and cannot do became an important field in the philosophy of science. The debate about scientific models as representations and idealizations significantly contributed to the understanding of how science works. In the 1960s–1970s, scholars of the social science and technology studies (STS) tuned to this debate while highlighting the importance of social, political and cultural factors that affect scientific research. More generally, there was a pragmatic, practice-oriented turn in various modelling accounts in philosophy and science studies. The focus shifted from analysing models as a means of representation to understanding them as pragmatic instruments of knowledge production, moving from the question of what models are to the question of what models can do for their users, and how.

The social studies of finance clearly drew on these discussions and readily followed the pragmatic, practice-oriented turn in order to apply their insights to financial models. The pragmatic accounts of modelling (partly reviewed in this chapter) highlighted the "fuzziness" of modelling and model use, the importance of contexts (audience, users, institutions and so on) and the various direct and indirect functions models can fulfil. Scholars of the social studies of finance particularly liked the idea that the importance of models as tools of scientific representation, explanation and calculation should be relativized; and they introduced the idea of performativity: models do not merely represent but also shape reality.

Nevertheless, I argue in this chapter that the social studies of finance remain too strongly anchored in science studies and the sociology of knowledge. Although answers to the question "Why and how are models used *in science*?" certainly provide some useful insights into the nature of model use in general, these insights are not directly applicable to the practice of financial markets. Indeed, financial models are created in universities by academics (although this is not the rule nowadays); but they are applied in the markets, and the market environment is not scientific in nature. Financial market participants are not interested in models that produce formal knowledge, but in instruments that help them to make (economically) successful decisions to make money; in other words, they use models for *non-epistemic goals*. Thus, there are differences between the scientific and market-related *cultures of model use*, and it might be helpful to address these differences more explicitly. Although the social studies of finance has made some steps to recognize these differences (as we will see in this chapter), they have still not managed to radically emancipate themselves from their heritage of science studies.

Indeed, while emerging from science and technology studies, the social studies of finance drew quite a strong analogy between *scientific production of knowledge* and *financial expertise*. Following the STS tradition, financial activities – and financial modelling in particular – were broadly analysed as epistemic practices (Knorr Cetina and Preda 2001; Knorr Cetina and Brügge 2002; Kalthoff 2005, 2011; Wansleben 2013). This analogy was justified because knowledge production seemed to be ubiquitous in the modern markets: in technology (computerization, big data and algorithms); in calculations; and in analyses, forecasts and strategies delivered by various professional groups. Since the 1960s, the processes of the scientization and quantification of finance have made knowledge the prominent feature of financial markets.

Following this observation, the social studies of finance claimed that, to be able to conduct financial transactions, market participants and organizations need coherent and credible knowledge about value, prices, assets and so on: "In every market actors *must know* how to value their products" (Aspers 2009: 111, my emphasis). This knowledge is mobilized in the form of judgment devices (Karpik 2010), "minting work" (Carruthers and Stinchcombe 1999) and, most notably, financial models (MacKenzie 2006; Henriksen 2013). Sometimes financial market participants are explicitly compared to scientists in laboratories who develop tools to acquire and share knowledge (Hägglund 2000). More generally, there has been agreement that, in well-functioning financial markets, "a crowd of *knowledgeable* buyers meets a crowd of *knowledgeable* sellers" (Carruthers and Stinchcombe 1999: 353, my emphases) who are able to calculate prices, categorize products and share beliefs. In this sense, valuation models, for example, contribute to the production of knowledge of the market value of assets and, thus, enable trading and the successful functioning of markets. Thus, knowledge work has been considered the crux for solving the problem of investability.

However, as discussed in the previous chapter, in markets of "nobody knows", knowledge production might not be the relevant focus because it cannot simply eliminate non-knowledge. To guarantee the functioning of markets, other mechanisms must be activated that allow buyers and sellers of assets to decide and interact in such a way that investments become possible. Knowledge production, and thus modelling in its STS understanding, might be just one – secondary – contributing factor. The primary goal of financial market participants is not to acquire knowledge, but to make an uncertain decision-making situation manageable and decidable. Thus, it is dissatisfactory to consider their practices as primarily "epistemic", science-centred practices.

CONTRASTING MODEL USE IN SCIENCE AND IN FINANCIAL MARKETS

Although implicitly or explicitly comparing market participants to academic economists or financial mathematicians seems to be a natural step, the difference between their *cultures of model use* should be clarified. In their recent work, Spears (2014) and MacKenzie and Spears (2014a) started to highlight the major issues in this respect:

> Much of the research on models in STS and philosophy of science addresses issues – for instance, whether modelling is a form of knowledge generation distinct from both theory and experiment (e.g. Dowling, 1999; Galison, 1997) or whether models are the crucial intermediaries between theory and reality (Cartwright, 1983) – that have no exact analogues in financial markets. Experiment – the relationship of which to modelling in science has been an important topic for scholars (e.g. Morgan, 2005) – is much less prominent in finance. Finance does have its experiments (see Muniesa and Callon, 2007), but they are generally looser affairs. Nor does "theory" occupy the prominent place in finance that it does in many sciences; for many financial practitioners, "theory" (option pricing theory, for example) simply is a collection of models, not something separate from models. (MacKenzie and Spears 2014a: 394)

Still, the major difference that necessitates a clear emancipation of the social studies of finance from philosophy of science and STS is the direct involvement of financial model users in the markets, their focus on fateful action-like decision-making and their situational engagement with the world. Knorr Cetina and Preda (2001) started addressing these issues in their concept of a "specular epistemology": market participants (for example analysts, economists and so on) produce specific research, for example, country reports, that is related to market observations and validated by the audience (for example clients). Being part of a reality they describe, financial "observing agents" – in contrast to scientists – are characterized by "reflexive self-inclusion". More specifically, Spears (2014) argued that scientists can live in the "small" world of their idealized models. The process of idealization (discussed below in detail) is a "sophisticated process of caricaturization" (Morgan 2012: 384) in which particular features of the target system are exaggerated and others are excluded in the process of modelling; importantly, the gap between models and reality is inevitable and *acceptable* for academic economists. The latter do not mind working with models that are caricatures of reality or just "credible worlds". The vast distance between their models and reality is not a central issue for them because economists (and scientists in general) are not directly involved in the world their models describe. Also, financial mathematicians are usually not involved in fateful action-like decision-making *themselves*. However, they develop models while taking into consideration the needs of "end users" (that is, deciders); still, models usually have to leave the realm of science and travel from academia to markets or from the "quant" division to the trading floor to become a part of action-like decision-making (Lépinay 2011; Wansleben 2013).

In contrast to scientists, users of financial models are part of financial markets; thus, they need models that guide them through the world and enable them to decide and act. This situation is principally different from modelling in science. Financial market participants understand their decision-making as a *constant process of discovery*, as fatefully *acting sensibly* and searching for productive methods to simultaneously calculate and suspend calculations. I do not think that we are merely talking about "the other kind of knowledge" – the specific "tacit knowledge" or "know-how" – but rather about a process where knowledge is just one component of true actions in the form of immediate involvement with the complex, constantly evolving world.

From this perspective, it becomes increasingly clear that financial practitioners set different priorities than scientists when confronting the "incompatibility principle", as formulated by Zadeh (1973: 28, my emphases):

> [A]s the complexity of a system increases, our ability to make precise and yet significant statements about its behavior diminishes until a threshold is reached beyond which *precision* and *significance (or relevance)* become almost mutually exclusive characteristics [. . .]. It is in this sense that precise quantitative analyses of the behavior of humanistic systems are not likely to have much relevance to the real-world societal, political, economic, and other types of problems.

While "acting sensibly", practitioners are often forced to choose *relevance over precision*. Financial agents are engaged in the "pursuit of relevance" (Graaf 2016); they need significant and relevant (and not necessarily precise) inputs for their decision-making, and models' results can be considered as only one such input. In other words, in complex, self-referential and reflexive financial markets it is not possible for models and other rules to deliver *precise* guidance (according to Derrida; see our discussion on financial decisions above), or they deliver insignificant guidance (according to Zadeh). Models in financial markets cannot truly maintain the status of being scientifically based, calculative guides to decisions; although, as discussed previously, they can participate in *decision-making at large* and help to stage or feign precision (see Chapter 5). As elements of financial, action-like decision-making, models have to be constantly connected to the markets in current situations; they calculate but are also *suspended, confirmed* or *questioned* with regard to their results in those immediate, real-time connections to the market. The empirical studies presented later in Chapter 4 demonstrate that this concept of model use tends to be the common denominator across many fields of financial markets.

But one might ask: what about the core concept of the social studies of finance, the performativity thesis? Does it not explicitly represent the idea that financial models, when they are used in the practice of markets, become a part of the market reality and shape it? In other words, does it not represent an adequate account of model use and effects of this use? Still, as I will show later in this chapter, the performativity concept investigates the movement of theoretical financial models into the realm of markets (that is, from "science"/academia to markets) without directly acknowledging that the context of model application changes from *epistemic* to *non-epistemic* during this move. In performativity debates, the practices of financial modelling are often conceptualized as "evaluation culture" that is clearly related – as MacKenzie and Spears (2014a: 395) acknowledge – to science study's notions such as "local scientific cultures" (Barnes et al. 1996), "experimental cultures" (Rheinberger 1997), "epistemic cultures" (Knorr Cetina 1999), "epistemological cultures" (Keller 2002) and "evidential cultures" (Collins 2004). Callon (2007) is prepared to go only as far as discussing "economists in the wild" – academics who not only develop but also apply or help apply theoretical ideas and models to solve some practical problems. Thus, in the performativity concept, the STS and sociology of knowledge heritage of the social studies of finance come to the fore and are not overcome.

Interestingly, in the recent book on investment chains by Arjaliès et al. mentioned earlier, a group of social study of finance scientists explicitly refers to their intellectual origins in the social studies of science and the necessity to go beyond them:

If you come to the study of market devices as one of us (MacKenzie) does, from the social studies of science, it is easy to focus too much on their cognitive aspects – on the way in which devices produce valuations and other forms of knowledge – and too little on their place in economic relations in a down-to-earth, grubby, monetary sense [. . .] Financial markets, after all, are not simply places in which "facts" are constructed and the objects being traded are valued, but also places in which money passes from hand to hand, especially along investment chains. [. . .] In studying trading's entanglements in the chains of finance we need to "follow the money", not just follow the operation of devices, the construction of facts, and the relations among traders – although all these aspects remain of central importance too. (Arjaliès et al. 2017: 100)

Following this programmatic statement, I will show in Chapters 4 and 5 how models are applied as *not purely epistemic devices* in the practice of *acting sensibly* in financial markets. However, first, in what follows, I would like to present *the state of the art* of modelling research by outlining its way from representative concepts in the philosophy of science to the extended performativity concepts in the social studies of finance and the follow-up discussions of cultures of model use.

MODELS AS REPRESENTATIONS AND IDEALIZATIONS IN SCIENCE

Traditionally, philosophy of science and social studies of science and technology have focused on modelling as a scientific activity. They have been particularly concerned with the question of how models help us acquire scientific knowledge about real-world phenomena (target systems). The focus of inquiry has been set on understanding representation: models represent real-world phenomena and, by doing so, give us knowledge or explain the world. However weak the connection between models and their target systems might be – for example *isomorphism* (van Fraassen 1980), *similarity* (Giere 1988, 2004, 2010) or *partial resemblance* (Mäki 2009) – representation is considered an important requirement for models to qualify as useful: good models should demonstrate some degree of accuracy in representing.

All representational accounts, however, have stumbled over one problem: the link between models and reality is very difficult to trace because there is always a *gap* between the complex, ever-changing world and formal models. In this sense, models are notoriously unrealistic and abstract entities. Particularly a prolonged discussion about the unrealistic assumptions of economic models and the poor correspondence of these models with the target system has been evolving over decades within the philosophy of science.

The two sides of modelling – the *necessity* to represent and the *genuine inability* to represent – eventually pointed to the so-called "puzzle of representation": "How can [models] represent, if they, well, misrepresent?" (Callender and Cohen 2006: 72). Related to this question, the philosopher of economics Julian Reiss discussed "the explanation paradox" of economic models: false models cannot explain. At the very beginning of his argumentation, Reiss (2012: 44) referred to the complexity of the economic systems which models strive – and fail – to explain:

> When phenomena are complex, and economic phenomena are, truth is hard to come by. Accounts given of economic phenomena are usually dramatically simplified and features we know affect a result are represented in a systematically distorted way.

In other words, economic models are predestined to be simplified, undercomplex and thus "false" entities, and it would indeed be a paradox to claim that they can deliver an adequate description or explanation of the real world. According to Reiss (2012: 49), the paradox consists of three statements:

1. Economic models are false.
2. Economic models are nevertheless explanatory.
3. Only true accounts can explain.

Reiss demonstrates that the usual strategy of philosophers of economics has been to relax one of the statements and thus avoid solving the paradox. Indeed, various accounts have been developed that explain how models succeed in bridging the gap between their imperfect (unrealistic, idealized) formal structure and the incomputable complex world, but they remain dissatisfactory. According to Reiss, all major concepts that have tried to establish a link between models and the world – such as *idealization, de-idealization* and *credible worlds* – have not managed to solve the "puzzle of representation" and the "explanation paradox" (Figure 3.1).

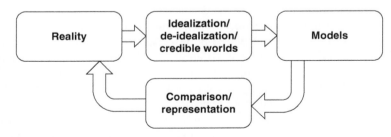

Figure 3.1   Bridging models and reality in science

Idealization accounts argue, for example, that the unrealisticness of (economic) models is not a problem but even an advantage. The concept of
"idealization" (Cartwright 1989, 1999; Hausman 1990; Mäki 1992, 2009)
generally states that "[m]odels are *true in the abstract*: they do not represent
what is true but rather what would be true in the absence of interferences"
(Reiss 2012: 50, my emphasis) – that is, in a stable world. Thus, if we are
happy with the assumption that the economic world does not change and
models successfully deliver an idealized account of this world, then models
help reveal some truth.

For example, according to Nowak (1989), in the process of idealization –
which he calls "reduction" – the set of properties of the investigated phenomenon is divided into the essential properties and those that remain. The
unessential properties are thus reduced and assumed to be non-existent.
Abstraction helps classify the essential properties and minimize the less
important properties so that the latter have no effect on (or are not a cause
of) the phenomena being explained. Thus, we can obtain knowledge if we
successfully reconstruct the essential *causal structure of the phenomenon*
(Nowak 1989) or isolate *tendencies or capacities* (Cartwright 1989; Mäki
1992, 2009). The world which models describe is purposely made "small"
and clearly structured.

However, there are problems with the idea of idealization, especially in
the case of economic models. The major problem is that causes, or capacities, often cannot be isolated cleanly. There is a genuine interdependence of
factors in economics (Alexandrova 2008: 391ff.); the ever-changing character
of the economic world should be taken into account (Boumans and Morgan
2001: 15). Based on an analysis of the work of applied economists (auction
designers), Alexandrova (2008: 391) suggests considering economic systems
as "holistic" in the sense of John Maynard Keynes: in a complex, changing
world, the inclusion or exclusion of additional causes would radically change
the picture and lead to different insights about the target system.

These considerations also undermine the idea of *de-idealization* as a possible solution for the representation paradox. De-idealization is supposed
to bridge the gap between idealized models and the complex reality by
moving in the opposite direction to idealization: the simplified models are
enriched – some flesh is put on the bones. This process can take the form
of both *relaxing the simplifying assumptions* (Hausman 1992; McMullin
1985) and *concretizing* or adding the excluded unessential properties back
(Nowak 1980, 1989; Cartwright 1989). As a result, models are supposed to
become more concrete and more realistic.

However, in light of the discussion above, one can easily see that the
de-idealization approaches confront similar difficulties to the concepts of
idealization (Morgan and Knuuttila 2012). Indeed, if factors in economic

models are interdependent and cannot be properly isolated, the reverse step of de-idealization seems to be an equally questionable solution. Moreover, it remains unclear as to why one should add the neglected factors back when, according to the idealization concepts, exactly this neglect made models useful epistemic tools in the first place. It seems that de-idealization makes models more complex without making them a better representation of a target system.

Confronted by all these dissatisfactory attempts to provide an incontestable description of the representational relationship between models and the world along the idealization/de-idealization axis, some philosophers have claimed that models can be useful even if they *do not* expose any direct connections to the real world. Accounts of models such as *credible worlds* (Sugden 2000), *parables* (Cartwright 2008), *fictions* (Godfrey-Smith 2009; Frigg 2010) and *make-believe* (Toon 2012) suggest that models are not created by observing a target system and stripping out complicating factors, but by imagining a model world that *could be* true. Sugden claims, for example, that to provide insights the model world must be *credible* (convincing, but not necessarily true), thus rejecting the third premise in the "explanation paradox" formulated by Reiss that only true models can explain. Within this framework, it is enough when models establish a link to the *imaginary*, not to the real world. Frigg (2010) and Toon (2012) applied the pretence theory of literary fiction as developed by Walton (1990) to depict models as instruments of imagination that help create a fictional world. Similar to readers of literary novels, modellers and model users know that the fictional world is not true; however, they *pretend* that they are discussing real-world objects when talking about models. Thus, according to Toon, modelling could be compared to being engaged in a children's game of make-believe where some objects (props such as tree trunks) count as something else (for example bears). In this game, everybody is required to imagine that this representation is true (that a tree trunk is a bear) and to behave accordingly. Thus, models are involved in generating *fictional* truth – note that we already referred to this idea when introducing Beckert's *fictional expectations*, and will come back to it in Chapter 5 when discussing financial models in decision-selling.

PRAGMATIC TURN IN SCIENCE STUDIES

But to what extent is it satisfactory for scientists to be confined to the fictional truth or to the abstract truth (which holds only when the world does not change and is simple)? Pages and pages of academic journals and books put forward arguments in favour of idealization, de-idealization and accounts of a credible world without really solving the initial paradox. The debate went on until the question was eventually re-formulated. Instead of asking *how do models represent?*, a different question was posed: *if models cannot represent and explain, why are they used in the first place?* In order to understand the ubiquity of model-based sciences *despite* models' inaccuracy and idealizations, there was a shift from focusing on models as specific formal items (their structure, methods and forms of idealization) to the analysis of *the concrete functioning of models*. It was a shift towards studying *modelling practices*. This discussion is interesting for us in this book because it is clearly analogous to the argumentation in the previous chapter: instead of dwelling on the insufficiency of financial models, I suggested analysing the cultures of their use.

This re-focusing towards a pragmatic, practice-oriented view on models was driven by the works of Morgan and Morrison (1999), Suárez (2004, 2010), Giere (2004, 2010), Frigg (2006), Morgan (2002, 2012), Mäki (2009) and Knuuttila (2005, 2011). For example, Morgan (2012: xvi) stated: "Asking: What qualities do models need to make them useful in a science? and What functions do models play in science? are more fruitful than asking What are models?"

Similarly, van Daalen et al. (2002) contrasted the new *contextual approach to modelling* with the "old" *validational* approach. The validational approach, as described above, focuses on the validity and truthfulness of models as the key issues (for example how well they represent). Within the contextual approach to modelling, however, "computer models are studied as a part of a wider social and political context, and are seen as both products and constituents of that wider context" (van Daalen et al. 2002: 223).

Hence, two issues have become programmatic for this practice-oriented, pragmatic view on modelling: first, *the context of model use matters*; second, *models are not passive; they might have effects*. Indeed, adherents of the pragmatic account claim that we will not be able to fully understand how models give us knowledge or serve us in any other ways if we continue to debate how accurately models correspond to their targets in the real world. Models are built and used to achieve specific results in particular contexts:

> The results orientation of modelling suggests that the starting point is more often than not the output and effects that the models are supposed to produce rather than a mechanism or a tendency to be isolated. Instead of directly trying to represent some selected aspects of a given target system – as has conventionally been assumed – modellers proceed in *a roundabout way*, seeking to build hypothetical systems in the light of the anticipated results or of certain general features of the phenomena they are supposed to exhibit. (Knuuttila 2009: 74, my emphasis)

Within the pragmatic research programme, this "roundabout way" is considered to be the key to understanding how models work. Following up, Knuuttila (2009) suggested paying attention to "model-based practice" as a more appropriate unit of analysis. Elsewhere, Knuuttila (2005, 2011) attacked the understanding of models as purely representational; in her view, models are rather "epistemic artefacts" which are purposely created to reach particular practical goals and are made productive by means of human intervention and manipulation. Thus, Knuuttila argued in favour of a shift from a two-sided relation "model–world" to a three-place relation "model–world–*user*". Not models *per se* but their users are result-oriented; they apply and manipulate models to achieve particular goals. The major point of this pragmatic, practice-oriented approach is the focus on what users do with models, particularly on how they *make models useful* or how they *make them count* (Alexandrova 2008). The definition of models as epistemic tools situates them as material objects that are not "ready-made" but are rather *unfolding elements of situational practices* (Knuuttila and Merz 2009; Knorr Cetina 1997, 2001; Rheinberger 1997).

More broadly, there has been a switch of focus from what happens *within the model* (for example stripping out and adding back the essential and inessential factors) to the way in which *auxiliary external factors* – such as users and their purposes, internal and external audiences, narratives and commentary, judgment and justification of results – *mediate* between models and reality. As a result, a plurality of links between models and reality emerges (Boldyrev and Ushakov 2016) which should be analysed in detail. Thus, while providing a more insightful picture of how models function and relate to reality, the pragmatic accounts of model use explain why models are useful tools despite their generic character, inaccuracy and tenuous connections with the real world.

SCIENCE AS A PRACTICAL ENDEAVOUR

The practice-oriented accounts of scientific modelling are supported by the observation that the goals of science have dramatically changed in the last decades: there has been a move from the pursuit of abstract causal understanding to solving practical problems. "Science is viewed today as an essentially practical endeavor" (Carrier and Nordmann 2011: 1) and should be considered in the context of its application. We observe a shift from "epistemic or truth-oriented research" to "application-dominated" research (Carrier 2011: 12). From this perspective, models are no longer understood as instruments of purely scientific inquiry; rather, they have become widely applied in various pragmatic fields for a range of *non-epistemic purposes*.

As a result, theoretical and empirical work on the application of models in politics and management has proliferated (Jasanoff 1990, 2005; Shackley 1998; Den Butter and Morgan 2000; van Egmond and Zeiss 2010), particularly in the fields of economic policy (Evans 1999; van den Bogaard 1999), climate policy (Shackley et al. 1999; Shackley 2001; Petersen 2008; Gramelsberger 2011; Gramelsberger and Feichter 2011, Frigg et al. 2013), flood risk management (Lane et al. 2011), health-care policy (Mansnerus 2015), energy scenarios (Dieckhoff 2015) and in financial markets (MacKenzie 2006). These recent studies emphasize that the traditional separation of science from the realm of pragmatic model applications by practitioners has relaxed. Many models are no longer created in the "ivory tower" of science and then transferred as fixed objects to practical fields in which they are mechanically applied. Rather, recent research on modelling demonstrates that, in many cases, the "scientific life" of models cannot be separated from their *working life* (Mansnerus 2015) which is external to science. Scientific and practical interests are often intertwined. In joint projects, scientists might be guided by the possibilities of directly applying models, whereas practitioners might be looking for a scientific rationale for their activities. This means that non-scientific activities – through their involvement in the creation and application of models – become grounded in scientific modelling. As a result, models influence political and economic *decisions* – and become connected to reality through this link. The move towards understanding science as a *practical endeavour* is not about a simple extension of science. Rather, we refer to the *politics of knowledge* (Landström and Whatmore 2014), to the true entwinement of models and various fields of practice: models are embedded in societally relevant decision-making processes and have the potential to change the world.

This blurring of borders between science and practice seems to have particular relevance for understanding modelling in the fields of economics and finance. According to Colander (2013), the pragmatic contexts in which economists work (and build their models) are not purely scientific but rather *engineering contexts* (similarly, Boldyrev and Ushakov 2016 put forward the concept of macroeconomic modelling as *social engineering*). Colander refers to Koen's (2003: 58) definition of the "engineering method" as "the strategy for causing the best change in a poorly understood or uncertain situation within the available resources". Here, it is not the abstract understanding and explanation that are paramount, but the usage of knowledge for decision-making and solving practical problems. Thus, scientific and pragmatic considerations blend; everything that can lead to a solution is used. Evidence and arguments of all kinds (scientific and non-scientific) are on the radar screen; they are oriented towards problem-solving and involve – alongside modelling – intuition, experience, historical knowledge and guesstimates (judgment) as well as considerations of time constraints and organizational aspects. Obviously, within this understanding of economic science, models are presented as just one resource for problem-solving (among many others).

FINANCE AS AN APPLICATION-DOMINATED RESEARCH FIELD

The social studies of finance were born out of this pragmatic research on modelling. Finance has been traditionally characterized by the striking proximity and entwinement of theory and practice (Bernstein 1992). Financial models have constantly travelled between, or simultaneously "inhabited", two worlds: academia and the financial industry. Indeed, some models – such as the Black-Scholes model (BSM) were created at universities and then adapted in the practice of markets. However, today, it is not unknown for models to be developed by practitioners. This trend became especially distinctive in the last decade of the twentieth century, when many academics trained in mathematics and physics were hired by investment banks as "quants" or financial engineers (Triana 2009, 2011; Patterson 2010). David X. Li is a prominent example of a person who moved from academia to the Canadian Imperial Bank of Commerce to model credit derivatives, and developed the notorious Gaussian copula formula (Salmon 2009; MacKenzie and Spears 2014a). Modern finance today represents a field where the borders between science and practice are nearly non-existent.

Similar to "economists in the wild" (Callon 2007), whose activities are no longer restricted to the academic "ivory tower", financial scientists in universities and business schools frequently come into contact with practitioners and markets. In my interviews, financial mathematicians constantly revealed parallel thinking in terms of two worlds. For example, a university finance professor in Zurich answered the question "What is a financial instrument?" as follows: "I have two explanations: it is a mathematical object and, on the other hand, it is a product that exists or might exist in the markets."

The research process in theoretical finance is described by informants as a "constant switch between two worlds", which often begins by considering a practical problem which is then translated into mathematical language to enable the search for a solution and then retranslated back into the language of the markets to address needs at the level of application. While preparing the presentation of their results, financial mathematicians have a "double standard" in their head: they know that they must communicate their findings not only to their peers but also to practitioners. Thus, the manner of explaining and presenting the results depends on the audience. Whereas academic colleagues are interested in the emergence and background of a created formula, practitioners want to know how it functions and *what can be done with it*. Financial scientists take the necessity of the latter pragmatic argumentation very seriously. In fact, it seems to constitute most of their everyday life in academia. The bottom line is that even in universities financial modelling is "a constantly revolving process" between science and practice. A financial mathematician from Munich described this process characteristically:

> It is not just about a theoretical solution; I have to demonstrate that it is also a real solution for practice. It is not about developing some formula and that's it; I have to ask instead: does anybody also need the formula?

This entwinement of theory and practice is enhanced by the constant "travelling" of both models and people between financial science and the investment industry. For example, PhD candidates often come from investment companies, and some of them stay at university and pursue academic careers. There is also movement in the opposite direction. Often, not only biographical interconnections but also institutional interdependencies can be observed between financial science and practice. One financial mathematician reported that he was on the supervisory board of a financial company that he founded – an example that is not an exception. There is also a lively exchange of ideas through channels such as journals and conferences.

All of these observations fit nicely into the concept of "application-dominated research" and, at first glance, suggest that finance can be fruitfully approached with the pragmatic concepts of modelling developed within the philosophy of science and social studies of science and technology. Thus, it is only natural that these accounts often serve as a point of departure for social studies of finance scholars. The latter analyse financial markets as *epistemic practices* where a specific kind of knowledge (for example valuation of financial securities) is produced. The social studies of finance are particularly inspired by the oeuvre of Michel Callon (1998, 2007) and Donald MacKenzie (2003, 2006), who applied the ideas of the social studies of science and technology to the fields of economics and finance. The most popular "transfer" is *the idea of performativity*.

SOCIAL STUDIES OF FINANCE: THE PERFORMATIVITY TURN

According to the performativity concept, financial knowledge is understood as genuinely *performative knowledge*. The "performative turn" is about further overcoming the "representational idiom" (Pickering 1995). Famously – and tellingly – the idea of performativity originated in a paper by Callon (1998) in which he stated that economics (as science!) performs the economy. This idea was then applied to financial markets by MacKenzie and Millo (2003). In their paper "Constructing the market, performing theory", they replaced economic science with the Black-Scholes model (as a scientific tool) and showed how this model did not merely represent, describe or explain market reality, but also actively shaped it. According to the performativity concept, the relationship between knowledge devices such as models, on the one hand, and economic reality, on the other hand, is not understood as passive (representation), but as active (Figure 3.2). Financial models *influence* or even *constitute* what is represented:

> [T]he tables have been turned, in the sense that from being *unrealistic*, theoretical models have been characterized as being *too realistic* – not in the sense of an accurate representation, but in the sense of generating the phenomena they describe. (Preda 2009: 119, my emphases)

Figure 3.2   Performativity

The question as to how economic theories and models perform and shape economic reality has come under particular scrutiny in the social studies of finance research. Although there are many different performativity concepts (see Muniesa 2014 and Boldyrev and Svetlova 2016 for an overview), it has become nearly canonical to refer to the strong form of models' influence on financial markets as "Barnesian performativity".

Introducing the term "Barnesian performativity", MacKenzie (2001) refers to Barnes's essay on bootstrapped induction where the latter uses the term "performativity" to describe instances in which an utterance "does something to a particular rather than describing it" (Barnes 1983: 526). Barnes is concerned with the differences between speech acts that categorize and refer to objects in the world (N-type in his parlance) and speech acts that, as described in the quotation above, change a given particular by virtue of (the inherent meaning of) the speech act itself (S-type). MacKenzie (2001) states that "finance is a domain of S-terms" as opposed to N-terms, and that financial models are an example of such self-referential and self-validating S-type utterances. Subsequently, MacKenzie (2007: 66) formulates:

> I use the term "Barnesian" simply as a label for a particular subset of the performativity of economics: the subset in which an aspect of economics is used in economic practice; its use has effects, and amongst those effects is to alter economic processes so as to make them more like their depiction by economics.

MacKenzie's prime example is the Black-Scholes option pricing model which (at least in the period after its introduction to the market) produced the effect that the real market prices came to approximate the prices calculated by the model (MacKenzie 2003, 2006). This happened because more and more market participants *used* the Black-Scholes model as a basis for their market positions. It means they started to integrate model calculations into their investment decisions and actions. Model calculations enter the market through participants' decision-making and, in this way, affect market reality. When a market participant uses a model to calculate an option price and acts as if this price were true, models can have effects. Thus, the influence of a model is strongly mediated by its use.

MacKenzie and Millo (2003: 123) describe how the BSM became "a guide to trading": initial doubts and concerns about the model were overcome so that traders started to believe in the model and use it to calculate option prices. As a result, the model's "use brought about a state of affairs of which it was a good empirical description" (MacKenzie 2007: 66).

There are also milder forms of models' effects that relate to *generic and effective performativity*, situations in which models do not bring a new world into being, but only influence economic events (MacKenzie 2007: 55).

The performativity concept has been celebrated as a significant *tour de force* in modelling research. While considering the link between models and reality, it continues to develop the pragmatic STS ideas discussed above: scientific theories and models cannot be analysed separately from the concrete practices in which they are embedded and applied. Economic knowledge is not the production of the mind that existed prior to its sociotechnical – often material – embodiment. Rather, many intermediaries and hybrids are at work in the struggles of "performation", which Callon (2007) understands as the co-evolution of linguistic statements, theories, models and their worlds. It is a complex interaction between human and non-human technical entities which makes it possible for economists to act as social engineers and for economics to perform itself. MacKenzie's research on the Black-Scholes formula illustrates exactly this.

CRITIQUES OF THE PERFORMATIVITY CONCEPT

Although the performativity concept has become a part of the DNA of the social studies of economic phenomena, it has simultaneously been an object of severe critique. This critique is important because it points to possible further directions for our thinking about models and the world.

First of all, it seems that performativity studies and representational accounts suffer from a similar problem: they focus too strongly on identifying an unambiguous one-way "theory to reality" link, and this endeavour often fails. All efforts to find another example of Barnesian performativity which is as straightforward as the Black-Scholes model have remained unsuccessful (see MacKenzie et al. 2007 for an overview). Furthermore, critics increasingly doubt the "automatic" character of the relationship between models and their worlds. Zuckerman (2012: 230), for example, claims that "past work on the performativity of economic theories does not venture an explanation for why a widely adopted theory may be performative in one case but not others".

Indeed, there are a lot of examples of cases where models are not believed or not used and still have severe effects on markets; or, even when used, they do not have any direct influence on market events. In other words, models vary in their ability to affect markets – and this variety should be accounted for.

Callon made an effort to remedy these theoretical defects. His idea of "performation" emphasises the *processual nature of performativity*. There is no mechanical link between theory and reality, no "jump" into a new reality when models get to work; rather, there is a long sequence of trials, rehearsals, failures and adjustments which is characteristic of models' "struggle for life" (Callon 2007: 332). What really matters for Callon and his followers is the back-and-forth, uncertain and staggering movement of performation, for which nothing can be guaranteed. MacKenzie (2007: 70) also does not subscribe to the "automatism" of the link, and concentrates on the "conditions of felicity" of the BSM model as conditions for Barnesian performativity in general: a model must have sufficient authority to warrant users' beliefs and possess sufficient cognitive simplicity so that it can be used easily and, above all, quickly, and be publicly available and supported by an appropriate technology so that a sufficient number of market participants can use it.

The processual concept of performativity and the focus on conditions of felicity support the critics' idea that the relation between the model and the world is a constantly renewed process of performation, particularly when we are concerned with "economics at large": Conditions of felicity outside science (when models leave the world of academia) principally differ from success conditions in purely scientific ("confined") contexts:

> The Black and Scholes formula or the theory of general equilibrium, confined to the academic world, can find their appropriate milieu, their felicity conditions. But when they move over to the Chicago derivatives exchange or to ministries responsible for economic planning, they may encounter or even trigger resistance, for their felicity conditions are not filled. The socio-technical arrangements that would have enabled them to survive in these strange worlds are not present or prove to be difficult to put in place. We can agree to call performation the process whereby socio-technical arrangements are enacted, to constitute so many ecological niches within and between which statements and models circulate and are true or at least enjoy a high degree of verisimilitude. (Callon 2007: 330)

Thus, Callon continues, what we find in the markets is *a wide spectrum of effects ranging from the perfect adaptation* to the *complete failure of models*. In other words, models are not always and automatically performative. Their effect and social conditions of felicity seem to depend on the practices of their use.

Here is an example from the literature: Millo and MacKenzie describe how the communicative and organizational effects of risk models in finance were created in the process of model use. Rooted in the Black-Scholes model, financial risk models have allowed for clearer communication between traders and trading organizations. They have provided the basis for effective technology in option markets, enabled the new practice of option trading ("spreading") and reduced the complexity of financial data. Investigating models' biographies, Millo and MacKenzie (2009: 651) demonstrate how an interesting interpretive process has evolved:

> The actors [practitioners] analyzed the practices in which the model took part, "distilled" from them the features that could be useful in their realm of practice and employed those features in the new set of applications.

The practices of model use also determine why, in financial markets, we frequently encounter the situations that Mackenzie (2006) labels as "counter-performative", namely situations in which the use of a model helps create the opposite of what the model describes. Zuckerman (2012) drew attention to an example of this phenomenon, namely to how the wide adoption of efficient market theory undermines its validity. Recently, MacKenzie and Spears (2014b: 436) also analysed the application of the

Black-Scholes model and the Gaussian copula formula in the practice of financial markets, showing that "there are multiple mechanisms of counter-performativity or, in other words, multiple ways in which the practical use of a model can undermine its empirical adequacy".

The examples of various ways of performation as well as of counter-performativity highlight that formal models may succeed, but can also fail (Esposito 2013) or become negligible due to their institutional environment and bureaucratic constraints (Svetlova 2012a; Henriksen 2013; Brisset 2014) as well as due to the irreducible importance of marketing and decision-selling (McFall 2011) or political considerations (van Egmond and Zeiss 2010; Hirschman and Popp Berman 2014).

Following up on those ideas, the most recent performativity research highlighted the understanding of performativity as a *performative practice* (for example Cabantous and Gond 2011) and the necessity to empirically investigate the mutual links between "models" and "economic reality" which cannot be understood as a mechanical, one-way influence. We should pay attention to "a flow of activity" (Cabantous and Gond 2011: 577) of which models are a part. There is no separate entity called "economics", or economic knowledge, that produces "effects" and exerts "influence". The understanding of performativity as performative practice rejects this simple unilateral causation.

SUMMARY AND CONCLUSION: POSSIBLE EXTENSIONS OF MODELLING ACCOUNTS

The pragmatic modelling accounts in the philosophy of science and STS, including the performativity concept, have been informative for my study. I have readily followed their suggestions not to focus on model "insufficiencies", but to analyse how models are used in various practices and, thus, how they are "made to count". The fact that those practices are multivariate and rich is also a very important insight: models are made useful when they are applied by their users, often in front of audiences in various institutional settings. Their success is not guaranteed, and the connection between models and reality is not a one-way street.

At the same time, I would like to explicitly stress that financial models are applied in the non-epistemic context of markets. They are elements of *specific professional practices* that principally *differ from scientific modelling*. The sliding and smooth "translation" of "economic theory" into "financial models" as epistemic devices by Callon (1998) might be more troublesome than it seems. In financial markets, not scientists but investment professionals of different kinds are at work – and, for them, financial

models are not "knowledge devices" but practical decision-making instruments. This is the step that the social studies of finance have made only
half-heartedly so far, although these insights are implied in some empirical
studies produced in the field.

In financial markets, the ultimate goal is not knowledge production
(explanation, understanding or representation) but successful decision-
making (which finally leads to making money). Hence, questions as to
how models structure decisions and actions as well as to which effects they
have on financial practice through this very "channel" of decision-making
are urgent. *Action-like decision-making* provides the connection between
markets ("reality") and models – although I do not really like the word
"connection" here. Models, their users, markets and audiences are a part
of action-like decision-making determines whether models are successful
(that is, widely used) and become performative or not. It is not so much
about the conditions of felicity of somehow "external" models, but more
about "acting sensibly" *with* models in various ways. In this book, I am
particularly interested in identifying and describing the various styles of
action-like decision-making.

Re-focusing on *the practices of model use* in decision-making might help
overcome the overemphasis on knowledge in performativity studies and
in the social studies of finance more generally. Indeed, we might become
less preoccupied with the theoretical and empirical search for a strong
link between knowledge objects, on the one hand, and markets, on the
other hand, and shift our focus to a detailed analysis of *cultures of model
use* in financial decision-making. Those cultures are not science-centred
but decision-centred. Investigations in this direction have already started.
For example, while observing that the efficient market hypothesis (EMH)
undermines its own validity, Zuckerman (2012) does not explain this phenomenon by simply analysing the EMH as a piece of scientific knowledge;
rather, he stresses that the extent to which the EMH is effectively rejected
or accepted in the decision-making of real investors in the real time of
"fuzzy" financial markets is of importance. It is not about what investors
think or know of prices and "fair" value, but about how they decide and
act upon their decisions. There are interesting empirical accounts that stem
from the social studies of finance and illustrate this point. I present some
of them in the next chapter.

Importantly, a detailed analysis of action-like decision-making might
more generally relativize the ultimate importance of models for what
happens in financial markets. The performativity thesis implies to some
extent that models unambiguously determine how model users make
decisions: if they believe in the model calculations, they inevitably follow
the calculations in a uniform way. Financial models are understood as an

inflexible structure from which all model users obtain similar results. For example, if each trader calculates the option price for a given contract according to the Black-Scholes model, all the market prices would simply be the Black-Scholes model's prices. In this way, the model produces the world that it describes. However, the analysis of cultures of model use in the next chapter shows that this rather radical view is often not justified. No doubt models play an important role in modern financial markets; however, this role is often not straightforward. This point was already touched upon in our discussion of the use of the Black-Scholes model in Chapter 2: instead of calculating the option prices "forwards" and getting uniform results, traders use "implied volatility" to incorporate their views on markets, and thus might get deviating prices. More generally, what we rather observe in the markets is a complex interplay between models, model users and the markets. There are various styles of model use that do not allow for the production of similar results even in one and the same market segment. Financial models are not the ultimate guides for decisions; they are used very tentatively and creatively.

Furthermore, emphasis on decision-making brings issues of *non-knowledge* to the fore: decision-makers in financial markets are constantly exposed to uncertainty that cannot be perfectly "framed" by means of models as calculative instruments (see Chapter 2). Thus, the central issue in pragmatic market contexts is not how knowledge is produced, but how *non-knowledge is coped with*.

Finally, re-focusing on models as practical decision-making instruments will happen in line with the turn towards the above-discussed "performative practices", supporting what Power (2016: 3) called "a more general 'turn to work' in management and organization studies". Power talks about "riskwork"; similarly, we could analyse "modelwork" as situated, concrete efforts to make models count in the pragmatic contexts of financial markets. Analyses of this kind will be presented and supported by rich empirical material in the next chapter.

4. Financial models in decision-making

In this chapter, I will discuss a number of empirical cases to illustrate *modelwork*, that is, how models matter for financial action-like decision-making – for example, for buying or selling securities, taking a trading position or stepping into the market with a forecast. I will specifically show how market professionals translate undecidable situations into decidable ones and solve the problem of investability for themselves.

The case studies in this chapter will clearly highlight that there is no separation between calculation, judgment, decision-makers and markets (Figure 4.1); rather, there are constant shifts of attention from models to markets and back again, as well as the constant formation of judgments and their application, of which models and markets are a subject but also a part. It is about judgment *with* models and *about* models, *with* markets (what do others think?) and *about* markets (what is my view?). Note that, although Figure 4.1 – for the sake of illustration – depicts markets, models and users as separate entities, they cannot be thought of and treated as such.

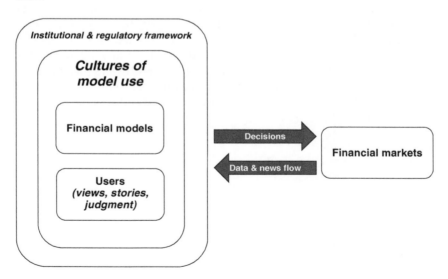

Figure 4.1   Models in action-like decision-making: an overview

The case studies in this chapter convincingly demonstrate that there is no "outside" position from which models influence market reality; models, their users and markets are united and interconnected in action-like decision-making. In the performative sense, while used in various modi, models are a part of the market; they provoke markets (Muniesa 2014) and create them as their own reference. There is a constant creative back and forth between markets, models and users within *cultures of model use*. The case studies refer to making models count in the processes of "qual-culation" and "effecting" calculations. The abstract concept of cultures of model use will be filled with life in this chapter.

In particular, I aim to identify and present various styles of "doing and undoing calculations" in different segments of financial markets. The presented empirical cases demonstrate that cultures of model use, or "calculative cultures" (Mikes 2009, 2011), differ from each other. The differences primarily refer to how models function as "qualculative" devices and reflect the degree of users' trust in models and the attitudes of users towards models' benefits and limitations. Thus, cultures of model use co-determine the extent to which a model influences final decision-making, ranging from cases in which models *determine the action* to situations in which models *are ignored*. Cultures of model use represent *gradations* within the range of *over-* and *under-calculative views*.

For instance, Power (2003, 2007) and Mikes (2009) demonstrate that, in the field of risk management, both examples of "model enthusiasm" (or "calculative idealism") and of "model scepticism" ("calculative prag-matism") can be frequently found. While risk managers with an "enthu-siastic" quantitative culture express unrestricted belief in formal models' ability to measure risk and apply formal models rigorously as guides for decisions, representatives of the same professional group in another bank use models very tentatively. Power (2003: 14) refers to "calculative pragma-tism" in this context – the "logic of practice" according to which adherents use numbers but do not expect them "to represent reality". Sceptics (or pragmatists) are convinced that particular tools, such as the Value at Risk (VaR) model, do not accurately represent underlying risk exposure and its dynamics because some risks are not quantifiable, and thus not explicable by probabilistic modelling. As a result, sceptical decision-makers "treat the model output as the starting point for further inquiries and the exercise of judgment" (Mikes 2011: 33). The models' results are compared with man-agers' expectations which feed into judgment; judgment is used to adjust the model outcomes.

This flexibility in the process of model use allows sceptical risk managers to account for non-quantifiable risks, to develop a holistic risk manage-ment approach and, thanks to this broader picture, to remain powerful in strategic decision-making within organizations. Interestingly, Mikes demonstrates that their *enthusiastic* colleagues – due to their focus on numbers – restrict themselves to the discussion of quantifiable risks and have no agenda-setting (strategic) power in the bank. Mikes's study is based on two real empirical cases, and illustrates that opposing "calculative cultures" may co-exist within the same field (for example risk management in banks).

This brief discussion illustrates that, indeed, in the practice of markets, models cannot be "the whole story". The empirical investigations presented below show that we never find instances of model use in isolation of human judgment, market observations and social considerations, which feed back into the model, help to adjust it or allow users to ignore it. In the next sub-section, I will discuss these issues in particular, using an example of active portfolio management. Afterwards, I will move on to the classification and detailed presentation of various cultures of model use.

AN EXAMPLE OF ACTIVE PORTFOLIO MANAGEMENT: HYBRID STYLES AND QUANTAMENTAL INVESTING

In the field of active portfolio management, one can observe an everlasting debate about the best way of combining quantitative and qualitative approaches and, as a result, diverse styles of investment-making. At the poles, we find the *fundamental* and the *purely quantitative* investment philosophies. Fundamental investing is based on qualitative processing of economic data (companies' financial statements, market position, quality of management and so forth). In this field, naturally, an ideal-type investment professional believes that exercising human judgment is the best way of identifying promising investment opportunities: "The fundamental investor is a journalist focused on crafting a unique story of a company's future prospects and predicting the potential for gain in the company stock" (Bukowski 2012: 92).

Quantitative portfolio managers, on the other hand, draw on mathematical and statistical procedures to find potentially outperforming securities. Based on observations of the past, they try to identify reliable stock-picking criteria ("factors") – for example, low multiples (for instance P/E, book/sales), profitability numbers and so forth: "The quantitative investor is a scientist, broadly focused, relying on historical information to differentiate across all companies, using statistical techniques to create a stock selection model" (Bukowski 2012: 92).

The co-existence of these two approaches mirrors the eternal "struggle against subjectivity" (Porter 1995: ix) in finance. The quantitative style is claimed to be objective and "unemotional" as it is based on formal models and, thus, better than the "soft" judgment-based fundamental methodology. These considerations were behind BlackRock's announcement that it was going to fire active human portfolio managers and replace them with machines.

However, in the practice of modern markets, we seldom encounter cases in which quantitative strategies are blindly applied without any human interaction or, conversely, cases in which a purely fundamental investment style dominates completely. Rather, *hybrid approaches* are used. Two surveys by Fabozzi et al. (2007, 2008) suggest that the asset management industry is still *in search of the optimal balance between judgment and models*. Describing the recent increase of interest in computer-driven hedge funds, and of money flowing into them (we have observed the doubling of their assets between 2009 and today), the *Financial Times* clearly highlights: "Even this understates the interest, as many traditional hedge funds and big mutual fund managers are all trying to blend more quantitative techniques with their traditional approaches" (Wigglesworth 2017b: 9).

The trend today – "quantamental investing" (Bukowski 2012; Lapierre 2015) as a combination of quantitative and fundamental analyses (the financial industry's equivalent to Cochoy's qualculation) – is the talk of the town. In the quantamental approach, past-based, repeatable processes of stock selection are combined with qualitative judgment which brings the future prospects of companies and economies into the process.

In the practice of asset management, the integration of computer-based and judgment-based approaches can take different forms. On the one hand, *fundamental managers* apply formal methods (screening, scorings, rankings and so on) in their investment processes in order to filter out promising, attention-deserving assets. On the other hand, *quantitative managers* cannot completely ignore or exclude human judgment from their decision-making due to the fallibility and blind spots of formal models already discussed in this book. "Quants" are aware that human asset managers are able to provide knowledge that cannot be delivered by models or cannot be directly incorporated into them – and this knowledge should be accounted for in order to connect models to the world.

First, the very process of model creation cannot be absolutely formalized: one needs *an idea* of which factors to test or which parameters to use as a filter for screening or a basis for an investment strategy; in other words, human creativity is required in the process of "crafting finance out of math" (Lépinay 2011). Some investment companies (for example Barclays Global Investors) have moved away from pure "data mining" and start by generating ideas for investing (not necessarily based on computing) and then test them (Economist 2008).

Second, during the process of crafting models, experts individually determine which data sources they utilize and which data they collect and process; Bloomberg reports that one of the most famous contemporary quant funds, Renaissance Technologies:

> spent heavily on collecting, sorting, and cleaning data, as well as making it accessible to its researchers. "If you have an idea, you want to test it quickly. And if you have to get the data in shape, it slows down the process tremendously," says Patterson [who spent ten years with Renaissance Technologies until 2001]. (Burton 2016)

The process of "getting data in shape" and creating clean data sets cannot be mechanized completely. Third, modellers make "human" decisions about input parameters – that is, about which factors to include in a strategy or a model, and how and what to do about the non-quantifiable factors (recall our discussion on the discounted cash flow/DCF model in Chapter 2). In other words, there is "fundamental" leeway in the process of "feeding" models. Finally (and this aspect has been particularly stressed in the book so far), flexibility often exists during the implementation of model-based strategies: the ways of connecting models to markets are not determined by formal rules; here, we are talking about heuristics, or cultures, of model use that might vary among individual market participants, investors' teams or organizations.

Often, we observe *a degree of discretion* with regard to deviation from model calculations and the application of judgment to the formal quantitative processes. Arjaliès et al. (2017: Ch. 4) describe how fundamental portfolio managers use input from their quantitative colleagues. This input can take the form of general research reports (which the fundamental managers can just delete from their mailbox) or reports on concrete, specific signals (which might guide but not determine the final decisions of portfolio managers due to so-called *advisory overlay*). Even in the case of purely quantitative funds, fundamental colleagues often have their say (they are asked to check the plausibility of data or weightings in the quantitative portfolios). Generally, there are still many elements and instances of human intervention and even human dominance in quantitative portfolio management. These interventions can be described as *model oversight* and *model overlay* (cf. Fabozzi et al. 2008).

Some quant managers ask their fundamental colleagues to perform a plausibility check on data when a big trade is planned or when an obvious data outlier is at hand – for instance, equity with an expected return of 100 per cent. In this case, we are talking about model oversight, that is, deviation of about 5–10 per cent from models or strategies is allowed. Model oversight is a control function exercised by humans to make sure that models do not make serious mistakes. Fundamental managers follow the market more closely and help their quantitative colleagues answer an important question: "Am I not aware of something?" They establish a connection between models, markets and quantitative model users. The extreme form of deviation is qualitative overlay, where fundamental managers are actively involved in constant checking of data and even making final investment decisions.

More generally, as one of my interviewees from a department of asset allocation suggested, fundamental input can come into quantitative models in three ways: first, in the process of pondering about the factors that might be included in the model; second, while "dialling up and down" various factors, which means that if the situation changes, some factors are given more (or less) weight in the model. Finally, the structure of the model is fixed but model users decide whether they accept the model's recommendations or not (that is, if they follow them in their decision-making). He called the first two cases *the dynamic approach to model use* and the third case *overlay*.

Thus, the variety of leak-ways in the process of acting *upon* models and *with* models allows asset managers – and financial market participants in general – to "sneak" their observations and interpretations of markets into the investment process. Although some quant funds claim that they fully rely on models, still (in one form or another) intuition, judgment, storytelling and metaphors principally supplement formal methods, either in the process of model creation or in the process of model application. In the industry, this situation is often considered to be inevitable. For example, the *Financial Times* quoted Michael Bernard, director of institutional clients at fund house Unigestion:

> Being a believer in the bright future of quantitative investment, he however is convinced "that there still needs to be a significant qualitative element". He said: "Computers can deal with a lot of data and have a very non-emotional view of the market, but a computer doesn't see things that you and I can see like the mood of [ECB president] Mario Draghi." (Fraser 2015: 3)

Some kind of qualitative connection to the reality of markets seems always to exist in practice. In a discussion of the application of model-driven investment strategies in markets, Triana (2009: 77) highlighted the importance of hybrid methods and fundamental overlay. He quoted a practitioner who said: "I expect that we will continue to use a fundamental overlay; it provides a common sense check. You cannot ignore real-world situations."

As a result, what we find in financial markets are investment professionals who – while being both a part of markets and simultaneously at their mercy – are searching for the most efficient ways of connecting models to the market by applying judgment, telling stories and so on. In the following sections, I will present concrete empirical examples from my research as well as from the social studies of finance literature to illustrate those connections. I will empirically identify and discuss *three general modes* of "bringing together" models, markets and users in the process of action-like decision-making (see Figure 4.1): "qualitative overlay", "backing out/ implied modelling" and "models as opinion proclaimers". In the case of qualitative overlay, the model results are compared with a pre-formed judgment and serve as an anchor but not as an ultimate guide for decisions. In the case of backing out and implied modelling, models are used to observe the markets and to figure out the mistakes in model users' estimates in order to correct mistakes or to identify new investment opportunities. Finally, models can be applied to express market participants' pre-formed opinions about the market or a security.

In all three cases, financial models are connected to the multifaceted reality of markets; their calculations might be noticed at one moment and suspended the next. These to-and-fro patterns of users' shifts between markets, models and judgments effectively illustrate the initial argument of this book: that models do not get the chance to become the ultimate guides to actions in the practice of financial decision-making, and, more often than not, play a rather subordinate role. Now, I will show in detail how their influence is mediated by cultures of model use.

QUALITATIVE OVERLAY

In the case of qualitative overlay (Figure 4.2), model calculations are *supplemented* by judgments that market participants form in the process of market observation, information processing, and communication with peers, brokers and analysts, while reading the financial press and so forth. Models' results are constantly compared to what model users observe in their complex reality. In this sense, models are subject to a *plausibility check*. Judgments take the form of a "holistic" view of the market and are considered to be more important than the models' calculations. Qualitative overlay refers to the method of model use according to which financial models are treated as an additional source of information; at the same time, they help to *structure* the decision-making process and *serve as anchors* for discussions and decisions. The qualitative judgment of model users has a priority in decision-making and is paramount for the final decision.

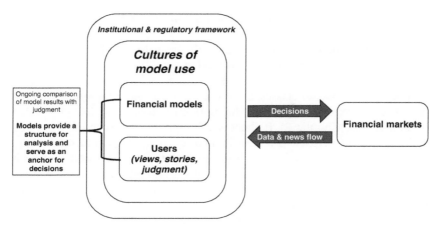

Figure 4.2   Models in action-like decision-making: qualitative overlay

The empirical examples of qualitative overlay I will discuss below are:

1. The application of the discounted cash flow (DCF) model in the wealth department of a big Swiss bank (based on Svetlova 2012a, 2013). In Chapter 2, we discussed in detail this model's insufficiencies; now we turn to understanding how the model is used and made to count in the practice of markets *despite* its problems.
2. The use of econometric forecasting models by foreign exchange analysts in a German bank (Wansleben 2013, 2014). Here, we will observe how this professional group (which is openly sceptical about model results) nevertheless integrates formal predictions into their idiosyncratic, qualitative "views" on markets; importantly, those "views" gain priority for the final decisions and actions.
3. The simulations of exotic equity derivatives in a French bank (Lépinay 2011). Lépinay describes how the models for valuating a capital guarantee product (CGP), a type of structured product, are frequently overlaid in the very process of model application by traders. He demonstrates how the way in which work is organized on the trading floor allows traders to connect formal models to market reality by running simulations and forming and applying judgment. Lépinay's study also perfectly illustrates how the attention of traders is permanently switched between models and markets, highlighting the temporal aspect of (un)doing calculations.

The Plausibility Check of Models: The Case of the DCF

This case study demonstrates how a particular valuation model – the discounted cash flow model (DCF) – is used in a wealth management department of a big Swiss investment bank to make decisions on the allocation of assets between asset classes. DCF is a classical valuation model which – from the theoretical perspective – helps identify (calculate) the "fair" value of an asset (see Chapter 2). If there is a discrepancy between the fair value and the current price, it is a case of market inefficiency and mispricing. As already discussed, active portfolio managers are convinced that such inefficiencies disappear with time and that the market price moves towards the fair value. There is a belief that if you know the fair value, you also know how the market price will develop.

In Chapter 2, we checked whether the DCF is efficient and reliable in calculating fair value. We identified a number of difficulties that asset managers experience when determining the inputs of the DCF model. Some factors cannot be accurately calculated; some are vague or non-quantifiable and thus cannot be considered by the model; and some are based on historical data, although they are related to the future. However, neglecting these factors can lead to an inaccurate calculation of the fair value, and thus to incorrect investment decisions.

The model users within the portfolio management department where I conducted my observations and interviews are fully aware of the inaccuracy of the inputs and of other *major handicaps of the DCF model* (for example the strong sensitivity of the estimated value of a company to small changes of input parameters). Nevertheless, the DCF model is one of *the most popular tools* in the field of fundamental security analysis and tactical asset allocation.

There is a particular culture of model use that allows for this popularity. When investors decide to use the DCF model for asset allocation, in the first stage they specify their own model; in other words, they translate the abstract theoretical construct into an applicable structure. The users specify the input parameters as well as how the cash flows and discount rate are calculated. This process involves many decisions about how to treat particular accounting numbers: for example, the way capital expenditures are defined and which numbers are applied to account for the relevant determinant factors – such as core consumer price index (CPI) or producer price index (PPI) in the case of the inflation rate. In other words, users decide which properties are essential and which are negligible. These decisions are grounded solely in the experience and convictions of portfolio managers, and not in the theory itself. Thus, to some extent, the process of model idealization is continued and completed in the concrete financial practices of model users. Here, *the model offers a flexible opportunity to give the world a structure* individually, according to one's convictions and experience (remember the *dynamic approach to model use* described by one of the interviewees). After the model's parameters have been determined, they remain unchanged for a number of years – the financial market professionals start to work with the model.

My focus is on the application of the DCF in the portfolio strategy and solutions group, which is part of the wealth department. This group is particularly concerned with the allocation of assets across asset classes, regions and industries. The process of DCF use here is structured as follows. There is a dedicated research group that "attends to" the model: the group makes assumptions about the inputs and calculates the "fair" values for various markets. Based on the DCF calculations, it produces a list that ranks all asset classes from the cheapest (the most strongly undervalued) to the most expensive (the most strongly overvalued). This list is sent to the portfolio strategy and solutions group to develop a concrete proposal for allocating capital in clients' portfolios to different asset classes, that is, for making decisions. The point of departure for the proposal is the list of the model's suggestions; however, some amendments are made at this stage. These amendments are essential for understanding the model's use and will be discussed in detail in what follows. The amended proposal is then sent to the investment committee which makes the final decisions on how to allocate money to different asset classes in all bank portfolios.

But how exactly does the wealth management department handle the DCF model? The following excerpt from an interview with a portfolio manager from this group provides some insight. He replied to my question "What do the numbers that come out of a model tell you?" as follows:

Ok, for example, for the past 1.5 or 2 years, the DCF has been saying that emerging market equities are overvalued. This statement is based on the fact that in the model the risk premium for emerging market equities is assumed to be higher than the risk premium for the developed countries. [. . .] Now, when you look at it and ask "should we really underweight emerging markets or not?", then you have the crucial question: "Is this assumption that emerging market risks are different true or false?" And in this case, for example [. . .] you could come to the conclusion that this assumption is not true because emerging markets have made significant progress in the last 10 years concerning corporate governance, concerning economic policy, stability and so on. [. . .]
The model always looks back [. . .] Many models claim they are forward-looking but their parameters come from history [. . .] The claim that the risk premium in emerging markets is higher comes from history. Then history is projected into the future and one says "emerging markets are overvalued". But now the discussion of a qualitative nature can begin. Is the history relevant now? Is it not? How

relevant is it? And if one comes to the conclusion that significant changes took place and one knows how it happened, one would not take this [model's] valuation signal seriously [. . .] This means we do not have enormous trust in models, but we know why this or that comes out of the model and we can use it as a basis for discussion. This is so with all valuation models. (head of the tactical asset allocation group, Zurich)

What the model delivers is a valuation signal. It suggests whether the asset is overvalued or undervalued. In this particular case, the model says that the asset class "emerging markets" is overvalued and thus should not be overweighted in bank portfolios. The interview excerpt demonstrates, however, that portfolio managers *do not perceive this valuation signal as the final word in their decision-making process.* When the people in the portfolio strategy and solutions group receive the list with recommendations, they question the model's advice. Why do they do this? Because portfolio managers *know* that the DCF model can deliver imprecise results (due to the erroneous inputs) which need to be corrected *in situ.*

However, errors in estimating the key parameters of the model do not prevent them from using this valuation methodology. It seems that pragmatic portfolio investors do not look for the perfect calculation or for mathematical truth (*precision*). They know that it is out of reach. They simply look for a *convenient instrument* that facilitates their decision-making process (*relevance*).

An interesting mixture of faith and mistrust in calculative instruments can be observed in the field. Portfolio managers allege that they have been using DCF very successfully for years, despite all drawbacks related to it: "[The DCF model] is not bad. It is surprising [. . .] Surprisingly, it is not as bad as one might think" (head of the tactical asset allocation group, Zurich).

What makes the use of this model a success? Two conditions were mentioned in the interviews: first, the user has to know the model and its handicaps; and, second, the model and its assumptions must be kept more or less fixed. At first glance, these assertions might contradict the statements about mistrust in models made in the interview excerpt that opened this section. In this interview fragment, the portfolio manager stated that the valuation signals delivered by the model and the assumptions behind them are questionable and that there is not an enormous amount of trust in the model. Why then use it at all?

The key to the puzzle is provided in the following fragment of a conversation with a portfolio manager from the observed group:

A: To be honest, model assertions [. . .] the rankings of markets are hardly questioned. Valuation itself is not questioned. The investment committee gets a bunch of numbers every month relating to the valuations of the asset classes. Maybe there is a discussion of whether one should take the valuation signal seriously or not. But the valuation signal itself is not questioned.

ES: But what is the difference between "questioning" and "taking seriously"?

A: I mean [. . .] here is an example where we were wrong. The model said a while ago, "Japanese shares are too expensive in comparison to the rest of the world." And still we said, "No, we don't believe that; there are structural changes; premiums will be adjusted and the return on equity will increase towards the world level, and it will happen quickly, and, and, and [. . .]" So we were against the Japan underweight, OK? In this case we were wrong. And there are such discussions.

ES: OK, then you question [. . .]

A: We don't question the model [. . .]

ES: But model assertions?

A: No, we say, *one should look not only at the model, but also at other things.* This is the message.

The model delivers valuation numbers and the related ranking lists of the asset classes. They are important; no one says, "They are just garbage." The model calculates correctly given the assumptions about the numerical values of its inputs. By translating the inputs into the "fair" value, it provides *a good point of departure for decision-making.* It is important that this decision basis is well understood and kept stable:

> In the model, one wants to change as little as possible. One wants to adjust the parameters as seldom as possible. This gives the whole thing a bit of stability and, in this sense, it is not a bad anchor. (head of the tactical asset allocation department, Zurich)

It is crucial to know the assumptions behind the model regardless of how unrealistic they are. When it comes to tactical investment decisions, these assumptions are discussed but seldom changed. According to the model users, risk premiums are "hardly ever changed"; growth rates are changed "very seldom" and inflation "from time to time". However, because experts know exactly what happens to the model's outcomes when inputs are varied, they can discuss the model's recommendations *qualitatively.* They know what is behind the numbers, and they are aware that not all relevant information is in the numbers. Investors have to "look at the other things", bring additional information into play. Using a model as a tool in its own right works quite well, but *it must be enriched.*

When using a model, market participants compare the model results with their own *judgment.* Specifically, they must decide whether the numerical assumptions and input data, which provide a basis for the valuation, fit with the qualitative views they hold concerning asset classes or companies.

If not, the subjectively perceived inadequacies of the model are corrected *in situ* or, as market participants say, they are *overlaid*.

In the interview extract at the beginning of this section, a portfolio manager reported that he doubted the assumption that the risk premium for emerging markets was high because he was convinced of some significant changes in the region. This statement implies a qualitative judgment. He said that emerging markets had made significant progress in the last ten years concerning corporate governance, economic policy, stability and so on. These changes influence the risk premium, which is an important element of the DCF model, but they are not captured by the model. As non-quantifiable factors, they enter the model through the risk premium parameter. According to the portfolio manager, the risk premium should be lowered to reflect the changes in emerging markets. Thus, the model's results that rely on historical risks rather than current risks are overruled by humans in the qualitative part of the decision, and this is called "qualitative overlay". "We say, 'OK, each phase is different, not like in the past' and 'What is different this time?' [. . .] This is, if you will, our judgmental part" (head of tactical asset allocation group, Frankfurt/Main).

This *judgment call is crucial for the final decision*. Note that the valuation signal of the DCF model to underweight emerging markets (mentioned in the first interview fragment in this section) was neglected in favour of the judgmental call. Similarly, in the case of the Japanese equity market, portfolio managers made a (wrong) judgment by powering down the model's outcome.

Here is another example of qualitative overlay: The DCF model was adjusted by non-quantifiable factors such as "management quality" and "investment sentiment" which – as "soft factors" – were not naturally taken into account by the model. Based on this adjustment, the model's recommendation about one of the major listed oil and gas companies in Russia was de-emphasized:

> It is important to know what is going on in a company. If a model recommends buying a cheap company, *I must know why it is cheap*. For example, Surgut is cheap; it has been cheap for a long time, but the reason for this is known: its management. Prosperity fund [a large shareholder] is planning a management change within the company. If that finally happens, if the previous managers are fired and a new team is hired, Surgut will double, and it will be a good deal. Until then it remains uninteresting, no matter how cheap it is. (portfolio manager, European emerging markets, Frankfurt/Main)

Thus, portfolio managers' decisions are not based on model calculations in the strict sense. Instead, they are the results of enriching the model with "other things" – that is, with other significant factors that cannot be captured by the model.

The procedure of qualitative overlay is based on an interesting phenomenon: the world is perceived as changed, but the model remains fixed. There is a perception among market participants that the ongoing adjustment of a model to a world that is constantly changing and is determined by too many variables is a hopeless endeavour. This is why no direct adjustment of the model takes place. Keeping the model stable enables users to observe the ever-changing world and orientate themselves in it. Valuation models do not help to "represent" or to "catch" market reality. They deliver a structure for analysis and for discussion among managers and across departments; they are an anchor or a benchmark with which the changing reality is subsequently compared. Thus, in the practice of markets, the DCF model is only *a supportive tool* for making decisions in the described investment process. The final decision is made by humans through the application of qualitative overlay.

On the Nature of Judgment in Financial Markets

However, what exactly is this notorious "judgment" which has been mentioned so many times on the last pages? Judgment in the empirical case of the DCF is a story, a commentary that is used to relate models to the real world and to re-grasp the world's complexity. Judgment reduces the distortion between the model and reality by taking most of the relevant factors and dynamics that were previously excluded from or not specified in the model and "bringing them back" into the decision-making process.

This understanding of judgment has been discussed in the literature about modelling. Already economists Gibbard and Varian (1978: 665f.) asked: "In what ways can a model help in understanding a situation in the world when its assumptions, as applied to this situation, are false?" and hinted that an economic model contains two interrelated elements – a mathematical structure and *a story*:

> A model [. . .] is a story with a specified structure: to explain this catch phrase is to explain what a model is. The structure is given by the logical and mathematical form of a set of postulates, the assumptions of the model. The structure forms an uninterpreted system [. . .]. Although the term "model" is often applied to a structure alone, we shall use it in another sense. In economists' use of models, there is always an element of interpretation: the model always tells a story.

Morgan (2002) agreed with Gibbard and Varian, and suggested that stories should be understood as a way of overcoming the problem of the notorious models' under-complexity. The idea is straightforward: modellers necessarily simplify the world while building models but *bring back complexity while interpreting model results*. These narratives, Morgan (2012: 362) argued, help "match" the model with the world. For example, she discussed how "the model situation" of the prisoner's dilemma game was translated into "the economic situation" of competition between firms and used to analyse companies' behaviour in a duopoly. This matching of models with specific economic cases by means of narratives might contribute to "collapsing the gap between the model situation and the world situation" (p. 363). Thus, combining mathematics and stories is a necessary step towards achieving a holistic view on the economy (see Alexandrova 2008).

Stories could be texts as well as (formal and informal) discussions that accompany the application of a model. Importantly, they are usually "supplied from elsewhere", as Cartwright (2008: 8) suggests in her "models-as-parables" account. *Narratives are not in the model*; they are developed externally and represent "a great deal of outside work, including much interpretation of other parts of the available text (model) and of the world itself and how it operates" (p. 8). This is the work of judgment which is – as we have seen – an integral part of model application.

However, if we insist on the fundamental difference between cultures of model use within science and financial markets, we should specify what judgment is in the latter case, in particular. Is it merely a one-off commentary or an ongoing process of discussing and storytelling? The empirical study on the DCF demonstrates that formation of judgment is a predominantly social activity that constantly evolves within teams of model users. The results of the DCF model within the wealth management group of a Zurich bank travel from the research team (the ranking list based on the model's calculations) to the portfolio strategy and solutions group (the amended ranking list based on judgment) to the investment committee (final investment decisions are made based on the amended list and further discussions). One portfolio manager from the portfolio strategy and solutions group stated:

> We prepare things [proposals for the investment committee]. But one should not imagine that everything is a one-way street. We hang around together in a confined space. This means that we discuss a lot with each other. And this means [. . .] it is not so that we do something in the black box and the [investment] committee doesn't know what was before and it gets only what it sees [spreadsheets with asset rankings according to the model]. But rather, they know everything; they know what is going on. They know what our models say. They know also what our opinions are because we talk about them every day on the floor.

This statement implies that if the investment committee looks at the model numbers in its monthly meetings and makes final asset allocation decisions, its opinion about those numbers has largely already been formed by the collective processes of information processing and story-telling on the floor. Thus, judgment as commentary is not a one-off event where narrative is used to "overlay" the model; it is rather an ongoing process of connecting the model to the constantly changing world around.

Furthermore, the commentary is not only a result of internal communication; it is also influenced by the experience of portfolio managers as well as their communications with other market participants. The head of the wealth management department in Zurich stated:

> We primarily adopt the DCF model results and do our qualitative overlay over the whole thing [. . .] it is, as I said, how seriously we take the model results with regard to a) – we have a bit of experience and b) – we intensively read and we talk to people in the world, outside of the bank.

"Experience" means that one has already worked with the model and knows its sensitivities and how to relate information from different sources to the model's outcomes. Written and oral communications in the market are also essential for shaping judgment. Financial investors use newspapers, research produced by brokerage houses, news agencies' screens (Reuters, Bloomberg) and charts as sources of information. There are also regular or sporadic conversations with brokers and other portfolio managers and discussions with hedge funds. For example, the portfolio manager from the observed Zurich bank said:

> Where we also have our contacts – but not so many – are the hedge funds where one feels that they have particular information advantages. For example, I'm going to talk tomorrow to the head of a big fund of funds in New York who has a lot of expertise [. . .] Thus, we try to listen to special sources to get additional elements of the picture.

Hence, judgment is an ongoing process of composing the puzzle picture of the markets by fitting together various elements – for example, rumours and stories, opinions of colleagues and competitors – as well as data from information services and hedge funds. Then, this holistic picture is connected to the model which is, naturally, detached from the market. The empirical research demonstrates that users have the structure of the DCF valuation in their heads as a template and constantly come back to the model and its variables in their discussions when introducing their commentary, which consists of the constructed whole picture. Sometimes, they discuss how a single model parameter – inflation or risk premium, for example – develops and how its potential changes (rise or fall) would influence the outcomes of the model, making particular assets cheaper or more expensive. In this crucial step of the model-based decision process, a decision is made by adjusting the model to the story. The narrative is an instrument for closing the gap between idealized models and a complex reality. This research suggests a particular understanding of how financial markets are "markets in stories" (Tuckett 2012) – stories *with* and *around* models.

Models and "Views" in Forex Analysis on the Trading Floor

An empirical study conducted by Wansleben (2013, 2014) describes the process of model-based foreign exchange (forex) forecasting in a big German bank in Frankfurt/Main. Interestingly, he discovered a similar culture of model use to that discussed in the previous section. Model calculations are delivered to the analysts from the economics department and are suspended in the process of *forecasting on the floor* – that is, *in situ* of markets. Also here, the model results are not the most relevant piece of information that determines the final decision.

The forecasting process starts in the economics department, where models are used to aggregate data about various macroeconomic phenomena – such as inflation, commodity prices, interest rates and so on – into the forecast of the euro–US dollar exchange rate and other important currency pairs. Economists who work with the model are explicitly sceptical about its capabilities. First of all, they know that there is no valid theoretical model that can be used to make precise forex forecasts. Thus, all forex models – including their own idiosyncratic models – have severe deficiencies. The definitive combination of factors that influence exchange rates is unknown; furthermore, the relevance of factors incorporated into the model changes over time – some of them possess an explanatory power today but can lose it tomorrow, when some other, often unforeseen, factors become crucial. Moreover, the factors are often of a purely qualitative nature and unquantifiable.

Still, economists use their model to generate the exchange rate forecasts every month; these forecasts "travel" to the forex analysts who are located on the floor among the traders and sales people, that is, their colleagues who stay in constant contact with the market. The task of analysts is to produce a forecast that can be used for taking action in the markets (for example trading) or for communication with clients. Thus, when the model's results arrive on the floor, they enter an environment which is characterized by a strong proximity to the market and is "non-epistemic" in nature. Here, models lose their immediate relevance. Wansleben (2013: 617) reports:

The analyst answering my question specified that the economist only runs models, while forecasting authority rests with the analyst team. Thus, analysts regard themselves as the primary authorities in the forecasting process. This becomes particularly evident in their attitude towards the economist's model. One analyst states, for instance: "The model result does not become our forecast directly. We always ask first: What does the model tell us in a particular situation?" [. . .]. In concrete terms, this means that the economist "delivers" the model forecast to the analysts who then treat this forecast as a resource with limited value for their own work.

Forex analysts share all of the concerns the economists have about their models (unrealistic assumptions, imprecise parameters and so on) but are particularly sceptical about the models' results because of the gap between models and markets. Analysts close this gap *in situ* while developing their so-called "view" on the market. This view takes into account both the economic model predictions and the analysts' judgment. Similar to the DCF example, judgment results from extensive observations and analyses of markets. The forex analysts talk extensively to other analysts, sales people and clients, constantly follow the news on the screen and listen to the traders' discussions on the trading floor. Their judgment also incorporates market "themes", that is, the news and issues that the majority of market participants are focusing on and are "playing" *at that time* – for example, the pending increase in interest rates or forthcoming inflation numbers. Thus, forex analysts constantly observe and interpret markets, making an effort not to lose contact with them.

Market observations are combined with model predictions in order to arrive at the official final view in a joint meeting in which analysts and economists participate:

> During this meeting, the following is discussed: what does the model "tell" [. . .] within a specific market situation, what other current developments must be taken into account and how to position the bank's view in relation to consensus [the average, calculated from all available forecasts] and the view of particular competitors. (Wansleben 2014: 617)

The final forecast is the view that results from these discussions. During the discussions, models serve as an "anchor", as a starting point for the development of a comprehensive narrative that takes into account market observations, themes and market emotions. Due to their market proximity, analysts have the power to overlay model results. Their decisions are fateful because traders who take and hedge risks might use them. Importantly, analysts have their "skin in the game" because they have to commit to their views (something that economists do not have to do). Analysts do not consider the forecasting of currency exchange rates as number production, but rather as "the act of committing to a particular view", to a particular story that can then be told to clients and other audiences (Wansleben 2014: 623). Certainly, models deliver important anchoring points for the stories, but are also enriched and overlaid in the process of the development of views.

Modelling and Trading Exotic Equity Derivatives

In his book *Codes of Finance*, Lépinay (2011) analyses the practice of model use in the field of exotic equity derivatives and offers another telling example of how models are adjusted by judgment. He describes how a capital guarantee product (CGP) was developed and modelled in a French investment bank. Interestingly, Lépinay demonstrates how the valuation model (designed by quants in the same bank) "travels" to the traders who have taken the new product into their portfolios. The model is supposed to become the traders' "road map", the "script" that helps them "anticipate" price changes of the product in order to hedge the portfolio successfully.

However, Lépinay's analysis shows that the traders are torn between two issues: the imperfection of the road maps they receive from quants, on the one hand, and the complex and ever-changing character of markets, on the other. Again, there is a need to reconcile these issues.

Indeed, traders know that they cannot entirely rely on models. Their quantitative colleagues develop models based on abstract price time series; however, the traders act *in the real markets* where prices are ambiguous. Moreover, when traders use a model to hedge a product, this hedging takes place at various geographical locations where prices might not be available or might be discontinued or split. The general problem is that when real market prices are fed into the model, they are changing at that very moment – they are moving away, so to speak. Thus, the model's calculation is hardly ever based on actual prices. Furthermore, the variances and risk correlations of products in a portfolio that traders manage also change constantly. The gap between models and markets is evident.

At the same time, the model is the only road map the traders get for "navigating" the hedging of a product in the market. They know that if they completely neglect the model, they will be exposed to uncontrolled risks. Similarly to Weick's mountaineers in the Alps – who held the wrong map in their hands but survived – the traders have to find a way to decide and act by becoming active and alert.

The solution that allows for action-like decision-making in this situation is *simulation*: the traders send small orders to the market and test the market reaction. At the same time, they observe the flow of real orders in the market, trying to get the whole picture. Thus, they "follow and test the script simultaneously" (Lépinay 2011: 79). At this stage, the distance between the model and the market is reduced. This process of "probing markets" is a good example of "acting sensibly", where models help to discover what is going on but do not serve as an ultimate road map. At the moment of making final decisions, models are combined with human judgment. It is not a coincidence that Lépinay pointedly called the section in the chapter where he described how models are applied by traders "From Scripts to Manipulations". The most fascinating part of the story is that, in this particular empirical case, the "manipulation" is more than a rich narrative. Rather, judgment is "lived" in the trading room in the communication and physical co-location ("the spatial distribution") of traders and their assistants.

Indeed, the reconciliation of models and markets takes place while the trader and his or her assistant work together at their desks. While the assistant runs the simulation of the hedge – and, by doing so, "steps out" of the market and kind of loses sight of it – the trader constantly keeps an eye on market fluctuations. The assistant communicates the newly calculated (simulated) levels of risk and discusses the numbers with the trader. The ongoing interpretation takes place, and judgment is formed and applied in this very tense interplay between market actors and technology:

> On the exotic desk, the trader and his or her assistant faced each other, separated only by a double wall of back-to-back monitors. The communication literally took place *in the interstices* of the screens and wires [. . .]. Talking in between the monitors, they moved sideways to find the new interstices that allowed them to make eye contact when the moment of passing orders came. Looking sequentially at their monitors and at their partners through the fence of monitors, the fine tuning of the hedge took place in a complex mix of interactions between the two operators facing each other, the simulated new pause/pose, and the fluctuating prices of underlyings. (Lépinay 2011: 81, original emphasis)

These ongoing discussions and interpretations are crucial for the final decision about how to hedge the portfolio. Because there is severe uncertainty about how a small fluctuation of an underlying will impact the portfolio as a whole, theoretical hedging cannot be applied "one-to-one". The decision has to be made as to *whether to rely or not rely on the model's advice*. Lépinay (p. 83) highlights: "Often, she [the assistant] decides not to follow this advice at all and, instead, trusts completely her own sense of the market and knowledge of the trends she recognizes."

Thereby, the assistant frequently "judges by instinct" (p. 83) and relies on her intuition and idiosyncratic knowledge of the markets. Certainly, Lépinay does not claim that the model is overruled all the time; obviously, sometimes the model's advice is followed (but never without critical scrutiny). What is crucial in these findings is the fact that there is no automatism in applying the model as an ultimate rule – there is always room for discretion in the process of model application.

BACKING OUT AND IMPLIED MODELLING

The second major pattern of model use that I would like to discuss is so-called "backing out" and the related process of "implied modelling" or "implied valuation". Models can be run backwards from a given (observable) market price in order to understand what the market "sees" (or implies) at a given time. In this process, the implied parameters such as "implied volatility" (recall our discussion about the Black-Scholes model in Chapter 2), "implied probability" or "implied correlations" are calculated. The "market view" is believed to be expressed by real prices and, by using models to back them out, the market participants can identify which expectations are implied in the current market price – that is, *what the other market participants expect*. By doing so, model users consider sociality of markets in their decision-making.

Backing out can also refer to some simple graphical or numerical representations of the market view (such as the "spread-plot" graph in the case of merger arbitrage or consensus estimates of financial analysts). The implied parameters can then be compared to the subjective (idiosyncratic) views of the market participants as the latter "check" and "unsettle" the market view; that is, as they find out where the market – or traders themselves – might be mistaken. This procedure helps answer important questions: have I missed something that the market has already discovered? Do I see something that the market does not see? Being a part of "implied calculations", models serve as a "linkage mechanism between the known and the unknown" (Triana 2009: 68) and help overcome essential uncertainties in the market. Backing out and implied modelling are not so much about calculation but more about well-reasoned agreement or disagreement with the market (Figure 4.3).

In this section, I will discuss two empirical examples: the first is the "plausibility check of consensus" in fundamental portfolio management (based on Svetlova 2010). This case illustrates how portfolio managers avoid forecasting while backing out the analyst consensus. The second example is "reflexive modelling" in the field of merger arbitrage traders (Beunza and Stark 2012). This very insightful case demonstrates how markets are observed through calculation of the implied probability of a merger.

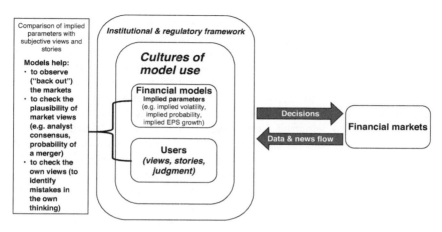

Figure 4.3   Models in action-like decision-making: backing out the market

Plausibility Check of Consensus and Reverse Engineering in Portfolio Management

In the field of active fundamental portfolio management, the procedure of backing out is frequently used to allow for the efficient interplay of models and markets. Famously, the gurus of active portfolio management Grinold and Kahn (1999: 7) explicitly stated that "active management is forecasting" and that active investing should be based upon forecasting ability that is better than the ability of the market average, and is proven to be sustainable and not random. At the same time, my interviewees in the field highlighted that they look for procedures that allow them to identify *what counts* and not to make precise forecasts. Portfolio managers generally understand the futility of financial forecasting and rather try to avoid it. They realize that the crucial point is not to deliver an exact numerical forecast but to achieve a better estimate of the situation (that is, to "see more") than the market (all other investors) and to take advantage of this – often non-numerical – estimate.

Backing out is the procedure that allows portfolio managers to circumvent forecasting because it starts with the numbers that *are known* (certain). Such numbers are, for example, *market prices* or *consensus (average) forecasts* of financial analysts – they are the officially published numbers and are readily available from Bloomberg and on the internet.

For instance, "reverse DCF modelling" is applied in the markets to "back out" the current market price of an equity. This approach was confirmed in my interviews with investors. Rappaport and Mauboussin (2001) also refer to the reverse DCF approach in their book *Expectations Investing*. In the first step, investors "read" (back out) the market expectations; that is, they estimate the shared expectations for sales, growth rates, cash flows, profit margins and so on which are implied in the market price. In the second step, they compare the implied numbers with their own views and expectations, trying to determine where and when revisions in expectations are likely to occur; in other words, they form expectations about potential (future) revisions – that is, about what the market might "discover" soon. Finally, investors make their decisions: they buy if they expect significant upward revisions and sell if they think the market expects too much. Thus, again, the "numbers" are not taken for granted but checked against common sense and reconciled with judgment. In this approach, judgment is considered to be correct and provides guidance for decisions.

A similar procedure of "backing out" the consensus estimates of financial analysts can be observed in the markets. The existing research on "markets for information" (Barker 1998) indicates that the analysts' consensus represents the averaged view of a security with which fund managers *agree or disagree*. Analysts' recommendations are:

> a benchmark against which fund managers can test their own private informa-
> tion, which is essential for both relative risk minimization and for the assess-
> ment of prospects for outperformance. [. . .] fund managers may not be able
> to outperform by using analysts' output directly, they nevertheless still need
> the analysts in order to have a measure of the consensus beliefs of the market.
> (Barker 1998: 16)

How do fund managers use this measure? Here is a reconstruction of the procedure based on my empirical material. In the first step, investors try to *understand* the average market forecast, that is, to identify which assumptions and interpretations underlie the number. For example, they can calculate which earnings per share (EPS) growth or cash flow growth is implied in the consensus estimate. In doing so, they can find out, for example, that the consensus assumes the cash flow growth of a particular company to be 25 per cent annually for the next five years.

The second step requires the application of judgment. At this stage, the portfolio managers start to ask themselves: do I agree with the market? Is 25 per cent future cash flow growth justified (realistic)? Can the company achieve this growth when keeping in mind its recent market position, the strength of its competitors, the quality of its current management and so on? Then, the decision is made about *whether and how to deviate from the consensus*. That is, the decision takes the form of comparing market expec-tations (which are the results of the backward calculation) with one's own expectations. Note that orientation towards the analysts' consensus does not mean blind acceptance of this commonly known view. Rather, the backing-out procedure helps portfolio managers to actively search for their individually justified ways of disagreeing with the market and expecting a surprise.

Let me illustrate this approach using an example from my empirical research. In 2008, a portfolio manager in a German investment boutique tried to estimate the investment prospects for the Royal Bank of Scotland (RBS). The key factor for the estimation of the bank's value at that time was the bank's exposure to the subprime sector. Thus, the portfolio manager in question tried to estimate whether he had a different opinion regarding this key factor. After the release of the RBS's trading statement, he observed that the consensus price was at a level of 70 pence per share. However, after gathering information and performing an individual analysis of the financial statement and the asset structure and, in particular, after estimating the depreciation requirements in his spreadsheet, he assumed an additional depreciation of 15 pence per share. Thus, he valued the RBS's share at approximately 55 pence per share due to its subprime exposure. Therefore, he disagreed with the consensus and was convinced that the consensus would be revised downwards significantly.

This "view" was based on his individual disagreement with the current average opinion of the market. Here, individual calculations are combined with a peculiar form of orientation towards the expectations of others. However, this orientation is not a form of imitation but a type of alertness or mindfulness towards what other market participants are doing. Thus, "backing out" to some extent allows the overcoming of social "blindness", the central problem of financial models as described by Esposito (2013).

Interestingly, Graaf (2016) describes how brokers enhance the sociality of their decision-making by developing a collective case of deviation from the market consensus: *reverse brokering*. Brokers understand that they will not attract clients' attention (and money) if they merely transmit the shared market opinion (consensus). Thus, what they do is actively support the fund managers' efforts to disagree with the market. Graaf describes how a broker created an investment case by applying reverse brokering. The broker crafted a pro forma model in which he deviated from the consensus with regard to only one parameter: the margin mix of the company. Then he sent the model to the clients he knew were interested in this particular company; in doing so, he offered an alternative, model-based view on the company, and thus made a proposal on how to disagree with the market. Then, the clients were free to do their own research and calculations and to come back to the broker with their own views, which the broker then incorporated into the model before sending the model around again, and so forth. Fascinatingly, here, the case of deviation from the consensus was developed in collaboration between brokers and investors;

the brokers benefited from their clients' idiosyncratic, detailed knowledge about the company and developed the model together with them. Thus, reverse brokering represents another interesting case of connecting models to markets by developing a *collective* case of backing out the consensus and deviating from it.

Reflexive Modelling in the Field of Merger Arbitrage

The other example of backing out the market refers to the calculation of implied probability and "reflexive modelling" described by Beunza and Stark (2012). The authors analyse how arbitrage traders decide to take position in a newly announced merger.

First, the traders form their own opinion about the probability of the merger. This is a crucial figure because – at the end of the day – the market prices of the companies involved in the merger are dependent on whether the merger effectively takes place or is called off. Thus, the merger arbitrageurs speculate on the probability of merger completion. They form a judgment about this probability by categorizing the companies, analysing accounting numbers and building analogies to past mergers and other similar deals. In this process, traders, on the one hand, mobilize their memories and professional associations and, on the other hand, analytically process information and conduct calculations using Excel spreadsheets and models. Nevertheless, traders are aware of the limits of their model-based views. Here, we are again confronted with the phenomenon of *calculative pragmatism*: "Arbitrageurs [. . .] are persistent but sceptical users of calculative devices" (Beunza and Stark 2012: 402).

To check the plausibility of their idiosyncratic views on the merger probability, traders need to compare their own estimates with what the market "thinks" about the likelihood of the merger being completed. To do this, traders use a so-called "spread plot" which graphically represents the difference between the stock prices of the companies involved in the merger. If the spread narrows, the market considers the merger as becoming more and more likely (and, accordingly, less likely if the spread widens). The spread plot represents *the aggregate opinion* of market participants about the likelihood of the merger. The implied probability of the merger can be "backed out" from the spread plot: "In using the spread plot, a key concept used by the arbitrageurs is 'the implied probability' of a merger. By implied, the arbitrageurs refer to the probability of the merger completion that rival arbitrageurs assign to the merger" (Beunza and Stark 2012: 400).

Then, the implied probability is compared to the traders' subjective views. If there is a disagreement ("dissonance"), traders start to ask: what am I missing, or what do my models not see? Thus, they are aware of the blind spots and fallibility of their models – they constantly reflect on them. After discovering dissonance with the market, traders start to search for additional information and do further analysis in order to make a decision on whether to maintain or dismiss their own judgment and whether to make corrections to their idiosyncratic models. At this stage, models are suspended or "undone". Beunza and Stark (2012) and also Stark (2011) refer to this process as "reflexive modelling":

> Such a reflexivity is not a narrative order and is emphatically not an intellectual exercise of transcending subjective experience. Neither is it "objective", but it is nonetheless objectified in the instrumentation, market devices, and material practices of merger arbitrage in the era of quantitative finance. (Stark 2011: 334)

Hence, also merger arbitrageurs value their models but are far from being "model dopes". They use models to determine the behaviour of other investors, to compare their own views with the views of others and to establish a position based on this *socially informed* calculation. "Thus, in place of models *versus* social cues, [we] observed traders *modeling social cues*" (Beunza and Stark 2012: 384, original emphasis). In this process of connecting models to markets, models are critically scrutinized and are treated as a supplementary element – but not as immediate guidance – for decisions.

MODELS AS OPINION PROCLAIMERS

Finally, not only the "market views" but also the pre-formed qualitative opinions of market participants (for example about the "fair" price of an asset) can be "backed out" in order to make a model proclaim what its users think is right. Investors play with parameters and numbers in the model until the model fits the subjective "fair" price or their subjective views more generally (Figure 4.4). This might seem to be a strange procedure but such (mis)use of models is quite widespread. *The subjective opinions of model users* that are formed independently ("outside") of the model *are expressed and supported* through their choice of variables in the model. Indeed, "models translate opinions into values" (Derman 1996: 3).

In this section, I illustrate this procedure by means of two examples: 1) I show how security analysts form *their views* about a company and then identify the numerical parameters that should be inserted into a model in order to support their pre-formed views; 2) I discuss a particular advancement of the Modern Portfolio Theory that helps its users find their voice in the process of portfolio selection, namely the Black-Litterman model (1992).

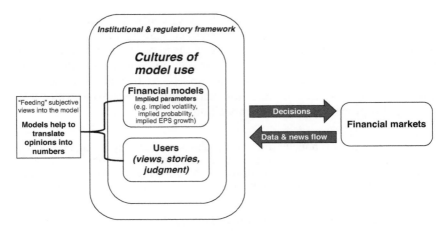

Figure 4.4   Models in action-like decision-making: models as opinion proclaimers

Securities Analysts

An interesting pattern of backward calculating can be observed in the field of securities analysis (Mars 1998; Hägglund 2000; Beunza and Garud 2007; Imam et al. 2008; Wansleben 2012). Securities analysts carry out research about individual companies, industries and regions; they analyse accounting data, regularly talk to companies' management, visit companies "in the field", participate in earnings presentations (conference calls after earning announcements) and observe economic news and industry trends. Based on this information, they produce valuation reports that present and explain the so-called "target price", that is, present what a particular analyst thinks the company's stock will be worth in the future and why. Importantly, securities analysts give recommendations (buy, sell or hold); in other words, they communicate and interpret their price forecasts to other market participants, and thus commit to their own views.

One might expect *calculating* a company's "fair" value, and thus making a correct forecast of the future price, to be the major task of a securities analyst. Recent research, however, has moved on from the understanding of analysts as "information processors" (Beunza and Garud 2007). The traditional "linear" view on analysts as modellers and price forecasters (Figure 4.5) has been abandoned.

Current research on financial analysts suggests that, in this field, models are not used to calculate forecasts, but rather to generate or to match *a story* about the company under scrutiny – the story or "view" that an

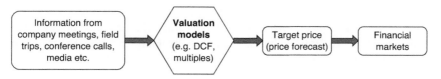

Figure 4.5   Traditional view: securities analysts as modellers and price forecasters

analyst has developed. Models can be considered as one element in this process, and thus play a subordinate role.

Imam et al. (2008) present three types of procedure that analysts use to reach a target price and a recommendation. The first two are "qualitative overlay" and a plausibility check in the form of "backing out" of the target price as just discussed above. Finally, analysts can use their pre-formed view of a company to determine the target price as "a subjectively determined percentage of premium or discount on the current price" and then apply the valuation model (for example the DCF) "to produce a number close to that price target" (Imam et al. 2008: 525). This is the procedure at the core of this section. Importantly, the authors stress the common characteristic of all three approaches:

> what is striking is the interplay between subjective judgment and formal analysis – the valuation is but one part of the process, and its role can be to "dress up" or communicate a target price that has in effect already been determined, as much as to be the mechanism by which the price is actually determined in the first place. As one media analyst put it: "how we *feel* about a stock is more important". (Imam et al. 2008: 525, original emphasis)

Let us discuss models as "opinion proclaimers" in more detail, however. In his extensive ethnographical work, Mars (1998) illustrates the importance of "how we feel", as described in the above quote, in great empirical detail. He shows how securities analysts first develop their story about a company and then adjust the numbers in their valuation models – which are usually idiosyncratic versions of the DCF model or the dividend discount model (DDM) – in order to fit the story. They gather information by talking to the CEOs and CFOs of a company, visiting the premises, following the ad hoc and regular news, analysing balance sheets, profit-and-loss accounts and cash-flow statements, and discussing a company's perspectives with competitors in the industry. Based on this information, analysts develop a "feeling" for the company, their judgment, and then spend days and nights attempting to "wangle" the numbers so that they fit into this personal picture. For example, if an analyst is convinced that a company is a "buy" (or a "sell") and that a target price should be at a particular level, he or she will *adjust the numbers in the DCF model* until the desired "target price" comes out as the "fair" value of the company. Here, models are important but passive tools for expressing the personal judgment of an analyst. Mars (1998: 137) calls this procedure "postgnosis" because it is directed from the imaginative future to today (not like the traditional *prognosis* from today to the future).

A good example of this approach can be found in Beunza and Garud's (2007) study on the disparity of opinions among securities analysts about Amazon.com Inc. in 1998. The authors demonstrate that the analysts who disagreed did not begin to form their recommendations by calculating revenues, operating margins and other financials of the company, but by making general assumptions regarding the company's business model – that is, by "framing" or categorizing the company. Here, the subjective expectations of analysts took the form of stories, which Beunza and Garud term "calculative frames". Whereas one analyst considered Amazon to be a start-up internet company with huge growth potential, another suggested that the company was a low-margin book retailer. It was only having developed the narrative that they began to numerically interpret the data by means of valuation models. In this phase, formal numbers were effectively used *to justify* the analysts' initial assumptions about Amazon's business model. The internet analyst at the Canadian bank CIBC Oppenheimer, Henry Blodget, concluded that Amazon was a start-up internet company with potentially high revenues and margins; this judgment justified a target price of $400. At the same time, an analyst with Merrill Lynch Cohen suggested that Amazon was a low-margin book retailer and recommended a target price of $50. No valuation model could justify such a difference unless the numbers had been adjusted. In this example, the secondary role of models is particularly striking. The analysts' judgments preceded and determined the model's outcomes. The valuation model was indeed suspended in the process of model use.

Hägglund (2000, 2002) delivers a similar empirical account of how securities analysts use valuation models. Analysts simply do not believe in the ability of models to forecast the "fair" value. Rather, Hägglund suggests, a model's numbers serve as an element for creating a specific object of analysis: a "quasi-company" or a fictional "investment object". At the time of Cohen's report, Amazon with a share price of $400 was such a fiction – a company that did not exist but was very useful as an "object" that could be presented to the market and discussed with clients. The "quasi-company" is a narrative that provides a holistic picture of a company; it is the story around the model that connects the model's numbers to the analysts' subjective view, to the market, to the past and the future: "The strength of a story is determined by how the plot brings the pieces and events into a

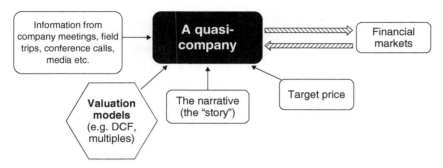

Figure 4.6   Models as an element of "quasi-companies" in securities analysis

larger, more meaningful world of human tasks. [. . .] it is all about bringing it into a meaningful *whole*" (Hägglund 2000: 328, original emphasis).

Instead of calculating a "fair" value, models give the analysts' narrative a structure and draw attention to the important details (for example sensitivities of the company's financial results to particular parameters such as oil prices or interest rates). As a result, *a discussion of scenarios* becomes possible: what will happen to the company's profit if the oil price goes up, or if interest rates go down? This flexible application of models is praised by Hägglund as the very condition of model usefulness (Figure 4.6). Analysts apply models because the latter do not keep them in the rigid cage of calculations, but allow them to develop narratives that stimulate communication with clients, enhance analysts' usefulness – and hence sales.

This procedure can be applied to both new and routine coverage of companies. New assets that come onto the market (for example in an initial public offering, IPO) should be performed as "stable investment objects" with their specific "sexy" story and attractive target price supported by a formal mathematical calculation of the value. At the same time, in the process of routine coverage, companies' stories, target prices and the related spreadsheets evolve as the subjective judgment of analysts changes.

Formal, model-based valuation is one of the possible technologies that helps stabilize an investment object, to "create" a company as an investment opportunity, as a sellable asset. Consequently, Hägglund (2002: 4) claims that we should "direct attention towards the formation of the investment object, rather than the calculation that is necessary to put a price on this object". Again, models play a role in decision-making, but not the leading one. They often help to create but also communicate and legitimize stories – the issues we will discuss in detail in Chapter 5.

The Black-Litterman Model

The Black-Litterman model was created in reaction to limitations of the Modern Portfolio Theory (MPT). The MPT was the first model that formalized the process of portfolio construction. This tool formally enabled asset managers to choose the weightings of securities in a portfolio so that the variance of the portfolio (associated with its risk) was reduced while keeping the expected returns unchanged. This so-called mean-variance optimization allowed the formalization of the idea of diversification ("never put all eggs in one basket") and provided a tool for building security portfolios based on only three sets of numbers: expected returns, variances and co-variances of the securities in the portfolio.

The so-called MPT optimizer – a computer program that "translates" inputs (for example expected returns, variances and co-variances of assets) into portfolio weights – was one of the first formal tools to be applied in the asset management industry. At the same time, as demonstrated by the empirical research, scepticism about the MPT has always been strong. In fact, active asset managers often do not rely on the MPT to structure their portfolios. Fabozzi et al. (2012: 17) summarize years of investors' experience with the MPT as follows: "many asset managers avoid using the quantitative portfolio allocation framework altogether. A major reason for the reluctance of portfolio managers to apply quantitative risk-return optimization is that they have observed that it may be unreliable in practice."

The asset allocation suggestions made by an optimizer are only as good as the expected returns, volatilities and co-variances "fed" into the tool. The model recommendations (the weights of individual assets in the portfolio) are highly sensitive to the estimated inputs, which are often not robust (they change over time); at the same time, small changes of inputs lead to dramatic swings in the model outputs (the proposed weightings).

Particularly the estimation of expected returns is a formally unsolvable problem. There is no mathematical algorithm that can effectively help to calculate the expected returns. One could rely on historical returns (Markowitz's original suggestion) or mean reversion; however, these methods are known to be imprecise because the market situation is constantly changing. In addition, correlations between assets are highly dynamic (not stable) and often change in an unpredictable manner. Especially in times of crisis, a sudden and significant increase in correlations is observed. As a result, investors face a so-called error maximization problem; in other words, they are left with inconsistent outcomes that are highly sensitive to the imprecise inputs: "A surprisingly small increase in the mean of just one asset drives half the securities from the portfolio" (Best and Grauer 1991: 315).

Furthermore, doubts have been expressed about whether the volatility of returns is an adequate measure of risk. For example, a focus on down-side deviations only (semi-variance) might make more sense for asset managers who do not mind upside deviations. But, more generally, volatility as a probability-based measure of risk is often considered to be too narrow to account for risks in financial markets. The famous discussion around "black swans" initiated by Taleb (2007) drew the attention of investors to the risks of extremely negative events (the risks "hidden" in the "tails" of return distributions and notoriously underestimated). The non-normality of the distribution of returns has been taken into consideration – that is, "fat" tails, skewness and kurtosis that do not apply to the normal (Gaussian) distribution. Moreover, Didier Sornette from ETH Zurich said that "Markowitz and Sharpe are blind to systemic risks and thus blind to the kind of huge losses of a systemic character [that can occur]" (Fabozzi et al. 2014: 38). Systemic events are not related to a one-off external shock, but are caused by the interplay of factors within the financial system: for example financial market participants observe each other's transactions and either panic, causing a massive sell-off, or blindly buy one and the same asset, bringing about a bubble; a bank run is another good example of systemic effects.

It is very difficult to determine the probabilities of systemic events; they are definitely not captured by the return distributions of individual assets. Thus, Sornette "believes that the concept of diversification is intrinsically inapplicable to financial markets because of their nonstationary nature" (Fabozzi et al. 2014: 33). Even William Sharpe, half a century after introducing the capital asset pricing model (CAPM), stated that: "It's dangerous, at least in general, to think of risk as a single number, whether it's a variance, a semivariance, or whatever" (Kahneman et al. 2005: 39). Thus, there is no adequate measure of risk that can be used in the Markowitz optimizer.

Due to all these deficiencies, the calculations of optimal portfolios generated in accordance with mean-variance analysis often suggest, first, extreme and, second, counterintuitive weights for assets (Fabozzi et al. 2012: 18); in other words, they suggest "crazy portfolios" (Bernstein 2007: 227). Indeed, the mean-variance optimizer often recommends rather concentrated (extreme) investments in a small number of assets; portfolio managers, however, are usually not happy with such non-robust solutions (especially if their performance is measured relative to a benchmark) and *overrule* the model by adjusting the weights – or do not use the model at all (Posner 2010).

More importantly, however, investors have a problem with the Markowitz optimizer because it frequently produces "counterintuitive" weights. The tool seems "to be taking risk positions that appear to be at odds with the strongest investment view" (Bevan and Winkelmann 1998: 1). In other words, an optimizer might recommend low weights of assets for which investors forecast a bright future with high confidence, or high weights of assets about which investors are sceptical or do not have a view at all. As a result, investors are not happy with the model recommendations because they *find it difficult to act against their own views and beliefs*. This is an issue we have already frequently encountered in this book. To be successfully applied, financial models should leave room for investors' *intuition, judgment and experience* – the very "instruments" that, in the eyes of professional investors, allow them to "beat" the market. Coleman (2014: 234) quotes a fund manager located in London: "Fund managers' whole belief system is that their judgment is right. Otherwise they couldn't be an active manager."

Thus, asset managers require models that allow them to incorporate their judgment and intuition. *They organize their practice of model use in such a way that allows them to entwine formal models and judgments.* Responding to these requirements in the 1990s, the original mean-variance tool was amended to be able to do exactly this – to incorporate judgment about assets into the optimization process and get a portfolio allocation that best *reflects the qualitative views* of users. This extension of the original MPT, the Black-Litterman asset allocation model, was published by Fischer Black and Robert Litterman in 1992.

To apply this model, investors take the so-called *reverse optimization approach*. In the first step, they assume that the market is in equilibrium and extract the implied "equilibrium" returns, that is, the returns that lead to clearance of the market; these equilibrium returns offer them a neutral reference point. In the next step, discrepancies between the neutral returns and the pre-formed subjective views of investors about individual securities or asset classes are identified. These discrepancies might appear because investors interpret the information available in the capital markets differently. Again, it seems to be crucial that a good (useful) financial model is able to accommodate the subjective judgments of investors. The Black-Litterman model does exactly this: the "expected returns [in this model] are a blend of the information available through the capital markets and information unique to a specific investor" (Bevan and Winkelmann 1998: 2). In the final step, a decision is made about how much weight to put on the implied equilibrium (neutral) returns and the individual investor's views, respectively. Bernstein (2007: 228) reports on Litterman's enthusiasm:

"Wow, this works!" Litterman exclaimed to himself. In an unconstrained context, the optimizer now recommends an optimal portfolio holding some capital in the market portfolio and some in portfolios representing your views. Furthermore, if you have equilibrium as your centre of gravity, you don't have to have a view on every single asset. When you do have a view on a single asset, the optimizer applies that view to an appropriate extent to every other asset correlated with it. That procedure prevents crazy portfolios. Now you can derive acceptable portfolios based on your confidence in your view and how much risk (size of positions) to allocate to your views. Now the optimizer is well-behaved! "No one trusted their optimizers," Litterman commented, "but we found out how to do that."

Now, investors seem to be pleased because they can apply the model to calculate their "view portfolios" which map their subjective judgments of the market information into the portfolio weightings, and portfolio weightings "behave well" because they do not contradict the investors' private opinions. Rather, *the model helps them express their opinions*. Indeed, the model functions as an opinion proclaimer.

SUMMARY AND CONCLUSION: CREATIVITY, CRISES AND MODEL RISK

In this chapter, we discussed how models enable individual investment decisions. Three modi of *modelwork* were presented: qualitative overlay, backing out (implied calculations) and the translation of users' subjective views into numbers. This analysis extends our understanding of how models enhance investability in markets, and why and how they are used despite their deficiencies. The case studies in this chapter have demonstrated that financial decision-making is *more than just calculation*. We have seen that the investability of markets is not established by rigorous acts of calculation and by merely telling "motivating stories" (Tuckett 2012), but by the creative process of combining judgmental stories and market observations with formal models. Model users make generic and idealized models work by exploiting the room for manoeuvre available in the flexible practice of model use. The case studies have shown how "qualculation" works in markets *in situ* and how calculative, technological and social aspects of financial modelling are interrelated.

Now, based on this discussion, we could come back to two questions posed previously in this book: why are some models performative and some not, and how are financial models dangerous?

Why Are Financial Models Not Omni-Performative?

While discussing the performativity concept in Chapter 3, we wondered why some models are more influential than others. Now, after having taken a look at the inside of the *performative practices* of model use, we can approach this question more insightfully.

The efficacy of models as a shaping force of markets depends on the active role of their users within the flexible practices of model use. The case studies in this chapter suggest that ability to provide for this flexibility determines the success or failure of models. If a model is sufficiently flexible to facilitate creative calculations, enable connections to markets and express the subjective truth of market users, the model might be effectively transformed into a useful – and performative – market tool. In other words, to become a widely used and influential financial instrument, the model should provide its users with scope for creativity.

The case studies in this chapter re-emphasize the notion of the creative usage of things and ideas in social practices. The concepts of social practice (Turner 1994; Schatzki 1996; Schatzki et al. 2001; Hörning 2001; see also Reckwitz 2002 for an overview) draw on the already-discussed Wittgensteinian model of ordinary language. While applying fixed linguistic structures and rules in everyday life, we undermine them and produce new meanings. Furthermore the idea of *bricolage* seems to be useful: A bricoleur brings about an innovation by providing unforeseeable and often unintended connections between readily available elements of practice (see Lévi-Strauss 1966; Weick 2001; Engelen et al. 2010 for the conceptualization of financial innovation as bricolage). These processes elude rational (calculative) logic. There is no such thing as "correct" or "incorrect" use.

In his related work, Michel de Certeau (1984: xiv) developed the idea of everyday creativity. While using supplied products, consumers develop "ways of operating" or "styles of action" which "intervene in a field which regulates them at a first level [. . .], but they introduce into it a way of turning it to their advantage that obeys other rules and constitutes something like a second level interwoven into the first" (p. 30).

In a similar vein, my studies show that financial models become for practitioners exactly what commercial products are for consumers, namely "the repertory with which users carry out operations of their own" (de Certeau 1984: 31). Like Indians who used colonizers' laws and religious practices for achieving their own unexpected goals, financial market participants utilize mathematical theories and models to "subvert them from within" (p. 32). In this way, they subvert calculative logic and develop the creativity of the market. The consequence of this creativity is the fact that a strong and automatic connection between models, decisions and markets cannot be simply presupposed and is occasionally difficult to detect. It is why models are not omni-performative.

The influence of models on markets is indirect and mediated by the styles of their use. Because there are many styles of model use and these styles depend on the flexibility that the model users enjoy, financial models vary in their ability to shape markets. This is why there is little evidence to support the strongest type of performativity: Barnesian performativity. Because models are primarily used as channels to transform the judgments of financial actors into numbers, there is no way that multiple users can manipulate models identically, derive similar results and create the world that the model describes – although my observations support notions of weaker forms of performativity (for example generic and, partly, effective performativity).

The other aspect of model use that weakens the strong performativity thesis is related to the organizational settings in which models are applied. The individual decisions of investors are usually framed by the organizations to which they belong. There are various styles of organizational framing in financial organizations that differ according to the manoeuvring room they provide for individual decisions. Organizations vary with regard to the extent to which model results are made binding for final decisions; that is, whether the model users are obliged to strictly implement model outcomes and recommendations or whether they enjoy flexibility in this respect. There is no single manner in which organizations deploy models. Instead, we observe various styles of model use in financial organizations, and these styles determine the degree or intensity of the influence of models on the markets.

My case study on DCF in this chapter shows how a large Zurich bank has adopted the model as the basis for its investment practice. Specifically, the DCF model provides suggestions for valuation as part of a well-structured investment process. I showed how, in the first step of the process, the wealth management research group makes assumptions regarding the relevant inputs for the DCF model. Then, the group calculates expected future cash flows for all asset classes for an indefinite time horizon, discounts them using a discount rate and determines the fair values for all the asset classes. A list that ranks all the asset classes – from the cheapest (the most strongly undervalued) to the most expensive (the most strongly overvalued) – is created. This list is sent to the portfolio strategy and solutions group to develop a concrete proposal on how to allocate the capital in client portfolios to different asset classes. The starting point for the proposal is the list of the model's suggestions. However, substantial amendments are made at this stage. I described how the DCF model is overruled by humans and used as a tool to obtain the results that its users consider to be correct (qualitative overlay). The amended proposal is then sent to the investment committee which makes the final decisions on how to allocate money to different asset classes in all the bank's portfolios. This procedure demonstrates how the institutionalized investment process is organized in such a way that the model is not the ultimate determinant of decisions and actions, but serves as a channel for transforming the judgment of the financial actors into a decision. The DCF model is only one element of the institutional decision-making process, which is clearly dominated by judgment. Thus, the DCF model can influence markets only indirectly because it is mediated by the organizational design.

How this mediation functions and how models are involved in decision-making in financial institutions is still poorly understood. The social studies of finance and accounting have only just started to open this black box. As already discussed at the beginning of this chapter, Mikes (2009, 2011) identified various "calculative cultures" in risk management that are not uniform but vary from bank to bank. The difference between them is the importance of judgment and interpretations; in other words, how the hybrid contexts of risk management are organized in each bank. The study by Hall et al. (2015) elaborates on Mike's findings: it presents two "calculative cultures", one based on risk models and toolmaking (the "Saxon bank") and one where interpersonal connections and individual experience serve as guides for decisions (the "Anglo bank"). Importantly, in both cases, the risk models have gained relevance for institutional decision-making in the process of interpretation of the model results and communication between risk officers and bank management about the models.

In the Saxon bank, where toolmaking is a central notion, the risk management instruments are influential because their results are constantly accompanied by qualitative interpretations and are involved in telling the company's ongoing story; they participate in the story. Also, the risk tools themselves (such as scenario analyses) are flexible enough to "absorb" and represent the views of most senior managers of each division. They have become successful "opinion proclaimers" in this particular organizational environment. In the Anglo bank, there are competing risk practices: the old and the new practice. In the end, the "old guard's" practice, based on individual experience and heuristics, dominates the "new guard's" expertise based on the relatively modern tool, namely the economic capital approach. The new tools, although implemented, fail to provide an efficient basis for inter-organizational communication and, as a result, have very limited influence on the business activities and decisions of the bank.

What I want to highlight with this discussion is the fact that, even if models are officially part of the organizational decision-making process, their role might be limited in the process of their organizational use.

Exactly as in individual decision-making, as discussed in this chapter, also the organizational cultures of "qualitative overlay" or "proclamation of opinions" might lead to the dominance of human judgment over models and make it possible that models become secondary decision-making tools or are even neglected, limiting their performative power.

This discussion has important implications for our understanding of the role of models in financial markets and society. Because the way in which models are used often prevents them from "performing" markets, the contribution of models to the last financial crisis and, more generally, the dangers they create for markets might be exaggerated and should be reconsidered. Now, we approach the next question of this section: how dangerous are models really?

Indeed, after analysing how financial market participants creatively use "inaccurate" models to make decisions, we still might want to follow Taleb (2010) and Triana (2011) and not celebrate this practice because it is dangerous and can lead to disasters, as observed in 2008. Here, we are confronted with the argument already mentioned in the introduction of this book: the crisis and other problems of the markets are caused by collective and thoughtless reliance on "wrong" models. Particularly, the regulators are to blame for providing market participants with inaccurate models – like parents, they should be made responsible for giving a dangerous toy to their children. Maybe, as Triana (2011) argues, it is better to have *no map at all* than to rely on the map of Saudi Arabia in the Himalayas; otherwise, everybody is running in the same – wrong – direction. Now, based on the discussion in this chapter, I will approach the accusations of models as villains from the modelwork perspective.

Model Risks

The rise of models in financial markets (as discussed in the introduction) is associated with various *model risks*. The McKinsey report on model risks specifies: "The use of models invariably presents model risk, which is the potential for adverse consequences from decisions based on *incorrect* or *misused* model outputs and reports" (Crespo et al. 2017, my emphases).

Thus, model risks can relate to two equally important issues: model deficiencies and model misuse. Model deficiencies can be of a "mechanical" or conceptual nature, as we have already discussed in this book. These are problems with unclear or unquantifiable input parameters, reliance on normal probability distribution (and thus exclusion of rare, black swan events), reliance on historical data and so on. As a result, models might come up with unworldly recommendations: they might overvalue or undervalue assets or underestimate risks (as is the case for VaR; see

Triana 2011). Furthermore, there are problems related to deliberate model manipulations or "incorrect" usage of models.

Note that such discussions presuppose that there are "correct" models that require "correct" usage. If their usage is "incorrect", it creates risks for the institution where the model is applied. The other possible consequence is that there are (only) inaccurate models, the application of which diligent market participants should avoid.

Furthermore, the common discussion of model risks highlights the fact that widespread thoughtless use of models creates specific risks that are relevant for the markets as a whole, namely *model herding*. If investors judge the market with the same or similar formal models, they will have the same or similar expectations and make the same decisions. This means that all of them will favour the same side of the market. In other words, they will want only to buy at the same time or only to sell at the same time. This will cause the other side of the market to thin out and threaten the market's existence. Such convergence of investors' behaviour can enhance the upward and downward market movements, contributing to bubbles and crashes.

For example, the implementation of similar stop-loss strategies for computer-controlled portfolio insurances was discussed as one of the factors that caused the stock market crisis in 1987 (Authers 2007: 9). Another example is the quant crash in August 2007 when some quantitatively managed hedge funds were simultaneously hit by market turbulences. A global quantitative equity fund of Goldman Sachs lost 30 per cent of its value within one week; many other computer-managed investment funds experienced the same fate, causing a drastic price fall in the market (Tett and Gangahar 2007: 7). One of the reasons for this event is related to model herding: quant companies mimicked each other's strategies and moved in unison:

> Companies learnt that whatever parameters they had been using to make their predictions, a host of their peers and rivals had been barking up precisely the same tree, meaning models they thought were exotic and cutting-edge were in fact mundane. This was partly because the pool of quantitative investment professionals who are truly at the cutting edge is still very small. Mr Alapat [from Amba Research, a Bangalore-based quant research house] says: "If a quant fund has a proprietary model that is successful, it gets mimicked very quickly." (Gangahar 2007: 7)

The widespread use of similar models creates additional risks described in the literature as "second-order dangers" (Holzer and Millo 2005), "model risk" (Esposito 2013) or "resonance" (Beunza and Stark 2012). Those risks relate to a distinct new form of interdependence among market participants which is mediated by models. According to Beunza and Stark (2012), there is a danger that market participants stop disagreeing with each other and suddenly start sharing the same model-based views about the markets. Thus, model herding is caused not only by the mechanical imitation of models by their users, but also by the fact that models are constantly related to the market in action-like decision-making. Beunza and Stark (2010, 2012) highlight this issue in their analysis of *reflexive modelling* (discussed in this chapter). While constantly observing and backing out the spread plot that represents the market consensus, merger arbitragers lock themselves into the thinking of the market and connect themselves to other financial actors. On the one hand, this procedure allows the inclusion of markets in decision-making; on the other hand, it gives rise to new risks:

> If a sufficiently large number of arbitrageurs simultaneously fail to see a merger obstacle ahead, the use of implied probability will provide traders with misplaced reassurance, leading them to expand their positions and suffer widespread, potentially catastrophic losses if the merger is cancelled. The reflexive use of models, in other words, creates systemic risk. (Beunza and Stark 2010: 6)

Hence, individual errors, interlocked in the process of model application, might be amplified and produce *resonance* of decisions. This resonance could become an external factor which cannot be taken into account by models. Financial models inevitably ignore effects that they themselves create (see discussion in Chapter 2). Because model use and its effects are constantly observed by other market participants, models unintentionally co-produce unwanted market phenomena – for example the misestimation of market risks in the case of the Long-Term Capital Management fund, LTCM (Holzer and Millo 2005), the GE-Honeywell merger failure (Beunza and Stark 2012) or the drastic price fall in August 2007 due to "quant quake" – and become themselves a part of the very phenomena they describe. As Esposito (2013: 118) states: "Financial crisis [. . .] occurred in a market that raised performativity to its highest levels, a market that was reacting primarily to itself and its expectations, a market driven by models led by the same expectations."

Recently, Borch (2016) stressed that, due to the increased importance of algorithms in financial markets, the herding tendencies have further increased. He contradicted Beunza and Stark's (2012) view that model use frequently generates dissonance, and claimed that the interdependences we observe in the high-frequency trading segment are interdependences among algorithms, and that human oversight and human control generally play a lesser role in the modern financial markets. Also, a recent *Financial Times* article on the "quant quake" in 2007 (Wigglesworth 2017b) revives old fears related to models: quant investing is rising; hedge funds are coming back; and the proliferation of similar quant strategies could again lead to a market meltdown.

This discussion points to very important risks related to modelling in financial markets. At the same time, if widespread model use in markets inevitably causes herding, one might wonder why bubbles and crashes have not become truly everyday phenomena – in other words, why we still observe "normal", "boring" days in markets (for instance without excess volatility). Indeed, we might want to understand both herding and *anti-herding* tendencies in markets, and pay attention to the production of both resonance and dissonance. Let us tackle these issues from the modelwork perspective.

Production of Diversity

The analysis of modelwork in this chapter allows for a more differentiated consideration of the risks related to financial models: models' insufficiency, misuse and herding. Concerning the first two risks – model deficiencies and model misuse – this book suggests that there are no "correct" models that can be used in a "correct way". All models are "wrong" in the sense that they do not perfectly represent reality, are merely imperfect idealizations and possess only limited predictive power. And every kind of model use is "misuse": there is no correct way of applying a model, just as there is no correct way of applying a language rule. For example, when people ignore grammatical rules or punctuation when using the WhatsApp messenger, it does not mean they are misusing the language – they are just using it in a particular way in a particular situation. In this sense, market participants are not "model dopes" (MacKenzie and Spears 2014b) or "F9 model monkeys" (a term used by Tett and Thal Larsen 2005), and do not "confuse illusion with reality" (Derman 2011) by blindly applying models. The different cultures of model use are about *coping with* model deficiencies and making insufficient models work. Every application of models is inevitably creative.

These considerations have consequences for the third type of model risk: model herding. The analysis of creative modelwork in this chapter relativizes the fear of a market collapse due to blind usage of similar models and points out the anti-herding tendencies created in the process of model use. As every decision is "incision" and implies the "undoing" of models, there is always a moment of flexibility in modelwork. The empirical examples in this chapter demonstrate that, while using models to structure decisions, observe markets or express opinions, investment professionals are free to follow or not follow the model prescriptions, to suspend or "game" them. There are many individually fashioned styles of using one and the same model. Just think of the DCF as applied by fund managers in the wealth department of a Swiss bank, by investors to "reverse engineer" the market and by financial analysts to express their judgment. Exactly because the styles of model use differ, there is no way that the different users can manipulate models absolutely identically and derive the same results. As we have seen in this chapter, strategies of model overlay and backing out are applied by market participants to *disagree* with the market or, at least, to question the market's views. Thus, the various strategies of model use give rise to forces that counteract herding tendencies. Cultures of model use do not automatically promote a particular behaviour in financial markets, but enforce disagreement.

The production of disagreement is enhanced in all phases of the model life cycle: model creation and model use. First, financial models are not created absolutely identically; there are proprietary variations of models developed in banks and investment companies. Remember that even in a field as strongly regulated as risk management, banks were allowed by the Basel Committee on Banking Supervision (BCBS) to use proprietary risk models (Lockwood 2015). Second, in the process of "crafting" models, there might be variations in the ways of identifying relevant data sources, collecting, cleaning and preparing data; quants compete for factors, signals and ideas which they incorporate into models, and this competition reduces the danger of herding:

> The rise of big data could lead to a new golden era for the industry, Mr Shen [the hedge fund manager] says. "The world is more complex and diverse now. That makes it harder [to perform], but it makes crowding less of a risk." QIS [Quantitative Investment Strategies arm at Goldman Sachs] is a case in point. While its quants might have tapped into only a dozen or so signals in 2007, they now use more than 250 with much less leverage. That means the dangers of crowded strategies that proved so toxic nearly a decade ago should be reduced. (Wigglesworth 2017b)

Furthermore, in data processing, cost considerations also play a role. Hardie and MacKenzie (2014) report that, in the highly sophisticated market segment of collateralized debt obligations (CDOs), a powerful cash flow model (Intex) was available prior to the 2008 crisis. This model allowed its users to analyse a variety of scenarios, to estimate the probability of default and to make informed decisions. However, the model was hardly used because such full analysis was too costly; investors rather applied various simplifying rules, or shortcuts.

Third, model users individually decide on the input parameters that are included in or excluded from models, as we have seen in our discussion of the DCF in this chapter. This is why there are no two absolutely identical

DCFs or VaRs in the market. Lockwood (2015: 742, original emphasis) describes how the VaR methodology is individually implemented by banks:

> The 1996 Amendment was careful to specify that "no particular *type of model* is prescribed" and that banks are free to choose their own parameters and distribution (including "variance-covariance matrices, historical simulations, or Monte Carlo simulations") for calculating their maximum possible losses. (BCBS 1996: 46)

It is crucial that banks are free to create their idiosyncratic models and to apply and interpret them in the way they want. Indeed – and this aspect has been particularly highlighted in this chapter – significant flexibility and creativity can be observed in the implementation of models and model-based strategies. The ways of connecting models to markets are not uniform and do not follow formal rules; they are indeed *heuristics of model use* that might vary among individual market participants, investor teams or organizations. In other words, the empirical examples in this chapter demonstrate that the diversity of decisions and opinions is generated in the markets and counteracts the crowding tendencies. Thus, the creative cultures of model use contribute to the production of "agreeing to disagree" (Morris 1995) in financial markets.

At the same time, this flexibility comes at a cost and bears its own dangers: it might contribute to the markets' instability and even potential collapse, but not through herding. I would claim that it was not the blind application of identical models that primarily caused the financial crisis in 2008, but the *inherent creativity* in modelwork. This creativity should not be understood as a deliberate misuse of models but rather as ways of making models work so that they open up new possibilities for users, but also create new dangers. Think of two examples: risk management in banks and credit rating agencies.

Risk Cultures

Risk management in banks has been frequently used as a prime example of models' failure during the last financial crisis. In particular, critics have focused on Value at Risk, a statistical measure of banks' potential losses. In the aftermath of the crisis, the model was frequently presented as a flawed and abstract mathematical construct. It was claimed that, due to its insufficient mathematical structure, VaR was predestined to underestimate risks in a turbulent situation. VaR is apparently "a peacetime statistic" (Nocera 2009): it presupposes normal market conditions based on historical data sets. Hence, if we use this formula to estimate the risks of new products (such as complicated structured instruments), we face a problem because these products have a short and unique history. Consequently, the model's parameters are unknown or uncertain. In the case of the VaR model, one such parameter is liquidity. According to Croft (2009: 21):

> VaR was not designed for illiquid products as it assumed the sale of products within 24 hours [. . .]. Putting really illiquid products into VaR, where you are looking at short-term moves in prices, is not appropriate because you will be locked in for a longer period and potentially suffer larger price moves. VaR will understate risk.

A very detailed discussion of VaR's deficiencies is provided in the book by Triana (2011), *The Number That Killed Us*. Note that this discussion focuses on only one model risk – inherent model insufficiencies – telling only a one-sided story. Concerning model application, usually a sweeping claim is made: VaR was used blindly and uniformly, and thus led to disaster. But was it really so?

The analysis of cultures of model use in this chapter suggests that the story about risk management might be more nuanced. Keeping in mind the various styles of modelwork, one would hardly expect risk management tools to be blindly applied, but rather to be involved in individual and organizational decision-making in a sophisticated manner. *Risk cultures* come to the fore in this discussion.

For example, managers working for the failed mortgage giant Fannie Mae first established a sophisticated risk-control system and then simply ignored the warnings that the system produced. The managers observed the market development and decided to continue assuming more risk. Following this human qualitative decision, they continued to buy hazardous mortgages, although the models advised against such transactions (Duhigg 2008).

A very detailed description of a similarly "weak risk culture" is provided in the Bank of England's report "The failure of HBOS plc" (2015). It again describes how the clear priority of fast growth over risk considerations was the dominating organizational policy. Although HBOS installed the appropriate risk management framework (the 3LoD model, that is, the three lines of defence approach), the system's warnings and "controls could be overridden when convenient" (p. 207):

> The June 2007 Blue Book [the internal document that summarized group's performance and key risks for the management] provided an example of where performance (in the form of fee income) took precedence over risk consideration (in the form of "internal hurdles"): *"Deals are agreed by Corporate Banking with pricing input from Treasury which do not meet our internal hurdles but which we expect to sell on to the market via a securitisation. This allows us to make fee income from deals we would have otherwise rejected."* (Bank of England 2015: 207–8, original emphasis)

The Bank of England report considered the major failure of HBOS to be related to its organizational risk framework, which gave insufficient priority to risk management, and to its failure to "instil an appropriate culture of risk within the organisation" (p. 208). Thus, again, it is not about having or not having sophisticated models, but about how their application is organized. The organizational *risk culture* (particularly its flexibility) is the key.

Apparently not all banks have made similar mistakes. For example, the Goldman Sachs bank was remarkably successful in managing its risks prior to and during the crisis. It did not blindly rely on the VaR framework, but constantly monitored and adjusted it according to its managers' judgmental calls:

> Judgment may also be recognized in a give-and-take debate, where decision makers weigh computer models against other factors. Goldman Sachs was one of the few financial institutions that profited from the subprime mortgage meltdown, and part of the difference was the judgment exercised by its leaders. The company shorted the ABX index [. . .], earning more than $1 billion in profits during 2007. During this period, senior executives were monitoring the value-at-risk (VaR, a statistical measure of potential loss) associated with the firm's mortgage position, as well as grilling the mortgage traders on the rationale for their bets. On separate occasions, the executives forced the traders to downsize their positions, even though the trades were profitable, in order to keep the VaR in check. At other times, they allowed the VaR to rise to an all-time high. (Posner 2010: 214)

Thus, it is the specific culture of model use and styles of judgment incorporated into decision-making within a financial organization that are essential for the success or failure of risk management. Models are always related to market events and judgments in the practices of model use, and an understanding of those practices is crucial for comprehending the causes of the crisis and other detrimental market events.

Credit Rating Agencies

The possibility of applying models as *opinion proclaimers* determines another interesting model-related phenomenon – and danger: models can be used to get the results their users want. A telling example relates to the practices of corporate rating agencies.

The existing literature convincingly demonstrates the prevalence of professional judgment in the production process of sovereign and corporate ratings (Columbano and Ezzamel 2017; D'Agostino and Lennkh 2016). In fact, ratings are opinions (Rona-Tas and Hiss 2011: 240); there is plenty of room for discretion although a formal rating methodology is applied. This issue has various consequences. One of them is the possibility of using statistics-based rating methodology not as a calculation device, but as an opinion proclaimer. Paid by product issuers, the agencies are compelled to produce the ratings wanted or required by the latter. Models enable them to assign high ratings to commercial papers that might in fact be high risks. This practice invites the suspicion that the broadly discussed deficiencies of rating models – including problems with omitted variables, normal distribution, correlated defaults and the Gaussian copula (MacKenzie and Spears 2014a, 2014b; Rona-Tas and Hiss 2011) – are in fact of secondary importance for understanding the role of rating agencies in the last financial crisis. Even if the mathematics were perfect, the models would have been used by the agencies to achieve the desired (predetermined) results, and this seems to be the key issue.

There is a terrific scene in the *Big Short* movie (2015) in which Mark Baum and Vinny Daniel ask the representative of Standard & Poor's why subprime bonds were not downgraded although the quality of the underlying loans was clearly deteriorating. The official starts by arguing about delinquency rates and models, and ends up stating that the rating agency simply had to keep its customers happy. The necessary link between the final product (the rating) and customer satisfaction is the model that is used as an opinion proclaimer: the rating agencies know which rating they want to produce and use the model to do it. Judgment can be used to undermine the model.

Penét explicitly illustrates the role that discretion and judgment play in the practice of the other rating agency, Moody's. Famously, the agency maintained its high "A" rating for Greece in 2009 although all indicators pointed towards a deterioration of the country's economic and debt situation, especially after the revision of its 2009 deficit projection from 3.7 to 12.5 per cent. Although the Moody's ratings are officially based on five pillars (macroeconomic fundamentals, government credibility, equivalent ratings, market prices and external support), these factors were judgmentally weighted so that only one factor – namely external European Central Bank (ECB) support – was given an absolute priority and allowed to justify the high rating. In 2009, Moody's wanted to demonstrate that the market fears over Greece were exaggerated, and easily achieved this goal using "backward reasoning": "Backward reasoning is a non-linear process by which a producer of anticipatory knowledge infers the meaning of new information in a way that vindicates former views, which are themselves embedded in the producer's present anticipations of a value outcome" (Penét 2015: 75).

In other words, the highly interpretative usage of new information and application of judgment allow credit rating agencies to achieve consistency of ratings and, more generally, maintain any rating they want. This is an important issue that points to severe problems for the stability and smooth functioning of financial markets. The over-optimistic ratings some investment vehicles such as CDOs received before the financial crisis might not be the result of erroneous models. It was not the models that underestimated the risks of those instruments, but humans who used the models to present the risks as lower than they really were. What is interesting here is, again, not the juxtaposition of calculation and judgment, but the real consequences of the fact that credit ratings are – in the final analysis – opinions based on *judgment about calculation*. This discrete and often not acknowledged dominance of judgment seems to be at the core of the debate on how to understand and regulate financial markets.

Consequences for Financial Regulators

The different practices of model use discussed in this chapter lead to the conclusion that the fundamental problem in financial markets does not seem to be the extinction of practical tacit knowledge due to increased rationalization and formalization (Oakeshott 1962; Porter 1995) and related overreliance on "wrong" unrealistic models. Rather, on the contrary, the – still ever-present – strong dependence on the informal, interpersonal procedures that inevitably accompany the application of models should be considered as crucial.

If we accept this view, then the traditional solutions for improving financial market stability – "better" models or "fewer" models – seem to be off target. Indeed, on the one hand, there are voices that require models' improvement. They suggest that if we manage to incorporate the missing mathematical elements (such as fat tails, for example) into the calculation, we will get an "accurate" model. However, according to the discussion in this book, this ideal is out of reach: "correct" models that perfectly represent and explain the world cannot exist. On the other hand, there are calls to "conquer" models as an evil, to ban them and go back to "intuition" (Derman 2011) and "common sense" (Triana 2011). Those solutions also seem questionable. First, it is unrealistic to eliminate models and algorithms from modern markets given their ubiquitous use. As we said, to model or not to model is not the question. Second, models in isolation are not the problem because in fact they do not dictate decisions. They are *always* combined with judgment and tacit knowledge; thus, there is enough – or, one might say, even too much – intuition in all sectors of financial markets. The problem is not about the re-introduction of human judgment into the nearly fully automated and formalized markets. We can hardly find a model or an algorithm used without a human component at one or the other stage: social elements are constantly "folded" into a market (Muniesa 2007).

Hence, the central challenge for regulators is how to govern the "qualculative" practices without conquering one of the two inseparable sides: formal models and judgments/interpretations. This governance requires an in-depth understanding of "qualculation", the issue that has started to get attention in the field of the social studies of finance and accounting, but has not been sufficiently developed to answer the important questions of financial regulation. It is important to differentiate between various qualculative practices and to understand the modi of differently combining judgment and modelling.

The analysis in this book has only made the first steps towards a necessary classification of practices of model use. Furthermore, the case studies discussed in this chapter suggest that there are major differences among various sectors of financial markets (asset management, risk management, proprietary trading and so forth) – and not only in relation to how models are applied. Thus, the investment chain mentioned at the beginning of the book could also represent a chain of cultures of model use. There are local peculiarities as to how formal models are *made to count* in each field – and those peculiarities are relevant for regulators as they determine the final decisions made by individuals and organizations.

Thus, the Borch (2016) vs Beunza and Stark (2012) controversy about herding (mentioned above) cannot be generalized and become a discussion about financial markets as a whole. The cultures of combining formal models with human judgment in a merger arbitrage department take different forms from those that they take in a high-frequency trading (HFT) company. They should be investigated and understood in their own right. The governability of modern markets depends on the proper understanding of cultures of model use which simultaneously produce order and disorder, resonance and dissonance. A "restorative regulation" – understood as the correction of technical malfunctioning of markets (Engelen et al. 2012) – can hardly be applied to them.

Thus, the ultimate challenge I would like to mention is that it is difficult – or rather pointless – to introduce rules that directly govern cultures of model use. The problem is that the introduction of formal rules or quantified norms into practices that are simultaneously formal and judgmental inevitably addresses only one side of them – the formal side. Gill delivers an in-depth analysis of genuinely judgmental decision-making practices in accounting, and points to "a gap between accountants' explicit discourse of rule-based factuality and their more tacit practices of fact construction". He demonstrates that, due to the interpretative approach that accountants usually take towards formal rules, "the more calculatively refined accounting knowledge becomes, the less compelling it seems in overall terms to those who create and use it, and the less likely it is to form the ultimate basis for their decisions" (Gill 2009: 136).

Thus, Gill suggests, there are *natural limits to the rationalization* of accounting and, I would say, to any practice in financial markets in general. Those limits are related to the fact that the formal rules that are introduced will be confronted by the inevitable scepticism of users and subverted from within. In this sense, regulation might defeat itself; and these processes of users' "natural fighting" rules in practice should be taken into consideration when governing financial markets.

Crucially, some innovative regulatory practices pay attention to the importance of qualitative aspects alongside formal issues such as calculation. For example, Coombs and Morris (2017) show how regulatory stress testing in the UK incorporates the process of narrativization in the obligatory calculation of scenarios: banks produce many pages of stories that accompany their risk modelling, explaining and communicating the results. Calculation and narrative are entangled in the formal regulatory process; they are not mutually exclusive but complementary logics. In the next chapter, we will continue and expand this discussion, analysing in more detail how models are used to communicate and justify decisions.

5. Models in "decision-selling"

In Chapter 2, I introduced two general modi of model use in financial markets: models as instruments of *action-like decision-making* (backstage) and as tools of *decision-selling* (front-stage). In other words, models are used by market participants to motivate either themselves (as discussed in the previous chapter) or others (this chapter) to overlook radical uncertainty and act.

Furthermore, we discussed financial *decision-making at large* as an ongoing and circular process (see Figure 2.1). We said that this process is about the production of promises and commitments which reach into the future but also "look back", while being constantly justified and explained. Indeed, on the one hand, there is the forward-looking process of creating alternatives, making incisions, undertaking commitments and developing convincing (often fictional) stories about and around those alternatives and commitments. On the other hand, there is the ongoing backwards-directed conceptualization of *incisions as decisions* and justification in the form of creating, negotiating and presenting the reasons behind what has been done: What were the alternatives at the moment of decision? Why was this particular alternative chosen and not the other one? Importantly, the forward-looking stories and retrospective justification are interwoven; usually, stories about decisions are constructed in such a way that simultaneous or subsequent justifications are possible.

Now we will discuss the role that models play in decision-making at large in more detail. We have said that they contribute to the persuasion and justification work which enables actions. But how exactly do models achieve this? The traditional way of explaining the persuasive power of models (as well as numbers and calculations in general) is to refer to the general positivistic pattern of objectivity, rigour and impersonality (the over-calculative view). In his book *Trust in Numbers*, Porter describes the pursuit of quantitative objectivity in science and politics as a way of excluding subjective discretion from decision-making. He shows how, after a long battle, judgment (as "counterweight" to calculation) is no longer considered as a unique strength of experts but rather a *weakness* that precludes uniformity, rigour and un-emotionality. Referring to Barnes (1986), Porter (1995: 98) emphasizes: "Quantification provided authority, but this is authority as Barry Barnes defines it: not power plus legitimacy, but power minus discretion."

This is the battle that models seem to win in the modern financial markets: the recent enthusiasm for automation, algorithms and modelling is related to the belief that formal procedures are capable of guaranteeing scientific objectivity and of emotionally defusing decisions. At the same time, as discussed in several places in this book, the models' calculative objectivity is hardly warranted. This observation leads to an important conclusion: although market participants are sceptical about models' ability to calculate, they readily make commitments and accept promises based on models because the latter provide the desired "power minus discretion" and thus the *symbolic* or "epistemic" authority (Kruglanski et al. 2005) for coping with uncertainties. This authority is by no means related to their immediate calculative power (which is constantly questioned and doubted) but is staged, or *feigned as calculation-based authority*, at the front-stage of financial markets. Let me explain this point.

As we discussed, in financial markets, we are dealing with a situation in which multiple unknown futures are thinkable, and thus "good" – logical or objective – reasons for investing do not exist. Models help create such reasons by producing and staging the necessary fictions. Unknown futures can be approached only by means of comprehensive fictions, that is, imaginative stories that are plausible but not necessarily true. To motivate investing, non-existing "objective" knowledge about the future must be *feigned and performed* as reliable and objective. In these performances, formal models play a crucial role which is at the core of this chapter.

I would like to draw particular attention to how models co-create and stage fictions in the process of convincing *other market participants* and selling decisions and "views" to them. When one group of market participants (for example financial analysts) presents imaginary future scenarios to another group (for example fund managers), it is crucial for the presenting group to establish a common ground for *shared beliefs* and to convince the other group to act in a particular way (for example to invest in the recommended stocks). In this *persuasive communication*, models play a crucial role.

In what follows, I will demonstrate how, first, models function as communication devices in markets in general and then, more specifically, how they persuade while helping to perform the objective knowledge at the front-stage. Here, we will be discussing one of the most important latent functions of financial models: models as participants in the theatre of financial markets. To illustrate this point, I will use the case study in which the economists of a Swiss bank presented the – fictional – "soft-landing" scenario for the world economy to the fund managers at the beginning of

2008, and explore the role that models and numbers played in this persuasive yet misleading communication.

FINANCIAL MODELS AS COMMUNICATION DEVICES

The social studies of finance have already pointed out that *enabling communication* is one of the most crucial contributions of models to the smooth functioning of financial markets (Millo and MacKenzie 2009; MacKenzie and Spears 2014b). Models often provide a language that is widely used in markets and, in doing so, coordinate actions and allow for innovations.

Let us discuss an example of the Capital Asset Pricing Model (CAPM) which was created – as its name suggests – to price financial assets. However, in its pure form, it has never been extensively used for this purpose due to its severe drawbacks. Still, the model has strongly shaped the way investors talk and think about financial markets.

The CAPM suggests that – at the market equilibrium – the expected returns come in two parts: the risk-free rate and the risk premium. The risk-free rate compensates investors for the fact that the same amount of money in the future will be worth less than it is today (the time value of money); the interest rate on ten-year Treasury bills is often used as a proxy for the risk-free rate. The risk premium rewards investors for investing in individual risky securities, and is calculated by multiplying beta (the measure of the security's volatility relative to the market portfolio's volatility) and the market premium (the excess return of the security over the market as a whole). Thus, the CAPM suggests that if investors know the risk-free rate, the beta and the market premium, they can estimate the returns of an asset.

At the same time, according to Coleman (2014: 231), who recently conducted interviews with fund managers around the globe, "most (88 percent) of the interviewees reported that they make little use of investment theory, many of them making specific mention of CAPM, portfolio theory and asset pricing."

What exactly are the reasons behind this situation? The CAPM framework "fails to survive contact with the real world" (Coleman 2014: 226) because it relies on unrealistic assumptions. The model assumes: that investors have homogenous expectations of asset returns and volatilities; that they are risk averse and can lend and borrow an unlimited amount of money at a risk-free interest rate; that there are no transaction costs; that investors can take any position (long or short) in any stock of any size without affecting the market price; and that there are no taxes. Markets that comply with this description simply do not exist. Thus, as Bernstein (2007: 172) gently confirmed, "CAPM in its pure form has never played much of a role in stock selection." In other words, the CAPM has not managed to develop into a widely used calculation device for asset pricing.

In this book, we have already referred to the issue of "unrealistic assumptions" several times. In this chapter, however, I would like to point out one important consequence of this discussion: models can be used as conceptual devices, as a language that shapes markets. Indeed, it would be wrong to claim that the CAPM – due to its "unrealisticness" – has had no applications in or effects on the investment industry. Although the model has generally failed to become a widespread calculative tool of asset valuation, at the same time it has established itself as a powerful *language* and *thought argument*.

Indeed, the CAPM – next to the Modern Portfolio Theory (MPT) and the Efficient Market Hypothesis (EMH) – has managed to become a widely accepted *way of thinking* and *talking about markets*. Milne (1995: 11, my emphases) outlined this contribution of the MPT-CAPM-EMH concepts as follows:

> The development of finance theory has been rapid [. . .]. These developments have been important in providing a coherent framework for thinking about existing financial markets and decision-making; and for creating ways of thinking about new financial products. It is ironic that abstract ideas developed in the 1950s and 1960s, which were thought to have limited application, should become *the common language of financial markets*.

Jovanovic (2012: 548) also highlighted that the contribution of Markowitz was not an insight into the importance of diversification *per se*, but the introduction and use of the common *mathematical language*, which is based on the modern probability theory. Indeed, one hardly finds a professional investor today who is not familiar with terms such as "expected returns", "mean-variance optimization" or "beta". The popularity of these terms is amazing. For example, Derman was impressed by the strong presence of the CAPM framework (despite all its fallacies) in the financial internet portals. He was searching for the volatility numbers of Apple and S&P500 on Bloomberg, Yahoo and Google; what he found, however, was beta. He stated:

> To my astonishment, there was no easy and direct way to obtain stock's volatility σ. All those websites give you easy access only to the stock's beta, the amount of market risk carried by the stock that is the hallmark of CAPM's view of the world. It is a sign of the political power of models that commercial websites publish the value of beta, a parameter in a model that doesn't work that well. (Derman 2011: 182)

Indeed, the CAPM (alongside the other core financial theories) has determined the modern language of financial markets. This language has become a repertory for the creative development of innovative products and investment ideas. For example, the CAPM attached importance to investing relative to a market portfolio. As a result, the benchmarking of investment funds has become common practice. One of the major ideas of the CAPM, that an average investor has no significant chance to out-perform the market, gave birth to the passive investment style and index funds; today, this is one of the fastest-growing segments of the market. The recent fashions in the investment industry – the search for alpha (an active excess return on an investment in comparison to a benchmark), "smart beta" and factor investing – originate in the CAPM framework. Performance measurement of investment funds also flourished because, with CAPM, it received a solid theoretical basis. And of course, the CAPM plays a prominent role in estimating a firm's cost of capital. Indeed, all those terms have shaped modern investors' language and their ways of thinking about the markets.

The other – less conceptual but more pragmatic – examples of *models as communicative tools* can be found in the derivative world. MacKenzie and Spears (2014b) describe how the Black-Scholes model and the Gaussian copula formula offer a common language – the markets' Esperanto which is absolutely necessary for their *successful functioning*. These models helped to structure the process of negotiation between traders and to coor-dinate actions – that is, to agree on the risk and price of financial instru-ments and, thus, reach a deal. In this sense, models function as widespread coordination devices and communication tools.

More specifically, MacKenzie and Spears (2014b; also Spears 2014) illustrate in rich empirical detail how the Black-Scholes model has pro-vided a language that has allowed the trading of options. This language is related to the process of "backing out", the implied volatility discussed in Chapters 2 and 4. To make a deal, traders determine and agree upon a volatility level. This has become a common practice:

> Two traders haggling over the price of an option could *talk* to each other not in dollars but in implied volatilities, for example with one trader offering to buy the option at an implied volatility of 20% and the other offering to sell it at 24%, and perhaps splitting the difference at 22%. (MacKenzie and Spears 2014b: 424, my emphasis)

This is why the Black-Scholes formula cannot be considered as a purely calculative tool; rather, the model-based calculations are used for talking and negotiating. Spears (2014: 121, my emphasis) summarized his inter-views with derivatives traders:

[Though] traders have largely abandoned the Black model as a tool of pricing and hedging options, the pricing formula produced by the model remains an essential tool with which options traders quote and *communicate prices for options.*

Interestingly, a similar communicative practice developed around the trading of collateralized debt obligations (CDOs). The Gaussian copula formula provided traders with the possibility to backward-calculate the "implied correlations", and this Esperanto managed to spread across the markets for a while. MacKenzie and Spears (2014b: 425) report that:

"implied correlation" became a standard feature of how participants talked about CDOs [. . .]. Otherwise, as an interviewee put it, "Like two people speaking two different languages, they can't really have a conversation." Only the Gaussian copula was used widely enough to serve as the necessary Esperanto. Whatever models different traders might privately prefer, "we communicate using the numbers implied by the Gaussian distribution," this interviewee told us.

In other words, practitioners needed a formula to organize their trading practice, and therefore adapted the Gaussian copula and tried to overlook its limitations. However, its limitations were severe. While applying the formula, traders confronted serious obstacles. The Gaussian copula model was less analytically straightforward than the Black-Scholes; it required a lot of ambiguous choices to be made by users. As different traders adapted different idiosyncratic versions of the model, the range of "implied correlations" they calculated was sometimes too huge to successfully coordinate actions.

As a result, the Gaussian copula formula caused more difficulties when striving to reach agreement on prices than the Black-Scholes model. Nevertheless, talking in "implied correlations" continued to be a common practice because it "provided a point of stability" (MacKenzie and Spears (2014b: 426), and *made complicated financial instruments discussable and specifiable, rendering markets investable.* Thus, the social studies of finance suggests that models are essential for the existence and functioning of markets – not as calculating machines, not as instruments of knowledge production, but *as tentative communication tools and, hence, decision-enablers.*

However, in this chapter, I would like to draw particular attention to models' participation in a specific type of communication, namely *persuasive communication at the front-stage* where one group of market participants initiates and sells decisions while persuading the other group.

MODELS AS PARTS OF PERSUASION ROUTINES

Already in 1995, McCloskey and Klamer highlighted that "one quarter of GDP is persuasion" and that financial markets are a good example of a place where people talk all the time in order to convince each other about potential deals, companies' prospects and so on. However, the role of models in this discussion was rather misrepresented:

> Efficient markets convey through prices all the information that a trader can expect to get publicly. No need to talk, since any informational advantage is reflected in price changes. Such efficiency would provide few rewards to talking if *the talkless model* were the whole story. The conventional story conjures up a silent film of people throwing darts or staring at computer screens, and typing (silently) their orders. Turn on the computers and retire to Rye. Something is missing, namely, the judgment part of knowledge, persuasion. (McCloskey and Klamer 1995: 194, my emphasis)

Here, the tendency is to consider judgment, narratives and human "talking" – in contrast to "silent" models – as the crucial element of persuasion work. Recently, Tuckett (2012) also argued that "financial markets are markets in stories", and demonstrated how fund managers solve the problem of acting under radical uncertainty through developing "convincing narratives" (Chong and Tuckett 2015: 310). Market participants produce confidence (as a collective belief state) or convince and motivate each other to act by telling stories about markets; the concept is closely related to the "animal spirits" (Keynes 1936; Akerlof and Shiller 2009).

However, this overemphasis on narratives and judgment in persuasion work in markets can hardly be sustained, if we follow the social studies of finance and consider models as persuasive communication devices. We clearly have to explore their role in the origin of shared beliefs and actors' confidence in those beliefs.

Particularly, as soon as investment professionals go front-stage and make efforts to convince others, they rely on models and numbers as sources of credibility for their stories. At the same time, as already discussed, we are often talking about "false precision" (Jasanoff 1991): here models function front-stage as elements of convincing fictional (*as-if*) narratives.

Those narratives can be considered part of the market routine. As Goffman (1959: 37) noted, "a given social front tends to become institutionalised in terms of the abstract stereotyped expectations to which it gives rise."

Indeed, there are conventions that help the audience orient itself while watching a performance. These conventional expectations are not formed for each individual performance every time anew; they are standardized and become part of the presentation routine. Primarily, the audience members expect a serious, unambiguous and consistent analysis from the professional presenters in financial markets (for example forecasters, analysts and so on); in other words, they anticipate the performance of "hard science" (Reichmann 2010; Wansleben 2014). As we will see in the case study on economic forecasting below, models and numbers are an important part of the convention of delivering precise, unambiguous predictions front-stage.

Here, the role of the audience becomes prominent (as already discussed in relation to pragmatic model accounts). The audience *expects* the presenters to use formal scientific language, especially the common language of economic theory and models, and to include graphical representations such as tables, charts and diagrams (Bourgoin and Muniesa 2016). The performers at the front-stage see themselves forced to adjust their presentation style to the audience requirements (searching for acceptance of their views, but also for status and recognition). Giorgi and Weber (2015) demonstrate that securities analysts, for example, consider their presentation style (that is, how they tell their stories) to be an important source of status and success. In particular, the authors show that the more the analyst's presentation style corresponds to the audience's requirements, the greater the analyst's status. In other words, market participants strive to make the style and form of their performances more formal in order to successfully execute "impression management" (Goffman 1959) at the front-stage. The delivery of numerical forecasts, frequent references to scientific theories and models and the usage of graphs and diagrams are routine parts of this impression management. In general, to stage professionalism and seriousness, the forecasting performers constantly use models and numbers to provide an idealized impression of omniscience which is, in fact, very often merely the staging of "false precision".

THEATRICALITY WITH MODELS

At the same time, presentations at the financial front-stage take place not only in order to "impress" but also in order to convince, to produce shared beliefs and to motivate others to act. One important aspect of this persuasion is *theatricality*: models help to *stage* decisions as being objective, serious, accountable and legitimate.

Here, I refer to the perlocutionary aspect of language and communication (Austin 1962). In contrast to illocution based on routines and conventions, perlocution makes things happen by means of theatrical persuasion, convincing staging and, thus, by making believe. The perlocutionary theatrical element of language is crucial for bringing about shared (collective) beliefs and expectations, with the latter being *staged as real* and the actors acting as if "the staged reality" were real. By participating in this staging (that is, in various types of presentations front-stage), models contribute to the production of "faith in markets" and thus to action-like decision-making, rendering markets possible. They participate in the act of social bootstrapping (Barnes 1983; Bloor 2000; Ortmann 2004); all institutional and, thus, also market realities are:

> created by references to these realities [. . .] [They are] composed of the corresponding acting, knowing, believing, assuming, thinking and supposing engaged in by everyone else [. . .] all the referring, thinking and orienting is part of a practice which is constituted by these very acts of referring, thinking and orienting. (Bloor 2000: 160f.)

Here, we discover clear similarities to the "make-believe" of Walton (1990) and "the act of feigning" (*Akt des Fingierens*) of Iser (1993). Fictions in the form of plausible stories (for example a novel or a theatrical play) are developed as common references, and gain their own reality while the spectators or readers slip into the story and adjust their beliefs. Crucially, they also start to behave (to decide and act) as if the fictions were true, and refer to them as true. This is exactly what Searle (2001: 37) meant when he wrote:

> One way to create institutional reality often is to act as if it already existed. This is how the United States was created. There was no way that a group of people could get together in Philadelphia, all of them subjects of the British Crown Colony, and declare themselves to be an independent nation. There was no institutional structure to enable them to do that. Well, they just did it. They did it and they got away with it [. . .]. You can create an institutional reality just by acting as if it already existed.

Only when people *act as if* new fictions – a new state, a new business relationship, a deal or a good firm – were real do those fictions become and continue to function as a new state, a new relationship, a deal or a good company (and *count as* in Searle's sense). It is exactly what the perlocutionary dimension of fictional stories describes: (fictional) utterances can become real if they are staged and produced by means of a theatrical performance, if they are told and re-told plausibly (*mimesis* in the sense of Walton). Financial models provide this plausibility while staging fictional beliefs and expectations as trustful and serious because they are number-based. In doing so, they deliver a common reference point that enables action-like decision-making.

For example, only when social agents stage, or fake, the successful game of trust, is trust produced (Beckert 2005). In the production of trust, not only pure signalling (with certificates, expert reports and so on) and self-presentation of the trust-takers are important; the particular behaviour of the trust-givers also matters. The latter act *as if* they trust (believe in the show staged for them by means of certificates and reports, but also by means of expensive suits and Rolex watches). In other words, they fake the "willingness to trust" and slip into the role of believers. Beckert (2005: 21) calls the self-representation of the trust-taker "performative commitment", clearly highlighting the importance of staging and "performance" for establishing a social relationship.

In this vein, models are used to produce such performative commitment while staging useful fictions (fictional expectations) that help convince others. They co-produce and co-present *shared imaginaries* and conduct a *seduction gambit* (Žižek 1993, 2001). Making a promise of marriage, Don Giovanni performed a seduction: he had to make sure "that the victim believed in the symbolic efficacy (that is, binding character) of his promise" (Boucher 2014). But because there was no given authority, or reason, to rely on in the situation, Don Giovanni had to *convincingly stage* it: by swearing to God (using this reference as a replacement for the lacking authority), but also by looking into eyes, holding hands, modulating his voice and so on. In persuasive communication in financial markets, models often play the role of "looking into eyes" and "holding hands", rendering their true calculative (in)ability rather unimportant. Models stage the reasons for believing in the presented version of the future (for example a forecast for a particular economy or company). As Beckert highlights:

> because it *appears* rational, calculation as a form of storytelling provides legitimated justifications for decisions *despite* the incalculability of outcomes. Hence, calculations in situations characterized by fundamental uncertainty have an entirely different role than the one assumed by the actors themselves: they are not instruments that make it possible to anticipate the future, but tranquilizers against the paralyzing effects of having to act in unpredictable environments. Calculations help in *overlooking* the profound uncertainty entailed in decisions by increasing commitment to what remains fictional expectations. (Beckert 2013: 234, original emphases)

Models provoke action-like decision-making by *faking and staging reasons* where there are no rational reasons for a decision whatsoever: *bootstrapping*. As discussed in Chapter 3, while introducing the term "Barnesian performativity", MacKenzie (2001, 2006) referred to Barnes's essay on bootstrapped induction and used financial models as an example of self-referential and self-validating S-type utterances. But what has not been highlighted strongly enough is that this self-referentiality and self-validity have a strong theatrical (perlocutionary) connotation: actors use models to perform (not to produce!) knowledge; and, by doing so, they develop and confirm their joint definition of the situation, refer to it as real and bring the situation into being, gaining the ability to decide and act and, as a result, to change the reality. Thus, a persuasive theatrical performance with and around models is the crux of the functioning of financial markets.

MODELS AS USEFUL FICTIONS: TWO EXAMPLES

Let us discuss two examples that illustrate models' functioning as useful fictions and instruments of persuasion: credit ratings and "quasi-companies". Indeed, one could consider the credit ratings produced by rating agencies to be useful fictions that significantly contribute to the functioning of markets (Esposito 2013). Ratings provide common and reliable anchoring points for valuations (MacKenzie 2011) and decisions, and thus enable actions. Their "reliability" stems from the usage of formal methodologies, which is particularly encouraged by the audiences, for instance by the European Securities and Markets Authority (ESMA): "There is the pressure from regulators and users to demonstrate that credit ratings are an objective product of robust statistical modelling" (Columbano and Ezzamel 2017: 1).

Rating agencies carefully maintain their "scientific" status. For example, they communicate their models in regular publications and are constantly involved in theoretical and methodological debates about how to model default risk, which probabilities to use and so on.

Still, as already discussed, the ability of rating agencies to reliably transform genuine uncertainties into calculable risks is a proclaimed goal – and an illusion. Nevertheless, those illusions are necessary to convince people to act, that is, investors to invest, by means of convincing stories, of which models and numbers are a part:

> Conviction is a mental state of the individual achieved through the creation of stories – what we term conviction narratives – which share a common structure. They comprised two parts: what we term "attractors" – elements that generate excitement and optimism often through associations with gain – and what we term "doubt-repellors" – elements that manage doubts and anxiety often through associations with safety. When narrativized together you have a story of the future which is convincing enough for the actor to find the impetus to act. (Chong and Tuckett 2015: 314)

Models function as such "attractors" and "doubt-repellors" in the process of persuading financial audiences. Like in the story of cocos (Chapter 2), they provoke a feeling of knowing and security and make the performance front-stage (decision-selling) successful. The same applies to ratings. At the front-stage of markets, where ratings are communicated and become important reference points for actions, the illusion of precision is convincingly performed every time anew with formal mechanisms (models, methodologies) functioning as necessary doubt-killers. In markets of *nobody-knows*, knowledge about the future of countries and companies can only be staged, not reliably generated. Formal models and methodologies – as "make-believes" – are essential components of this staging. At the backstage, however – that is, in the internal practices of fabricating ratings – rating agencies vigorously defend the fuzziness of the procedure and maintain the application of judgment (Columbano and Ezzamel 2017). Ratings are, in fact, judgment-based opinions; however, they will never be presented as such front-stage. Thus, models' roles as calculative tools in the presentation modus (front-stage) and in the production modus (backstage) are limited significantly, but in different ways: backstage, models are *overlaid by judgment*; front-stage, they are instruments for *staging precision*.

Another telling example of a useful model-based fiction is the "quasi-company" (Hägglund 2000), which has already been discussed in Chapter 4. Securities analysts meet investors and present stories about companies to them. Those stories are developed around valuation models and multiples. Hägglund suggests that all involved market participants – analysts and their clients, for example portfolio managers – know that the presented numbers and calculations are imprecise estimates (fictions). At the same time, the numbers allow them to tell interesting and useful stories with many details; in other words, they enable and enhance persuasive communication between analysts and investors. Here, a valuation model, for example the DCF, serves as "an icebreaker at the financial party" (Hägglund 2000: 324) where everybody should be – but in fact is not – "frozen" by uncertainty. The uncertainty is "conquered", or "overlooked" (but not reduced), because various market participants find themselves "glued" around one fictional object – the quasi-company. Those fictions are based partly on models and partly on imaginative interpretations and narratives created by security analysts. One important role of models and numbers here is to justify the narratives, make them credible, remove the doubts. Referring to the accounts of models as "make-believes", one can suggest that models serve here as "props in discursive process, providing justifiable accounts of value that help to create convictions about future price developments in the inherently uncertain conditions of financial markets" (Beckert 2016: 148).

Models – as props – help provide legitimatization for the quasi-companies.

Both analysts and fund managers *pretend* to believe in the modelled fictions and discuss them seriously, *as if* the quasi-companies (for example Amazon at a target price of $400 in 1998) were real. In the end, it is not the calculated target price of a company that is interesting; the detailed, model-based – and thus justified or "plausible enough" – story which is presented to audiences and is developed in permanent discussions with them is what matters. Security analysts and their audiences analyse, adjust and question models and, in doing so, co-develop the patterns of the story's justification – they co-create shared reasons to believe the story.

THE FAILURE OF MODELS AS FAILURE OF PERFORMANCE

Importantly, there is no automatism in the success of the front-stage performances in financial markets. Recall the Blodget–Cohen controversy about the valuation of Amazon in 1998: both analysts used models and multiples to construct their stories; however, only one version (Blodget's) became accepted by the market participants (Beunza and Garud 2007). An analysis of this controversy suggests that performed stories (or quasi-companies) can be accepted or rejected – there is always a seed of failure in every performance. In this respect, the discussion of perlocution and fictions sheds new light on the previously discussed phenomena of *model failure* and *counter-performativity*: some financial models are used but do not produce effects, or they produce effects opposite to what they describe. This happens because the performances, of which models are a part, are always evasive and unforeseeable: "Performance contains the experience of powerlessness" (Krämer 2014: 229).

Like in a real theatre, where actors cannot count on a positive reaction from the spectators, the decision-sellers at the financial front cannot be sure that they will manage to convince their audiences. Models are not a guarantee. In other words, if model-based fictions are not performed successfully (that is, not believed or even ignored in the process of staging), models fail to develop performative effects and might produce unexpected results.

Hence, while focusing on performance and perlocution, we should not exclude the unpredictability and contingency of the social. On the contrary, we should make them part of the concept, because there is no guarantee for success. The concept of perlocution as performance helps explain how this guarantee is faked – and might become real but also fail. This is exactly the point made by Butler (2010: 153) when she wrote:

My worry is that the cultural constructivist position thinks performativity works and that it imputes a certain sovereign agency to the operation of performativity that foregrounds the illocutionary over the perlocutionary. If the theory presumes efficacity, then it fails to see that breakdown is constitutive of performativity (performativity never fully achieves its effect, and so in this sense "fails" all the time).

This preoccupation of perlocution with failure is more profound than Austin's (1962) theory of misfire of performative utterances, with its focus on the routine conditions of felicity to which Callon and MacKenzie primarily pay attention. Recalling Austin's most popular example – marriage – we can say that a wedding always succeeds if it is ritually performed in a particular institutional setting (for example in a church) in front of an adequate audience (two witnesses). Performative events, however, are devoid of any planning and control; they are unique and unrepeatable – and thus to some extent always unpredictable and surprising. In the case of perlocution and performance, there are no pre-defined circumstances in which a performance succeeds.

Moreover, the conditions of success are created while the models and their surrounding stories are presented at the front-stage. In the following case study on forecasting in a Swiss bank, I will show that a model's (and numbers') relevance can change while the story is presented to and discussed with the audience. Hence, it is not only at the backstage that models can be overlaid, ignored or creatively used (see Chapter 4). Also at the front-stage, we find examples of the performative "undoing calculations". The case study on economic forecasting below shows how models and numbers are connected to market events front-stage. On the one hand, economists follow conventions to present a scientifically justified and unambiguous definition of a situation based on numbers; in doing so, they downplay and largely exclude major uncertainties and potential surprises that are imminent at the very time of presentation (February 2008). Among many possible scenarios, only one is selected and presented.

On the other hand, in extreme situations (for example pre-crisis), model users cannot stay disentangled from what is going on in markets and economies; thus, they decide to disregard the predictions of some formal models and to lend weight to possible uncertain events that have already distorted and might further distort the model results. In other words, the relevance of model-based fictions can be radically undermined in order to account for uncertainty and surprises. Thus, when the model results are presented to the audience, they can be downplayed so that they do not influence final forecasts and decisions. Models can be *made to not count* in a concrete situation of social interaction and performance in financial markets. In other words, although models are an official constituent of the investment process or of a professional presentation, it does not mean that their calculations are always effectively taken into consideration when financial decisions are discussed and made. Models might be a part of *convincing stories* that fail.

Interestingly, in the process of staging model-based stories, the very responsibility for failure, or how responsibility is shared, can be created. The already-mentioned fascinating case study on "reverse brokering" by Graaf (2016) is a good illustration. Brokers developed an investment case and wanted to make their clients buy into the story (decision-selling). To do so, they co-created a story *together* with their clients. They calculated the initial pro forma model and then sent (presented) this model to the selected customers whom they knew were interested in the company in question. Importantly, this process of "reverse brokering" not only initiated dialogue with clients, but also allowed them to simultaneously develop *justification* for the investment case. It was particularly important because brokers suggested deviating from the consensus, committed themselves and took a reputational risk. By constantly co-working on and communicating about the model, clients co-developed the arguments as to why this investment case was interesting (recall *decision-making at large* as a simultaneous process of making promises and delivering justifications). Through this cooperation (which is similar to theatrical happenings), the brokers not only developed the acceptance of the quasi-company by their clients but also *shared responsibility with them*. Graaf shows how they also managed to avoid blame when the investment case later collapsed due to the unfavourable development of the oil price (a macro-phenomenon which was not in the model). The clients, as active participants in the financial happening, were reluctant to blame themselves.

This discussion suggests that models succeed and fail not only as calculative devices but also as performative devices. Models and numbers are part of the performative market theatre, and thus their success is always fragile.

Let us now expand these considerations using a concrete example. In the next section, I will present a case study (based on Svetlova 2012b) on how economic forecasting was performed in a Swiss bank just before the financial turmoil in 2008, and how tentatively models and numbers were treated on this occasion.

ECONOMIC FORECASTING IN A SWISS INVESTMENT BANK

The argument presented in this case study is based on field research conducted in several German and Swiss investment companies and banks in 2007 and in the first half of 2008. At that time, the world was experiencing the first wave of economic turmoil. The subprime crisis had already hit the banking system. It was becoming apparent that various structured financial products – such as asset-backed securities, collateral debt obligations and structured investment vehicles – contained securitized loans of different qualities (including very low-quality loans), but their distribution among financial institutions was unclear. The burst of the subprime bubble in the US in 2007 caused considerable problems for some banks; they announced significant losses and wrote off substantial assets. However, the extent of outstanding write-off was difficult to estimate. There was speculation that some big banks might go bankrupt. It was considered possible that monoline insurers that had suffered losses from insuring structured products would not maintain their high (mostly AAA) ratings. Due to these uncertainties, liquidity in the interbank trade became scarce. Risk premiums skyrocketed. In addition to the banks, the construction sector suffered from the subprime crisis. The US Fed reacted with severe interest rate cuts of 2.25 per cent which were enacted in five stages between September 2007 and January 2008. Moreover, an extensive fiscal package of USD 150 billion (1 per cent of the GNP) was provided by the US Government (Bergheim et al. 2008: 3).

In this situation, economic experts faced the following questions: would the financial crisis be successfully overcome in the foreseeable future? Would it spill over to the real economy? In other words, would the economy plunge into a recession in the US and then in Europe? The exact forecast of further developments was crucial for the investment decisions of portfolio managers, especially for decisions about asset allocation between shares, fixed-income securities and cash. If the financial crisis could be absorbed and the real economy did not suffer significantly (that is, a "soft landing"), riskier assets (for example, equities) should be overweighted; otherwise, in the case of a "hard landing", bond or cash holdings would be preferable.

To inform themselves of the situation, portfolio managers formed the audiences of various investment meetings at which forecasts were presented. For example, on 14 February 2008, an economist, an equity analyst and a bond analyst from the Swiss bank presented *the house view* on the global economy and the financial markets in an internal investment committee meeting. They delivered formal presentations to diagnose the confusing state of the economy at the beginning of 2008 and to provide *a persuasive account* of what was happening and what they predicted was going to happen. This meeting provided many interesting materials for an analysis of front-stage performance with respect to economic predictions.

Staging the "Soft Landing" in February 2008

As already discussed, forecasting and the presentation of forecasts at the social front are subject to particular routines. The audience members (in our case, portfolio managers) expect a serious, unambiguous and consistent analysis from professional forecasters. The seriousness and scientific character of forecasts should be supported by *a particular style of presentation*.

First, the audience expects a prediction expressed in numbers (that is, an exact numerical specification of an expected event should be given): for example, "inflation will be 4 per cent at the end of the year" or "the target price for the share in 2008 is $101". Second, the presentation of only one possible scenario – the so-called "house view" – is a norm. The expression of confusing scenarios (for example both recession and no recession are possible) is avoided front-stage – the presenters have to commit themselves to one view. Third, the audience expects the presenters to use formal scientific language and, especially, models. The outcomes of models as trustworthy scientific tools support and justify the presented unambiguous scenarios.

Let us now look at how precision and respectability were performed in the investment committee meeting at the Swiss bank in mid-February 2008. I will concentrate on the argumentation delivered by the bank's internal economist. He opened his presentation with a clear statement concerning the pressing question of the possibility of a recession:

> Our official forecast is no recession in the US. I formulate it differently: we expect no deep, really prolonged recession with much more than two-quarters of negative economic growth. However, we expect a very weak first half-year of 2008, and then a quite steep increase in GDP and, subsequently, high growth by the end of 2008 and in the first quarter of 2009.

This is a clear forecast: the economist predicted the so-called "soft-landing" scenario as the only possible development. All other possible scenarios were ruled out. Furthermore, the presentation was accompanied by predictions of exact values for GDP growth, interest rates and inflation. For example, the economist forecasted 2.2 per cent growth for the US economy in 2008.

A combination of the following formal forecasting methods was used to *justify* the "soft-landing" scenario:

- *Trend extrapolation.* The economist from the Swiss bank started his argument for the "soft-landing" scenario with an economic textbook definition of recession. According to this definition, recession occurs when a decrease in consumption expenditure is accompanied by a high level of investment. Then, he argued that "consumption has been strong *so far*" and that "*as of now* we have not seen over-investments in the US" – implying that these "so-far" and "as-of-now" developments were reasons enough to expect a continuation of both trends. Thus, no recession was expected according to the definition.
  The economist continued by arguing that the industrial sector had been doing well *so far* (with the exception of the construction sector), and forecasted that this development would continue. Thus, as the industrial sector would continue to be strong, there was no reason to expect contagion of the real economy by the already weak financial sector; hence, fears of a recession were groundless.
- *Analogy from previous historical situations.* In his arguments for a "soft-landing" scenario, the economist stressed that the US government had reacted very aggressively to the recent turbulence in the financial markets; as mentioned above, the US Fed had cut rates five times, and a significant fiscal package had been provided. He argued that, in the past, fiscal packages *had* increased consumption by an average of 1 per cent in the following quarter. Thus, this development should occur this time around as well; due to the fiscal programme, consumption would rebound and thus support the economy, preventing a recession.
  Furthermore, the economist argued that the US Fed had *always* historically supported banks in trouble and could thus be reasonably expected *to continue* to function as the "lender of last resort". Hence, the fears of bankruptcy by one or two big banks and, as a result, of systemic financial crisis with severe consequences for growth were not justified.
- *Early or leading indicators.* The indicators are based on statistically significant correlations between two events which are usually represented as sets of data. The idea is that it is possible to causally infer the appearance of one event from the appearance or particular development of another event. Indicators are often constructed by institutions with distinguished reputations, enhancing the trustworthiness of indicator-based predictions and helping to stage a sense of seriousness and reliability.

In this way, the Swiss bank's economist argued in his presentation that, for example, incoming orders were "a classic early indicator" of the development of the real economy. As this indicator had developed rather positively in the last few months, this was a clear signal of the favourable development of activities in the real sector and, thus, that a recession was not expected.

Now, let us briefly review and note that the performance of the "no-recession" story was supported by the following reasoning: the industrial sector was still doing well, although some weakness in the banking and construction sectors could be observed. Banks threatened by the liquidity crunch would always be supported by the Fed, as they had been in the past. As usual, the monetary and fiscal measures would produce positive effects on consumption and investments. Thus, a rapid economic recovery could be expected in the second half of 2008; a "hard landing" was ruled out.

This discussion illustrates how presenters at the front-stage bend the truth to satisfy the audience's expectations and deliver only one exact forecast. They consciously exclude alternative scenarios, even if they are aware of uncertainties, contradictory arguments and warning signals. By doing so, they produce the – albeit illusory or fictional – security of "business-as-usual" and, by reducing fears (using various formal "doubt-repellors"), induce readiness to act on the side of investors. They *perform* the knowable situation of risk where calculation-based decisions are possible.

Neglect of Uncertainties and Exclusion of Lack of Knowledge

Because the economic forecasters at the Swiss bank knew they had to produce only one view, they stuck to the "so-far-everything-is-ok" reasoning. The story of the "soft landing" was staged as coherent, consistent and scientifically justified by means of numbers and models. Irreconcilable arguments, even if they were supported by evidence, were often downplayed to keep the story free of contradictions.

Let us discuss two examples of when obvious warning signals were dismissed. The first relates to the ISM Manufacturing Index, the second to the ten-year US Treasury yield model.

The bank economist presented a graph that showed the development of the Institute for Supply Management (ISM)'s Manufacturing Index. This index is a popular indicator of economic activity; it is calculated and published every month by the ISM. An index value above 50 indicates that the economy is generally expanding; a reading below 50 means it is contracting. The crucial mark is 43. If the index is below 43, the economy is undergoing a recession.

Before February 2008, the ISM Manufacturing Index for the US fell below 50, and the portion of the index calculated solely for the service industries came close to the dangerous mark of 43. The bank economist could not ignore these developments when presenting the state of the global economy because the ISM index is regarded as a reliable – and conventional – recession indicator and is closely watched by the investment community. At the same time, the sharp drop in the index did not fit into his story of a "soft landing". Thus, the economist commented on it as follows:

> I think we should not over-interpret this drop [. . .] The weight of financial institutions and insurance companies in this index is high, and the fact that the mood is bad there does not surprise anybody, I think. The ISM index jumped below 50, and I think it will oscillate around this level in the next months. However, we do not envisage it to drop significantly below 43; the manufacturing industry is still doing too well to expect that.

Obviously, this reasoning is very weak. The idea of trend extrapolation ("the manufacturing industry is still doing well") was given more weight than the evidence provided by an indicator, although there was no rational reason to neglect an important warning. The only reason to argue this way was *the front-stage necessity of maintaining a coherent story* and of making it more convincing for the audience.

Another insightful example of the suppression of warning signals is how the quantitative model's predictions were treated in the economist's presentation. Long before the crisis, the economic department of the Swiss bank developed sophisticated regression models to forecast the ten-year US Treasury yield, the three-month money market yield, the ten-year swap spreads and some other important market figures. The graphs that represent the model forecasts had become compulsory and routine components of the bank economist's presentation at the investment meetings. However, their role was downplayed in the front-stage argument against recession in February 2008.

One of the models delivers a forecast for the ten-year US Treasury yield in the form of a range (+/− one standard deviation). The actual realization of the yield is plotted over the forecast range in a presentation slide to show whether the yield is following the forecast. In February 2008, the ten-year US Treasury yield did not fall within the predicted range. This required the economist to decide either to stick to the model or to explain why the model was not working and neglect its results at the front-stage for the sake of consistency. The economist argued as follows:

> What about the 10-year Treasury? I think that *we cannot stick to econometric models in the recent environment* because they are simply not good in times of

financial turmoil. At least in our short-term expectations, *we deviate significantly from our fundamental model* and expect the 10-year Treasury to sink to the level of 3.5%. This comes down to the fact that too much is still unclear. Not all banks wrote off, especially small banks [. . .] and there are monoliners; it is unknown if monoliners will be downgraded or if they will keep their AAA ratings. If they are downgraded, this could contribute to further turmoil in the financial markets, and the 10-year yield will come down further.

Obviously, in this particular case, the economist decided to disregard the predictions of the formal model and to give weight to uncertain events. Thus, "qualitative overlay" of models is also possible front-stage: the results of calculations and modelling can be overruled or neglected; they can be downplayed so that they do not exert any influence on the final forecast, as in the discussed case. In other words, models can be rendered unimportant (fail) in the very situation of forecasting performance.

The Role of Surprises

As we now know, the "soft-landing" scenario did not materialize in 2008 – *it was a fiction*. The major reason for this was the occurrence of large-scale surprises. The volume of bad loans in the banking system and of the subsequent write-offs exceeded all expectations. Furthermore, the US Fed behaved surprisingly inconsistently during the evolving crisis in 2008. As the banks found themselves in increasingly great difficulty, the market participants were still convinced that the central banks would continue to act as lenders of last resort. In late summer 2008, mortgage companies Fannie Mae and Freddie Mac were rescued, and the belief that the US Fed would continue to intervene in individual cases was strengthened. The real surprise came when Lehman Brothers was left to go bankrupt, with disastrous consequences for the global economy. As a result, an extreme liquidity squeeze and a credit crunch occurred.

In addition, there was no decoupling of the real economy from the financial sector. The growth rate in the industrial sector and the entire economy was catastrophic. According to the US Bureau of Economic Analysis, the growth rate of the US economy was zero and, in contrast to expectations, the last two quarters were especially weak. The ISM index dropped dramatically to 32 points. The fiscal package was unable to stimulate consumption. It was a genuinely "hard landing" for the world economy.

The possibility of these surprises was excluded by forecasters front-stage in order to perform *the knowledgeability and predictability of markets –* that is, to *stage non-knowledge as knowledge*. The forecasters satisfied their audiences' requirements of delivering an unambiguous, coherent and numerical view; in other words, they presented a situation of risk when, in fact, the economic participants faced a situation of uncertainty that could not be reduced to risk. At the same time, this strategy helped overcome the genuine uncertainty of the situation and motivated portfolio managers to make an investment decision, that is, to stay in the market and not to sell immediately. This example illustrates how the situational necessity of bending information to meet the audience's expectations resulted in significant mistakes and a low quality of forecasting which was indeed merely a fictional, yet useful, story.

Backstage and Its Connection to Front-Stage

The nature of forecasting backstage is different. Here, actors can drop the roles that they play at the front-stage, as the audience is not admitted to the backstage. As we saw in Chapter 4, this means that an impression of omniscience, precision and perfect foresight does not need to be produced. Indeed, backstage discussions about the future are characterized by a less formal atmosphere and are not strongly constrained, allowing for the presentation of a situation as a situation of Knightian uncertainty. Here, financial market participants treat economies as non-stationary and complex; for them, economic events are unique and do not repeat themselves. Thus, such events cannot be predicted by extrapolating established patterns into the future or relying on models and calculations. Changes occur in the economy all the time, and market participants are aware of this and frequently address potential surprises backstage. The use of models for decision-making incorporates these views (see Chapter 4).

When discussing future economic developments with their teams backstage, portfolio managers express scepticism about the significance of models and do not attempt to calculate precise forecasts because they consider them too "subtle" or too "specific". Instead, they are satisfied with something rougher, such as the direction of a price development or trend (as we saw in the study on the *plausibility check of consensus*). Generally, in my interviews, portfolio managers stated:

> I try to move at different aggregation levels. I want to know if the market goes up or goes down. How many percent points? I don't know. (portfolio manager, Frankfurt/Main)
> Forecast is [. . .] not a particular number but a particular dynamic. (independent financial advisor, Frankfurt/Main)

It is important to stress that this dynamic is not determined by simply extrapolating the identified trends but, rather, by scrutinizing these trends. For example, the head of the tactical asset allocation team in Frankfurt said that his team had developed a phase model that shows in which phase of the business cycle the economy and the market are. After answering the question "Where are we now in the cycle?", portfolio managers usually ponder:

> We say "Ok, each phase is different, not like in the past" and "What is different this time?" [. . .] this is, if you want, our judgmental part [. . .] In this qualitative part, we ask: "What is different this time?", "Why is it different?", "Will it have different consequences?" (head of the tactical asset allocation group, Frankfurt/Main)

This statement clearly reminds us of the question that was crucial for foreign exchange analysts according to Wansleben (2014: 617): "What does the model tell us in a particular situation?" Here, the uniqueness of market events is stressed. Similarly, portfolio managers discuss what might surprise the market in this very specific situation. A bond portfolio manager from Zurich phrased it as follows: "What I estimate or try to estimate is simply, 'Are there any surprises upwards or downwards?'"

At the backstage, awareness of changes and surprises allows for the development of various *parallel scenarios* about how the future might unfold. There is no pressure from the audience to produce one sole concise scenario. Portfolio managers backstage develop multiple scenarios in the form of fictional expectations. Backstage, forecasting is treated as a process of coping with Knightian uncertainty and not as a formal prediction under risk. Empirical material suggests that this imaginative element plays quite a prominent role as a basis for exploring alternatives and discussing possible surprises.

Furthermore, market participants address their doubts and market uncertainties much more openly backstage – they frequently confess to doing business in markets of *nobody-knows*. In an internal discussion in February 2008, the head of the portfolio management team in the observed Swiss bank said: "I think our main problem is that we do not have a distinctive scenario on which we orient our strategy. We sway between 'recession' and 'no recession'. The picture is absolutely not clear."

Such a statement could not be made in a front-stage presentation. Again, in the absence of an audience, confusing and unclear statements are admissible and even necessary because they facilitate discussions about alternative scenarios and surprises, thus supporting a more realistic forecast.

Considering these observations, one might ask: why do the doubts, uncertainties and provocative thoughts discussed backstage not leak to front-stage forecasting? Goffman (1959: 115) stressed that the backstage is cut off from the front "by a partition and guarded passageway". This partition is meant to keep the audience away from the backstage, as well as to allow front-stage performers to relax and drop their role. At the same time, the above discussion suggests that the barrier between front-stage and backstage also functions as a filter for information and views. The need to present just one quantified view at the front-stage forces forecasters to narrow the broad range of scenarios, doubts and uncertainties produced backstage. A situation of perceived uncertainty in the Knightian sense is simplified to a situation of risk. This socially established funnel is so powerful that, even in a time of crisis, as we have seen, it continued to work perfectly and was not shaken.

Although the fascinating process of translating various forecasts and arguments into a "house view" could not be observed explicitly during the study at hand, there are further hints suggesting that a complicated whirl of backstage opinions and positions is blocked by the barrier between the front-stage and the backstage. In an informal conversation that took place in the corridor after the presentation described above, the Swiss bank economist admitted that he and his colleagues had had extremely heated discussions about the future of the world economy in 2008 while preparing for the meeting; in fact, he said, "they have not had such heated discussions in ages". The team was aware that the times were very difficult and unstable; thus, there were various scenarios defeated by different team members, and various forecasts were floated. The economist said that it was very hard to agree upon one view.

As some further empirical studies (Mars 1998; Abolafia 2005; Reichmann 2010) suggest, this process of compulsory agreement on a house view is determined by negotiating conflicts and by searching for compromises that are often not substantially content-based, but rather politically motivated. Thus, which scenario "wins" and reaches the front-stage presentation is often not the result of fact-bound discussions based on models, but of the power relationships within a group or a bank. Nevertheless, because the team members of the Swiss bank knew they had to form a house view, they managed to leave alternatives, uncertainties and doubts behind the scenes and thus came up with the "soft-landing" scenario, which was presented as an official forecast. The "soft-landing" scenario was a necessary fiction to keep markets going at that time.

SUMMARY AND CONCLUSION: ILLUSIONS OF CONTROL AND FINANCIAL STAGING

In this chapter, we discussed how models (and, more generally, numbers) participate in the staging of false precision, which is necessary for the market to function as it produces decidability and willingness to invest. Precision can be – and frequently is – simulated by models for a purpose:

it serves as a source of credibility for the communicated stories or as a basis for the reputation of the storytellers. The example in which a fictional "soft-landing" scenario was produced illustrated how models and numbers provide plausibility to stories in direct, face-to-face interactions between financial market participants. In addition, we argued that the participation of models in such social interactions at the front-stage mediates their influence. Models' importance can be diminished or increased in the very process of presenting persuasive fictions in the investment chain; this observation relativizes the strong performativity thesis and brings counter-performativity to the foreground. In this chapter, I argued that models might produce results that are contradictory to what they describe/forecast, not just because people – when managed by formal tolls – tend to "game" the system. "Gaming" means working towards improving the numbers in this context. For instance:

> consumer credit rating models lead borrowers to behave in ways that improve their credit score while leaving their financial situation unaltered, making estimates of credit risk less accurate. Similarly, VaR encourages practices that keep predicted losses low but do not necessarily make a portfolio less risky. (Lockwood 2015: 737f., referring to Rona-Tas and Hiss 2011)

Such practices clearly undermine models' results, making them counter-performative (see also Esposito 2013); however, in this chapter, I primarily referred to the possibility of subverting models in the process of using their outcomes for communication and staging.

In this context, a particular societal model risk should be mentioned. By presenting uncertainties as calculable risks in staged "as-if" stories, models might produce a false sense of security – a dangerous, model-induced illusion of control. The prime example discussed in the literature is the Value at Risk model. Its wide acceptance allowed banks to authoritatively claim that they were able to control and limit future losses by measuring risk, and thus created "a perception of control" where absolute control was clearly not possible (Lockwood 2015).

As already mentioned in the introduction, this issue is usually widely related to the "love affair" with formal models. While blindly relying on VaR, banks ignored the relevant incalculable *uncertainties*, became overconfident about their ability to control and foresee risks and took on too many risks, jeopardizing the financial system as a whole (Triana 2011). However, those accusations are built upon the assumption that VaR users are "model dopes" who are blind to the limitations of their models. I think this discussion can be further refined based on the findings in this chapter.

Indeed, the distinction between front-stage and backstage allows for a subtler view of the use of financial models and their effects. As we have seen, at the backstage, users are rather sceptical about the abilities of their models; at least, there are cultures of model use that *vary* depending on the degree of this scepticism (again, Mikes 2009, 2010 illustrates this point for the risk management cultures in banks; see also Chapter 4). However, doubts about models are frequently "played down" when the players move from the backstage to the front-stage. At the front-stage, model users are rather ostentatiously enthusiastic about their models because the latter provide them with authority, enabling them to convince their audience or to comply with formal requirements. Note that model users are enchanted with formal tools front-stage because, here, they have to perform this *calculative enthusiasm* to achieve their goals and follow the convention. Lockwood (2015: 745, my emphasis) refers to VaR:

> Those inside the financial industry are, as we have seen, not unaware of [those] limitations of VaR [. . .]. However, the VaR numbers that are *disclosed to investors, regulators, and the public* convey no information about possible losses that fall outside the predictions of the model. Because VaR enjoys an exceptionally privileged place in public evaluations of financial risk, it tends to crowd out other, non-probabilistic methods of anticipating crisis, leaving banks – and the citizens who are asked to bail them out – unprepared for losses that VaR cannot predict.

Between backstage and front-stage, two parallel logics are at work – "economic logic" and "authoritative logic" (Lockwood 2015) – that are often confused in discussions about financial models. Models are usually criticized from the point of view of "economic logic" (that is, they ignore incalculable uncertainties, are based on historical data and so on), whereas their critics disregard the fact that they are also – importantly – a part of the theatrical practices that are characterized by "authoritative logic", the logic of presentation, persuasion and compliance. The constraints of "authoritative logic" frequently suppress "economic logic", rendering the latter less important for understanding the effects of models on society. Thus, the general criticism that financial models (for example, VaR) damage the markets because they crowd out the non-calculative approaches to risk and uncertainty such as "subjective judgment" or "professional experience" (Lockwood 2015) might apply to the front-stage, but not to the backstage. In other words, the front-stage phenomena where "authoritative logic" dominates (theatrical performances, rhetoric, make-believe tricks and so on) should be investigated in their own right in order to fully understand the influence of models on society.

Thus, as models play a key role in financial market communication, we need to consider that models' results are framed by formal constraints and the specific goals of theatrical performances. It is also possible that, backstage, each group of professionals sees and addresses different limitations of one and the same model and suppresses them with distinctive styles at the front-stage.

These observations have consequences for our understanding of communication in financial markets, for example, between regulators and banks. There is no reason to depict regulators – as is often the case in the press – as exceptionally blind and mindless "model dopes" who force insufficient and useless models on the financial system. Rather, financial policy-makers – as a very well-informed professional group – might merely see different limitations of VaR, for example, to those seen by the banks that use the same formula; also, regulators may not communicate the limitations clearly enough in the presentation modus when they have to persuade potential users (front-stage) – for instance, when introducing particular models as regulation tools to market participants (just think of the strong lobbying for VaR described in Triana 2011). Vice versa, the model-based reports and analyses delivered to regulators are not merely the products of model calculations but also the result of particular styles of "doing/undoing" calculations and making-believe front-stage. In other words, "reading" financial communication should involve taking into account the inevitable rhetoric aspects of it and the related distortions of model outcomes. Clearly, more research is necessary here to further our understanding.

6. Conclusions and discussion

The impetus for this book was the observation that financial models are frequently blamed for various mischiefs that happen in financial markets. The book analyses the pressing question of how reasonable those accusations are. It investigates the diverse *cultures of model use* in financial markets and argues for a more differentiated view of models. Depending on how they are used, financial models vary in their ability to shape markets. The extensive empirical studies in this book demonstrate that the influence of models on markets – and on society more generally – is *mediated* in the very contexts of the models' use. In the diverse practices of decision-making and decision-selling, financial models can be considered the tools of formal calculation, storytelling, communication and theatrical performance. While assuming those different roles, financial models support a diversity of decisions and expectations of financial market participants and generally contribute to the markets' stability rather than destroying them.

At the same time, the study at hand makes some conceptional suggestions that might have consequences for further research, for example in decision-making theory, valuation studies, ignorance studies and ethics of financial markets. These implications are primarily related to the concept of *symmetrical ignorance*, which is central to the argumentation in this book. In financial markets, I argue, ignorance refers to "unspecified non-knowledge" which cannot be conceptualized as missed information or not-yet-knowledge and, importantly, cannot be fully eliminated through any kind of knowledge work. Non-knowledge about the future in financial markets is a good example. Indeed, there are no experts who know the future currency exchange rate or the future price of an asset. Regardless of how long and how intelligently market participants calculate, imagine, represent, structure and communicate possible scenarios, they cannot be sure about the future. Importantly, as we have seen throughout the book, financial non-knowledge also refers to elements of the current market situation, for example to the "true" financial state of a company or the *present* "fair value" of an asset. Thus, the ignorance that is characteristic of communication among financial market participants is indeed ubiquitous and symmetrical. As highlighted in this book, a meaningful discussion about the unknowns should be related to expectations, beliefs, imaginations, stories and other "intellectual constructs with which [society but also financial markets] can endure the unobservability of the world and make its opacity productive" (Luhmann 1992: 220, my translation).

Two intellectual instruments for coping with non-knowledge are discussed in the book in particular detail: *calculation* and *staging of illusions of knowledge*. It is shown that calculation and financial models as calculative tools are not sufficient for bridging genuinely symmetrical non-knowledge. For this reason, financial models are conceptualized as both *formal* and *theatrical* tools that do not necessarily produce knowledge, but more generally enable decisions and actions. Particularly, the book demonstrates that *action-like decision-making* is facilitated by connecting models (calculations) to the realities of markets, on the one hand, and by producing illusions of knowledge by means of formal models, on the other hand. Thus, the book identifies *symmetrical ignorance, action-like decision-making, calculation* and *performing the illusions of knowledge* as the cornerstones of the discussion about the applications of financial models and their effects. Let me now highlight in more detail some consequences of this thinking for further research.

IGNORANCE STUDIES OF FINANCIAL MARKETS

This book brings *ignorance studies* to the forefront of the discussion about financial markets. This truly interdisciplinary research field, which has started consolidating itself over the last three decades (Smithson 1989; Proctor and Schiebinger 2008; Boschen et al. 2006, 2010; Gross and McGoey 2015), pays attention to the crucial role non-knowledge plays in modern societies, and investigates ignorance not only as an important challenge for scientists and politicians but also as a resource for successful action. Importantly, scholars in the field argue in favour of developing the systematic study of ignorance in its own right. Nevertheless, they pursue this endeavour within the tradition of social studies of science while conceptualizing non-knowledge as socially constructed within particular *epistemic* cultures. They focus on the strategic production of culturally induced ignorance, and investigate efforts to construct, present and communicate (or conceal) non-knowledge by particular interest groups, for instance, efforts by the tobacco industry to obscure the risks of smoking (Proctor 2008).

Relating to this research, the implications of the *symmetrical ignorance* concept are twofold. First, the insights of ignorance studies can be fruitfully applied to studies of financial markets. Second, those applications should take into consideration the move from a science-centred to a decision-centred understanding of financial markets, as advocated in this book. It means that investigations into ignorance go beyond the notion of "epistemic cultures" and are extended to non-scientific or non-epistemic contexts of financial markets.

Indeed, the work of financial intermediaries within the "chains of finance" can be widely understood as work on *non-knowledge*. From this perspective, various *judgment devices* (Karpik 2010) – for instance, brands, guides, rankings and ratings, as fabricated by diverse intermediaries such as rating agencies, audit companies and marketing agencies – cannot be understood solely as aids for producing knowledge in the face of radical uncertainty. Indeed, the findings of this book suggest considering most judgment devices in financial markets (for example credit ratings, share price forecasts or risk estimates) as necessary *illusions of knowledge*, plausible presentations of *non-knowledge as knowledge*. This staging seems to be one of the central intellectual constructs of bridging non-knowledge in financial markets. The *pseudo-knowledge* work in financial intermediaries deserves to be analysed in its own right, although the term "pseudo-knowledge" is not intended to have any negative connotation.

Importantly, work on non-knowledge in financial intermediaries does not necessarily have to be conceptualized as "strategic ignorance", as deliberate deception – although communication within the links of the investment chain is frequently represented in this vein. For example, if a financial advisor presents radical uncertainties as calculable risks to a client (as discussed in the case of cocos in Chapter 2 and in the case of the economist's presentation of a "soft landing" in Chapter 5), strategic ignorance is produced. This actively created ignorance of risks helps market participants compensate for their limited knowledge of the exact mathematical value of assets (as in the case of cocos, for example) and jump over the gorge of non-knowledge, allowing markets to function. In this way, ignorance can be considered as a resource, "a productive force" of markets (McGoey 2012). At the same time, willing investors who are "made" to ignore risks become exposed to severe financial losses: Strategic ignorance is dangerous.

However, while conducting ignorance studies on financial markets, researchers might not primarily pay attention to the issue of strategic production of non-knowledge. Note that strategic ignorance means that knowledge is known to one party but concealed from another (as in the case of Akerlof's "markets for lemons", from which this book clearly distanced itself from the beginning), and is thus non-symmetrical. If both parties are *equally ignorant* about the key issues of a situation, the unintentional, routinely performed and carefully communicated *illusions of knowledge* gain particular importance.

In this book, we have seen that formal models play a role in both the production of strategic ignorance and the performance of non-knowledge as knowledge. Thus, to some extent, *cultures of model use* can be understood and investigated as "cultures of non-knowledge" (Boschen et al. 2010). Indeed, the diversity of cultures of model use draws attention to the variety of ways in which different groups of model users produce and communicate heterogeneous types of non-knowledge; furthermore, for each culture, different types of unknowns are relevant and there are different ways of recognizing them and coping with unforeseen developments that come up. The concept of a non-knowledge culture might provide a new angle for analysing modelling cultures in financial markets – and the work of financial intermediaries more generally. In particular, such a non-knowledge-centred view could deliver new insights into what happens at the finance–society front-stage: what is communicated and how it is communicated, what is concealed and why it is concealed. This book has only taken some initial steps in this direction.

DECISION-MAKING THEORY AND ECONOMICS

I hope that the discussions in this study have the potential to initiate a dialogue between the social studies of finance (SSF) and decision-making theory (taken in its own right but also as part of microeconomics), the dialog which has been nearly non-existent so far. Particularly, this interdisciplinary exchange might relate to our understanding of the basic decision-making situation in economics, the micro-foundations of macro-events and the formation of expectations.

The connecting points between the two fields of research should have become obvious, as the book generally highlights the importance of genuine uncertainty, endogeneity, reflexivity and the sociality of the economic world not only for economic sociology and SSF but also for the current economic debate. Indeed, these topics increasingly occupy economic research in areas such as global coordination games (Morris and Shin 2003), endogenous risk (Danielsson and Shin 2002; Danielsson et al. 2009), epistemic game theory (Brandenburger 2008), reflexive expectation formation (Ehrig and Jost 2012), interactive unawareness (Heifetz et al. 2006), adaptive rationality, heuristics and recently the "big world" problem (Brighton and Gigerenzer 2012), imperfect knowledge economics (Frydman and Goldberg 2007) and "animal spirits" (Akerlof and Shiller 2009). This research moves primarily in two directions: either it facilitates even bigger efforts to formalize the unknowns – for instance, the state space in the Savage matrix (see Svetlova and van Elst 2015 for an overview); or the focus is shifted to the non-calculative tools of decision-making – for example intuition and heuristics (Brighton and Gigerenzer 2012) or judgment (Karpik 2010).

However, as this book argues, the most pressing issue of decision-making theory today is to understand the *interplay* of calculation (formalization) and judgment (intuition). On the one hand, because the market actors on various politically relevant terrains where non-knowledge dominates (for example environmental change, terrorism, the prevention of infectious diseases, financial market regulation and so on) recognize the limits of formal rules, programming and calculability, they turn to judgment and intuition. On the other hand, judgment and intuition, although important for bridging the gorge of the unknown, are subject to constant criticism for being arbitrary, unsystematic and, thus, are not serious procedures that are able to deliver an ultimate justification for decisions. In other words, as this book suggests, intuition cannot be eradicated by calculation, and calculation cannot work without intuition and judgment. Thus, the central question of decision-making theory today – as well as within some important practical societal fields such as security – is how decision-makers calculate the incalculable (Amoore 2014) and make decisions *without* the ultimate justification. Or, as we ask in this book: how do financial market participants form expectations and decide under conditions of radical uncertainty, that is, in circumstances in which expectations and decisions are fundamentally groundless? What endures and what matters? These problems are linked to Taleb's (2007) question: "How do we live in the world we don't understand?" Decision-makers in financial markets (but also in other societally relevant fields) constantly "jump" from non-knowledge to knowledge by allowing intuition to flow into mathematical calculations or by presenting decisions as calculations; they perform the jump which, however, ultimately never succeeds, and they find themselves floundering on the edge of the gorge of non-knowledge.

Importantly, decision-makers do not fall into the abyss because they "bootstrap" themselves, meanwhile, by using models. *Action-like decision-making* in financial markets, politics and economics is supported by technological tools, and this insight has theoretical and methodological consequences not only for science and technology studies (STS) and the social studies of finance, but also for decision-making theory and economics.

First of all, in light of this discussion, the basic concept of decision-making can be adjusted. The analysis in this book helps us to recognize that the nature of (financial) decision-making has fundamentally changed and cannot be approached using the "naive" Savage matrix and its variations. The major challenge for decision-makers today is not to get the probabilities right but to project the possible (genuinely unknown) state space. These projections are made by means of formal models which enable the formation of expectations (as we have seen in this book). Investors develop and apply ways of decision-making that are not purely analytical or purely intuitive, while presupposing that the world is a "big world" characterized by endogenous risks, sociality and self-referentiality.

The "big world" concept, symmetrical ignorance and the importance of technological equipment have supported the theoretical insight into a diversity of ways in which financial market participants (and economic actors more generally) make decisions and form expectations. This diversity is not trivial from the economic science perspective. Maybe surprisingly, in economics and finance, the nature of expectations remains an insufficiently resolved question. The rational expectation hypothesis (Muth 1961; Lucas 1972) that has dominated economics and finance until recently is based on representative agents who rely on one, fully predetermined model to form their – thus homogeneous – expectations. Agents are presupposed to update their prior beliefs (probabilities) in light of new information in a similar manner (using Bayesian updating). Thus, expectations are assumed to be common knowledge because they result from a shared calculating strategy – the "communism of models" in the words of Thomas J. Sargent (Evans and Honkapohja 2005).

However, under conditions of radical uncertainty, this strictly calculative approach and the resulting homogeneity of expectations are questionable. Rather, the diversity of views and decisions is observed and requires explanation. The celebrated authors of *Imperfect Knowledge Economics*, Frydman and Goldberg (2007: 8), suggest that:

> individuals are not constrained to view the world through the prism of a common model [. . .] [M]arket participants, who act on the basis of different preferences, constraints and causal factors, will adapt different strategies in forecasting the future as well as the consequences of their decisions.

Frydman and Goldberg argue against the "communism of models", which impedes economic discussions on "differences among people's models" (Sargent in Evans and Honkapohja 2005).

My book supports the view of Frydman and Goldberg, which is that, as a consequence, it does not make sense for economists to search for one overarching model that guides human decision-making, and that heterogeneous individual expectation strategies matter and cannot be pre-specified by any theory. Importantly, the analysis in the present book explains the heterogeneity of expectations that might be of interest to economists. This heterogeneity results not only from discrepancies in the information level of market participants but also from the uniqueness of the interplay between calculation and judgment, material elements of decision-making (such as spreadsheets and models), sources of information (the Bloomberg data service, newspapers, other market participants and so on), the social context (for example discussions with brokers, analysts and CEOs) and organizational constraints. This complexity of decision-making frames – as a unique combination of calculative, social, temporal, material and organizational elements – has been neglected in economics so far, although it significantly determines how agents decide and form expectations.

However, despite the described heterogeneities, I infer from my research that there are particular regularities, or structures, behind individual strategies for making decisions and forming expectations. Thus, I consider "animal spirits" – as rather erratic, emotional, purely story-based replies to the uncertainty issue and the "big world" problem (Akerlof and Shiller 2009) – to be an insufficient description of human decision-making. My studies suggest that market participants do not often change their expectation strategies based only on rumours and fears. Also, unlike Gigerenzer, for example, who claims that heuristics is the method of decision-making under uncertainty because it facilitates radical simplification and processing of less information, the book suggests that the circumstances are more complex. Understanding expectations and decisions cannot be reduced to the analysis of heuristics or mental models – it is rather about the *heuristics of model use*. In this book, I present two concrete empirical examples of the forms that model-based expectations can assume in the markets: *the plausibility check of consensus* and *the plausibility check of models*. Certainly, further model-based decision-making strategies will be identified by follow-up research.

Importantly, the forms of expecting and deciding described in this book enable investors to deviate from the consensus. Expectations do not answer the question "Where will the long-term cash flow be?" (forecasting) but reflect on questions such as "Where do I disagree with the market?", "What does the market not perceive?" and "What will the market perceive next?" Thus, expectations take the form of the Keynesian (1936: 156) idea of "what the average opinion expects the average opinion to be" and are accompanied by a search for instances of *individual disagreement* with the current average opinion of the market. As the book demonstrates, this disagreement is model-based. As instruments for professionals to cope with complexity and uncertainty in markets, models, spreadsheets and other technological tools significantly contribute to the understanding of regularities in the formation of expectations. They generate insights upon which economists and decision-making theorists might want to build. If economics takes these findings seriously, it might return to the problem of "genuine microfoundations", the development of which was interrupted by the rational expectation hypothesis (Phelps 2007: xx).

Furthermore, I would argue that my research has methodological consequences for economics. The pressing question is: How can we do meaningful research on "groundless" decisions? One could follow Wittgenstein (1958: 156), who famously said: "If I have exhausted the justifications, I have reached bedrock and my spade is turned. Then I am inclined to say: 'This is simply what I do.'" I think that economics and decision-making research should more consistently investigate this "simply what I do" by applying *qualitative* methods of empirical research such as interviews and participant observations. Indeed, one of the major means of enriching the theory of decision-making under uncertainty is observation. Modern economics already requires theory to align more closely with observation (Akerlof and Kranton 2010). My book demonstrates how this alignment can be achieved, while subscribing to the statement by Frydman and Goldberg (2010: 23):

> In modeling individual behavior [. . .] economists must make use of empirical findings about how individuals actually behave. This necessity undermines the common belief among economists that contemporary economics can rigorously explain the findings of other "soft" social sciences [. . .] [I]n order to represent purposeful individual decision-making, economists must draw on the findings of other social scientists.

These findings, I would argue, are produced by qualitative empirical research which has been widely dismissed by economists so far, the notable exceptions being Bewley (1999), Piore (1995, 2006) and Tuckett (2011, 2012). Still, I believe – like Frydman and Goldberg (2007: 17) – that "in searching for empirical regularities that might be useful in modeling an individual's decisions, economists will need to look beyond laboratory experiments and insights from psychology".

My book demonstrates how the social studies of finance approach can contribute to this search. Indeed, it shows how the central challenge of connecting formal and informal methods of decision-making is solved in the everyday practices of financial market participants ("This is simply what I do"). The empirically identified patterns and regularities of model-based decision-making and expectation formation might inform economic theory.

VALUATION STUDIES

Alongside ignorance studies, valuation studies are the other emerging interdisciplinary field of research. This field investigates the processes of valuing and evaluating in various domains (Beckert and Aspers 2011; Mennicken and Sjögren 2015; Kornberger et al. 2015). Although the question of valuation is not in the centre of my study here, the book's insights might still be of interest to valuation scholars. This is thanks to the fact that valuation studies make the *impossibility of formal valuation* their point of departure, exactly like the concept of *action-like decision-making* pre-supposes the *impossibility of calculation* and refuses to see formal rules as a relevant basis for decisions. Thus, both valuation studies and this book point to similar opposite movements: on the one hand, the search for ways of "objective" valuation/decision-making (e.g. for satisfactory modelling); and, on the other hand, the recognition of mental, social, organizational and cultural factors that play into valuation and decision-making pro-cesses. Think about the discussion on the use of one of the most popular valuation models – the DCF model – in this book. In Chapter 4, we saw that this model is just part of the dynamic valuation process that takes place around it *in situ* of markets.

Thus, based on the cultures of model use, financial market research-ers and valuation studies scholars might want to identify and compare *the various regimes of valuation* that can be observed in markets. Those regimes differ depending on which assets are valued, who values them and how models are used (ignored, overlaid, believed and so on) – that is, depending on how models are made to count for valuation. Figure 6.1 illustrates this point.

All four valuation regimes in Figure 6.1 are different. As discussed in this book in detail, equities are made valuable while they are constructed as "investment objects" by means of models *and* stories; however, models' results are frequently guided by the imagination and narratives of their users. Bonds' valuation is contrasted to that of equities in the financial market aphorism "Bonds are mathematics, equities are stories"; thus, one would expect bonds' valuation to be based solely on strict calcula-tions. However, although straightforward mathematical models are indeed available in the field of government bonds, for example, the influence of politics here is so strong that formal models are frequently rendered irrel-evant. In the field of complex financial products (as discussed in different parts of this book), financial models might be available but not used due to computational intractability (Hardie and MacKenzie 2014), the unreli-ability of input parameters (MacKenzie and Spears 2014b) or the routine shift of valuation efforts to the rating agencies (MacKenzie 2011). Cocos

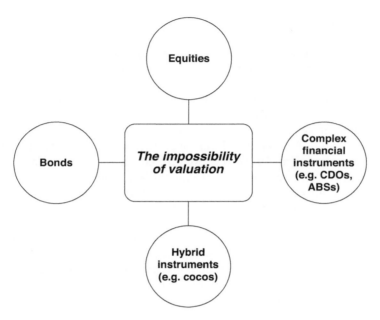

Figure 6.1   Valuation regimes

(contingent convertible bonds) represent the most curious case of valuation where only heterogeneous idiosyncratic models are available so that the consumptive, marketing-driven regime of valuation dominates (see Chapter 2). Certainly, more distinct valuation practices will be identified and described in the due course of future research. It would be helpful to classify valuation regimes according to parameters such as personal trust in models by users, organizational requirements (to blindly follow or overrule a model), typical narratives and unknowns, as well as methods of models' de-idealization *in situ* of markets.

What is important, however, is that the descriptions of those practices and the related valuation regimes should accompany formal presentations of financial models in finance textbooks. This would make (potential) model users aware not only of models' formal limitations but also of the ways in which even the most perfect mathematics can be made irrelevant or in which a very humble model can be blindly believed and become a widely used valuation tool.

Furthermore, I would like to note that the role of models in various valuation regimes is not fixed. As highlighted in this book, models have their "working lives" and biographies: they travel within organizations (think about the DCF and forex models in Chapter 4) and among intermediaries (e.g. "reverse brokerage") and, in doing so, change their status and functions.

Also, the concept of *decision-making at large* as a process that simultaneously includes model construction and model use to make and justify decisions stresses the centrality of a biographical approach for understanding the roles of models in valuation and decision-making. Until now, the common denominator of this approach has been an interest in tracing the circulation of *epistemic* factors and ideas across various, primarily scientific, contexts and uses (Appadurai 1990; Rheinberger 1997; Daston 2000; Howlett and Morgan 2011). However, the consideration of models in the framework of financial decision-making at large and as part of valuation regimes requires us to expand the biographical approach because financial models distinctly transgress the understanding of them as epistemic objects. Spears (2014) highlighted and showed empirically that financial models are sometimes designed for a very different set of purposes from those for which they are later used. Also, think about the "transformation" of the Black-Scholes formula in the practice of markets discussed in Chapter 2. Moreover, keeping in mind the discussion on decision-selling in this book, one might ask whether it is possible that particular models sometimes develop from being purely calculative tools to serving solely as marketing tools during their "working life". This and other paths of financial model biographies could be investigated in more detail.

Finally, while combining both the concept of "chains of finance" and that of model-based valuation regimes, one could come to understand valuation as a "chain" phenomenon. Valuation does not happen in isolation in one of the boxes in the chain, but rather is distributed among its boxes and links. As we have seen in this book, models facilitate communication and the co-production of asset values among various intermediaries. For example, analysts and brokers discuss their models with portfolio managers; and in this discussion they co-construct the value of equities, which only then become valuable "investment objects". The fact that models travel among financial intermediaries is important for our understanding of value creation in financial markets. Thus, in my opinion, this "chain" view of valuation deserves further consideration.

FINANCE ETHICS AND THE QUESTION OF RESPONSIBILITY

The discussion about cultures of model use in this book has consequences for how issues of ethics and responsibility are addressed in financial markets and in society more broadly. Finance ethics is inevitably related to a particular understanding of the financial system. So far, ethical discussions about finance have referred to the traditional conceptualization of markets: that of an isolated actor who makes rational decisions and has the capacity to show perfect foresight (rational expectations). This concept implies that economic actors can foresee all implications of their decisions, and thus can be explicitly made responsible for their decisions and actions. This understanding of economics and finance suggests considering consequentialist ethics and responsibility ethics as the most appropriate ethical concepts. Within those concepts, ethics is about perfectly anticipating the consequences of actions and making individuals or institutions responsible for them (accountability) (Mitchell 2009: 109; Muniesa and Lenglet 2013; Owen et al. 2013).

In light of the study at hand, however, this understanding of finance ethics exhibits significant weaknesses. It does not take into consideration the "big world" concept, symmetrical ignorance, feedback loops, the reflexivity and sociality of markets or the idea of technologically equipped action. In modern financial markets, the book argues, the knowledge of actors always remains restricted due to the unintended, unforeseen and often uncontrollable effects of their actions; thus, determinism, perfect foresight, accountability and consequentialism are questionable. The growing interdependence of actors, the reflexivity of markets and technologization (the rise of models and algorithms) have rendered it impossible for individuals to have complete knowledge of the consequences of their actions and to entirely control them. In this respect, the literature on economic and finance ethics refers to "epistemic insufficiency" (DeMartino 2013), the "responsibility gap" (Owen et al. 2013) and the "impossibility of business ethics" (Woermann 2013).

At the same time, in various domains of fateful, action-like decision-making, a new form of responsibility is emerging – the responsibility *to calculate the incalculable*. Amoore (2013) refers to the trial of several Italian seismologists and volcanologists who were blamed for failing to arrive at a reasonable calculation of the likelihood of a future earthquake. The scientists failed to warn the public and, thus, the earthquake of L'Aquila struck unexpectedly in 2009. Importantly, this was a clear case of symmetrical ignorance, and even the judge acknowledged the impossibility of knowing how likely a future earthquake was to occur. Rather, the scientists were found guilty "for failing to infer, intuit, imagine and extrapolate from available data" (Amoore 2014: 424). In other words, they were expected to calculate the incalculable by means of all available formal and informal tools (e.g. by modelling but also through intuition and imagination). Thus, our understanding of how "qualculative" methods of dealing with ignorance are applied is crucial for the meaningful discussion of responsibility and accountability in financial markets and in other societal domains. The empirical insights into practices of calculating the incalculable show how tentative and vague those calculations are, so that deterministic ethics becomes rather meaningless. Also, the functioning of models as tools of performance – particularly, as tools of staging *false* certainty and security – should be taken into consideration in ethical debates.

However, one should note that the book clearly focuses on decision-making at the individual level, whereas, in modern financial markets, the responsibility is frequently assigned to systemic events (at the macro level) – for example, responsibility for systemic risks. Nevertheless, also in such situations, adequate ethical concepts should incorporate insights that the actors operate with incomplete knowledge, that technology cannot be entirely controlled and often plays a secondary role, and that collective outcomes are often not intended.

All in all, I hope that this book provides valuable insights into how models interact with decision-makers, financial markets and society and contributes to a more differentiated view than that of models as villains. If the book provokes new thoughts on how modern financial markets work, my goal is achieved.

References

Abolafia, M. (2005), 'Making sense of recession: Toward an interpretive theory of economic action', in V. Nee and R. Swedberg (eds), *The Economic Sociology of Capitalism*, Princeton, NJ: Princeton University Press, 204–226.

Akerlof, G. A. (1970), 'The market for "lemons": Quality uncertainty and the market mechanism', *Quarterly Journal of Economics*, **84** (3), 488–500.

Akerlof, G. A. and R. Kranton (2010), *Identity Economics: How Our Identities Shape Our Work, Wages, and Well-Being*, Princeton, NJ: Princeton University Press.

Akerlof, G. A. and R. J. Shiller (2009), *Animal Spirits: How Human Psychology Drives the Economy, and Why It Matters for Global Capitalism*, Princeton, NJ: Princeton University Press.

Alexandrova, A. (2008), 'Making models count', *Philosophy of Science*, **75** (3), 383–404.

Alvesson, M. (2013), *The Triumph of Emptiness: Consumption, Higher Education, and Work Organization*, Oxford: Oxford University Press.

Amoore, L. (2014), 'Security and the incalculable', *Security Dialog*, **45** (5), 423–439.

Appadurai, A. (1990), 'Disjuncture and difference in the global cultural economy', *Public Culture*, **2** (2), 1–24.

Arjaliès, D.-L., P. Grant, I. Hardie, D. MacKenzie and E. Svetlova (2017), *Chains of Finance: How Investment Management Is Shaped*, Oxford: Oxford University Press.

Arthur, W. (1994), 'Inductive reasoning and bounded rationality', *American Economic Review*, **84** (2), 406–411.

Arthur, W. (1995), 'Complexity in economic and financial markets', www.iwp.jku.at/born/mpwfst/02/wiphil2kff/texte/BAComplexity.pdf, accessed 13 June 2017.

Aspers, P. (2009), 'Knowledge and valuation in markets', *Theory and Society*, **38** (2), 111–131.

Austin, J. (1962), *How to Do Things with Words: The William James Lectures Delivered at Harvard University in 1955*, Oxford: Oxford University Press.

Authers, J. (2007), 'The anatomy of a crash: What the market upheavals of 1987 say about today, *Financial Times*, 19 October.

Ayache, E. (2007), 'Elie Ayache, author of the Blank Swan', *Wilmott Magazine* (October), 40–49.

Ayache, E. (2010), *The Blank Swan: The End of Probability*, Chichester: John Wiley & Sons.

Bank of England (2015), 'The failure of HBOS plc (HBOS)', a report by the Financial Conduct Authority (FCA) and the Prudential Regulation Authority (PRA), accessed 13 June 2017 at www.bankofengland.co.uk/pra/Documents/publications/reports/hbos.pdf.

Barker, R. (1998), 'The market for information: Evidence from finance directors, analysts and fund managers', *Accounting and Business Research*, **29** (1), 3–20.

Barnes, B. (1983), 'Social life as bootstrapped induction', *Sociology*, **17** (4), 524–545.

Barnes, B. (1986), 'On authority and its relation to power', in J. Law (ed.), *Power, Action, and Belief: A New Sociology of Knowledge?*, London: Routledge, 180–195.

Barnes, B., D. Bloor and J. Henry (1996), *Scientific Knowledge: A Sociological Analysis*, Chicago, IL: University of Chicago Press.

Beckert, J. (1996), 'What is sociological about economic sociology? Uncertainty and the embeddedness of economic action', *Theory and Society*, **25** (6), 803–840.

Beckert, J. (2005), 'Trust and the performative construction of markets', MPIfG Discussion Paper, 05/8, accessed 13 June 2017 at www.mpifg.de/pu/mpifg_dp/dp05-8.pdf.

Beckert, J. (2013), 'Imagined futures: Fictional expectations in the economy', *Theory and Society*, **42** (3), 219–240.

Beckert, J. (2016), *Imagined Futures: Fictional Expectations and Capitalist Dynamics*, Cambridge, MA: Harvard University Press.

Beckert, J. and P. Aspers (eds) (2011), *The Worth of Goods: Valuation and Pricing in the Economy*, Oxford: Oxford University Press.

Bergheim, S., B. Gräf, M. Lanzeni and S. Schneider (2008), 'Die Weltwirtschaft in 2008: Verlangsammung aber keine Rezession', Deutsche Bank Research, accessed 13 June 2017 at www.dbresearch.com/PROD/DBR_INTERNET_EN-PROD/PROD0000000000221134/Die_Weltwirtschaft_in_2008%3A_Verlangsamung%2C_aber_ke.pdf.

Bernstein, P. L. (1992), *Capital Ideas: The Improbable Origins of Modern Wall Street*, New York: John Wiley & Sons.

Bernstein, P. L. (1996), *Against the Gods: The Remarkable Story of Risk*, New York: John Wiley & Sons.

Bernstein, P. L. (2007), *Capital Ideas Evolving: The Improbable Origins of Modern Wall Street*, New York: John Wiley & Sons.

Best, M. and R. Grauer (1991), On the sensitivity of mean-variance-efficient portfolios to changes in asset means: Some analytical and computational results, *Review of Financial Studies*, **4** (2), 315–342.

Betz, G. (2006), *Prediction or Prophecy? The Boundaries of Economic Foreknowledge and Their Socio-Political Consequences*, Wiesbaden: Deutscher Universitäts-Verlag.

Beunza, D. and R. Garud (2007), 'Calculators, lemmings or frame-makers? The intermediary role of securities analysts', *Sociological Review*, **55** (s2), 13–39.

Beunza, D. and D. Stark (2004), 'Tools of the trade: The socio-technology of arbitrage in a Wall Street trading room', *Industrial and Corporate Change*, **13** (2), 369–400.

Beunza, D. and D. Stark (2010), 'Models, reflexivity and systemic risk: A critique of behavioral finance', paper presented at the conference Re-embedding Finance, Paris, 20–21 May.

Beunza, D. and D. Stark (2012), 'From dissonance to resonance: Cognitive interdependence in quantitative finance', *Economy and Society*, **41** (3), 383–417.

Bevan, A. and K. Winkelmann (1998), 'Using the Black-Litterman global asset allocation model: Three years of practical experience', Fixed Income research, Goldman Sachs, accessed 12 June 2017 at https://faculty.fuqua.duke.edu/~charvey/Teaching/IntesaBci_2001/GS_Using_the_black.pdf.

Bewley, T. (1999), *Why Wages Do Not Fall during a Recession*, Cambridge, MA: Harvard University Press.

Black, F. and R. Litterman (1992), 'Global portfolio optimization', *Financial Analysts Journal*, **48** (5), 28–43.

Bloor, D. (1997), *Wittgenstein, Rules and Institutions*, London: Routledge.

Bloor, D. (2000), 'Collective representations as social institutions', in W. Pickering (ed.), *Durkheim and Representations*, London: Routledge, 157–166.

Bogle, J. (1999), *Common Sense on Mutual Funds: New Imperatives for the Intelligent Investor*, New York: Wiley.

Boldyrev, I. and E. Svetlova (2016), 'After the turn: How the performativity of economics matters', in I. Boldyrev and E. Svetlova (eds), *Enacting Dismal Science: New Perspectives on the Performativity of Economics*, New York: Palgrave Macmillan, 1–27.

Boldyrev, I. and A. Ushakov (2016), 'Adjusting the model to adjust the world: Constructive mechanisms in postwar general equilibrium theory', *Journal of Economic Methodology*, **23** (1), 38–56.

Borch, C. (2016), 'High-frequency trading, algorithmic finance and the flash crash: Reflections on eventalization', *Economy and Society*, **45** (3–4), 350–378.

Boschen, S., K. Kastenhofer, L. Marschall, L. Rust, J. Soentgen and P. Wehling (2006), 'Scientific cultures of non-knowledge in the controversy over genetically modified organisms (GMO): The cases of molecular biology and ecology', *GAIA; Ecological Perspectives for Science and Society*, **15** (4), 294–301.

Boschen, S., K. Kastenhofer, I. Rust, J. Soentgen and P. Wehling (2010), 'Scientific non-knowledge and its political dynamics: The cases of agribiotechnology and mobile phoning', *Science, Technology & Human Values*, **36** (6), 783–811.

Boucher, G. (2014), 'The Lacanian performative: Austin after Žižek', in B. Chow and A. Mangold (eds.), *Žižek and Performance*, Basingstoke: Palgrave Macmillan, 13–32.

Boumans, M. and M. Morgan (2001), 'Ceteris paribus conditions: Materiality and the application of economic theories', *Journal of Economic Methodology*, **8** (1), 11–26.

Bourgoin, A. and F. Muniesa (2016), 'Building a rock-solid slide: Management consulting, PowerPoint, and the craft of signification', *Management Communication Quarterly*, **30** (3), 390–410.

Brandenburger, A. (2008), 'Epistemic game theory: An overview', in S. N. Durlauf and L. E. Blume (eds), *The New Palgrave Dictionary of Economics*, Basingstoke: Palgrave Macmillan.

Brighton, H. and G. Gigerenzer (2012), 'Are rational actor models "rational" outside small worlds?', in S. Okasha and K. Binmore (eds), *Evolution and Rationality: Decisions, Co-Operation and Strategic Behavior*, Cambridge: Cambridge University Press, 84–109.

Brisset, N. (2014), 'Economics is not always performative: Some limits for performativity', *Journal of Economic Methodology*, **23** (2), 160–184.

Brodie, L. (2012), 'Doug Kass: Kill the quants before they kill us', accessed 5 July 2017 at www.cnbc.com/id/48470448.

Bukowski, P. (2012), 'Basics of quantitative equity investing', in F. Fabozzi (ed), *Encyclopedia of Financial Models*, vol. 2, Hoboken, NJ: John Wiley & Sons, 89–106.

Burton, K. (2016), 'Inside a moneymaking machine like no other', Bloomberg Markets, accessed 13 June 2017 at www.bloomberg.com/news/articles/2016-11-21/how-renaissance-s-medallion-fund-became-finance-s-blackest-box.

Butler, J. (2010), 'Performative agency', *Journal of Cultural Economy*, **3** (2), 147–161.

Cabantous, L. and J.-P. Gond (2011), 'Rational decision making as a "performative praxis": Explaining rationality's éternel retour', *Organization Science*, **22** (3), 573–586.

Callender, G. and J. Cohen (2006), 'There is no special problem about scientific representation', *Theoria*, **55** (1), 67–85.

Callon, M. (1998), 'Introduction: The embeddedness of economic markets in economics', in M. Callon (ed), *The Laws of the Market*, Oxford: Blackwell, 1–57.

Callon, M. (2007), 'What does it mean to say that economics is performative?', in D. MacKenzie, F. Muniesa and L. Siu (eds), *Do Economists Make Markets? On the Performativity of Economics*, Princeton, NJ: Princeton University Press, 311–357.

Callon, M. and F. Muniesa (2005), 'Economic markets as calculative collective devices', *Organization Studies*, **26** (8), 1229–1250.

Carrier, M. (2011), 'Knowledge, politics, and commerce: Science under the pressure of practice', in M. Carrier and A. Nordmann (eds), *Science in the Context of Application*, Dordrecht: Springer, 11–30.

Carrier, M. and A. Nordmann (eds) (2011), *Science in the Context of Application*, Dordrecht: Springer.

Carruthers, B. G. and A. L. Stinchcombe (1999), 'The social structure of liquidity: Flexibility, markets, and states', *Theory and Society*, **28** (3), 353–382.

Cartwright, N. (1983), *How the Laws of Physics Lie*, Oxford: Clarendon.

Cartwright, N. (1989), *Nature's Capacities and Their Measurement*, Oxford: Oxford University Press.

Cartwright, N. (1999), *The Dappled World: A Study of the Boundaries of Science*, Cambridge: Cambridge University Press.

Cartwright, N. (2008), Models: Parables vs fables, *Insights*, **1** (11), 2–10.

Caves, R. E. (2003), 'Contracts between art and commerce', *Journal of Economic Perspectives*, **17** (2), 73–83.

Cheng, E. (2017), 'Just 10% of trading is regular stock picking, JPMorgan estimates', accessed 5 July 2017 at www.cnbc.com/2017/06/13/death-of-the-human-investor-just-10-percent-of-trading-is-regular-stock-picking-jpmorgan-estimates.html.

Chia, R. (1994), 'The concept of decision: A deconstructive analysis', *Journal of Management Studies*, **31** (6), 781–806.

Chong, K. and D. Tuckett (2015), 'Constructing conviction through action and narrative: How money managers manage uncertainty and the consequence for financial market functioning', *Socio-Economic Review*, **13** (2), 309–330.

Cochoy, F. (2008), 'Calculation, qualculation, calqulation: Shopping cart arithmetic, equipped cognition and the clustered consumer', *Marketing Theory*, **8** (1), 15–44.

Colander, D. (2013), 'The systemic failure of economic methodologists', *Journal of Economic Methodology*, **20** (1), 56–68.

Coleman, L. (2014), 'Why finance theory fails to survive contact with the real world: A fund manager perspective', *Critical Perspectives on Accounting*, **25** (3), 226–236.

Collins, H. (2004), *Gravity's Shadow: The Search for Gravitational Waves*, Chicago: University of Chicago Press.

Columbano, C. and M. Ezzamel (2017), 'Sovereign credit rating: Modelling, valuation and professional judgement', paper presented at the Interdisciplinary Perspectives on Accounting Workshop "Valuation, Technology and Society", University of Leicester, 21–22 April.

Coombs, N. and J. Morris (2017), 'Narrating imagined crises: Bank stress tests and cultural reform in finance', paper presented at the conference "Chains of Value: How Intermediaries Evaluate Financial Instruments", University of Edinburgh, 4–5 May.

Corbin, J. and A. Strauss (2008), *Basics of Qualitative Research: Techniques and Procedures For Developing Grounded Theory*, Los Angeles: Sage.

Crespo, I., P. Kumar, P. Noteboom and M. Taymans (2017), 'The evolution of model risk management', McKinsey & Company, accessed 13 June 2017 at http://www.mckinsey.com/business-functions/risk/our-insights/the-evolution-of-model-risk-management.

Croft, J. (2009), 'Modeling adapts as catastrophic clouds clear', *Financial Times*, 5 October, 21.

D'Agostino, A. and R. Lennkh (2016), 'Euro area sovereign ratings: An analysis of fundamental criteria and subjective judgement', European Stability Mechanism (ESM) Working Paper Series 14, 1–34.

Danielsson, J. and H. Shin (2002), *Endogenous Risk*, accessed 13 June 2017 at www.ucd.ie/t4cms/danielsson.pdf.

Danielsson, J., H. S. Shin and J.-P. Zigrand (2009), *Risk Appetite and Endogenous Risk*, accessed 13 June 2017 at www.cemfi.es/ftp/pdf/papers/wshop/riskappetite.pdf.

Daston, Lorraine (ed.) (2000), *Biographies of Scientific Objects*, Chicago: University of Chicago Press.

De Certeau, M. (1984), *The Practice of Everyday Life*, Berkeley: University of California Press.

DeMartino, G. (2013), 'Epistemic aspects of economic practice and the need for professional economic ethics', *Review of Social Economy*, **71** (2), 166–186.

Den Butter, F. and M. Morgan (2000), *Empirical Models and Policy Making: Interaction and Institutions*, London: Routledge.

Derman, E. (1996), Model Risk. In Quantitative Strategies. Research Notes, Goldmann Sachs, accessed 13 June 2017 at http://www.emanuel derman.com/writing/entry/model-risk.

Derman, E. (2011), *Models. Behaving. Badly. Why Confusing Illusion with*

Reality Can Lead to Disaster, on Wall Street and in Life, New York: John Wiley & Sons.

Derrida, J. (1994), 'Force de loi: Le "fondement mystique de l'autorité"/ Force of law: The mystical foundation of authority', accessed 13 June 2017 at http://is.muni.cz/el/1422/jaro2007/MVV012468K/um/3241828/ Derrida_-_Force_de_Loi.pdf.

Dewey, J. (1915), 'The logic of judgments of practice', *Journal of Philosophy, Psychology and Scientific Methods*, **12** (19), 505–523.

Dieckhoff, C. (2014), *Modellierte Zukunft: Energieszenarien in der wissenschaftlichen Politikberatung*, Bielefeld: transcript.

Dowling, D. (1999), 'Experimenting on theories', *Science in Context*, **12** (2), 261–273.

Duhigg, C. (2008), 'Pressured to take more risk, Fannie reached tipping point', *New York Times*, accessed 12 June 2107 at www.nytimes.com/2008/10/05/ business/05fannie.html?_r=1.

The Economist (2008), Better than beta? Managers' superior skills are becoming harder to prove, accessed 14 June 2017 at www.economist. com/node/10715918.

Ehrig, T. and J. Jost (2012), 'Reflexive expectation formation', accessed 5 July 2017 at www.mis.mpg.de/fileadmin/jjost/ehrigjost2011.pdf.

Engelen, E., I. Ertürk, J. Froud, A. Leaver and K. Williams (2010), 'Reconceptualizing financial innovation: Frame, conjuncture and bricolage', *Economy and Society*, **39** (1), 33–63.

Engelen, E., I. Ertürk, J. Froud, S. Johal, A. Leaver, M. Moran and K. Williams (2012), 'Misrule of experts? The financial crisis as elite debacle', *Economy and Society*, **41** (3), 360–382.

Esposito, E. (2011), *The Future of Futures: The Time of Money in Financing and Society*, Cheltenham, UK and Northampton, MA, USA: Edward Elgar Publishing.

Esposito, E. (2013), 'The structures of uncertainty: performativity and unpredictability in economic operations', *Economy and Society*, **42** (1), 102–129.

Evans, G. and S. Honkapohja (2005), 'An interview with Thomas J. Sargent', *Macroeconomic Dynamics*, **9** (4), 561–583.

Evans, R. (1999), *Macroeconomic Forecasting: A Sociological Appraisal*, London: Routledge.

Fabozzi, F., S. Focardi and C. Jonas (2007), 'Trends in quantitative equity management: survey results', *Quantitative Finance*, **7** (2), 115–122.

Fabozzi, F., S. Focardi and C. Jonas (2008), *Challenges in Quantitative Equity Management*, Charlottesville, VA: Research Foundation of CFA Institute.

Fabozzi, F., S. Focardi and C. Jonas (2014), *Investment Management:*

A Science to Teach or an Art to Learn? Charlottesville, VA: Research Foundation of CFA Institute.

Fabozzi, F., H. Markowitz, P. Kolm and F. Gupta (2012), 'Mean-variance model for portfolio selection', in F. Fabozzi (ed.), *Encyclopedia of Financial Models*, vol. 1, Hoboken, NJ: John Wiley & Sons, 3–20.

Fraser, I. (2015), 'Man group boss says computers are future for asset management', *Financial Times* (FTfm), 16 March, 3.

Frigg, R. (2006), 'Scientific representation and the semantic view of theories', *Theoria*, **21** (1), 49–65.

Frigg, R. (2010), 'Models and fiction', *Synthese*, **172** (2), 251–268.

Frigg, R., D. Stainforth and L. Smith (2013), 'The myopia of imperfect climate models: The case of UKCP09', *Philosophy of Science*, **80** (5), 886–897.

Frydman, R. and M. Goldberg (2007), *Imperfect Knowledge Economics: Exchange Rates and Risk*, Princeton, NJ: Princeton University Press.

Galison, P. (1997), *Image and Logic: A Material Culture of Microphysics*, Chicago: University of Chicago Press.

Gallo, A. (2014), 'Regulators must act on coco bond risks', *Financial Times*, 7 May, accessed 12 June 2017 at www.ft.com/content/dbef9b1a-cede-11e3-8e62-00144feabdc0?mhq5j=e2.

Gangahar, A. (2007), 'Do not compute: How misfiring quant funds are distorting the markets', *Financial Times*, 10 December, 7.

Gibbard, A. and H. R. Varian (1978), 'Economic models', *Journal of Philosophy*, **75** (11), 664–677.

Giere, R. N. (1988), *Explaining Science*, Chicago: University of Chicago Press.

Giere, R. N. (2004), 'How models are used to represent physical reality', *Philosophy of Science*, **77** (5), S742–S752.

Giere, R. N. (2010), 'An agent-based conception of models and scientific representation', *Synthese*, **772** (2), 269–281.

Gigerenzer, G. (2007), *Gut Feelings: The Intelligence of the Unconscious*, London: Penguin.

Gigerenzer, G. and P. M. Todd (1999), *Simple Heuristics That Make Us Smart*, Oxford: Oxford University Press.

Gill, M. (2009), *Accountants' Truth: Knowledge and Ethics in the Financial World*, Oxford: Oxford University Press.

Giorgi, S. and K. Weber (2015), 'Marks of distinction: Framing and audience appreciation in the context of investment advice', *Administrative Science Quarterly*, **60** (2), 333–367.

Godfrey-Smith, P. (2009), 'Models and fictions in science', *Philosophical Studies*, **143** (1), 101–116.

Goffman, E. (1959), *The Presentation of Self in Everyday Life*, London: Penguin.

Goffman, E. (1969), *Where the Action Is: Three Essays*, London: Penguin.

Goffman, E. (1974), *Frame Analysis: An Essay on the Organization of Experience*, Cambridge, MA: Harvard University Press.

Graaf, J. (2016), *The Pursuit of Relevance: Studies on the Relationships between Accounting and Users*, PhD dissertation, Stockholm University.

Gramelsberger, G. (2011), 'Generation of evidence in simulation runs: Interlinking with models for predicting weather and climate change', *Simulation & Gaming*, **42** (2), 212–224.

Gramelsberger, G. and J. Feichter (eds) (2011), *Climate Change and Policy: The Calculability of Climate Change and the Challenge of Uncertainty*, New York: Springer.

Grinold R. C. and R. N. Kahn (1999), *Active Portfolio Management: A Quantitative Approach for Providing Superior Returns and Controlling Risk*, New York: McGraw-Hill.

Gross, M. and L. McGoey (eds) (2015), *Routledge International Handbook of Ignorance Studies*, London: Routledge.

The Guardian (2017), 'We are unlikely to spot next financial crisis, Bank of England official says', accessed 5 July 2017 at www.theguardian.com/business/2017/feb/21/we-will-miss-the-next-financial-crisis-predicts-bank-of-england.

Hägglund, P. (2000), 'The value of facts: How analysts' recommendations focus on facts instead of value, in H. Kalthoff, R. Rottenburg and H.-J. Wagener (eds), *Facts and Figures: Economic Representations and Practices*, Marburg: Metropolis, 313–337.

Hägglund, P. (2002), Making a stable investment object: The importance of having good connections in the stock market, paper presented at the New York Conference on Social Studies of Finance, Columbia University, 3–4 May, accessed 12 June 2017 www.coi.columbia.edu/.stage/ssf/papers/hagglund.doc.

Hall, M., A. Mikes and Y. Millo (2015), 'How do risk managers become influential? A field study of toolmaking in two financial institutions', *Management Accounting Research*, **26** (1), 3–22.

Hardie, I. and D. MacKenzie (2014), 'The lemon-squeezing problem: Analytical and computational limitations in collateralized debt obligation evaluation', *Competition and Change*, **18** (5), 383–401.

Harrington, B. (2007), 'Capital and community: Findings from the American investment craze of the 1990s', *Economic Sociology: The European Electronic Newsletter*, **8** (3), 19–25.

Haug, E. G. and N. Taleb (2011), 'Option traders use (very) sophisticated heuristics, never the Black–Scholes–Merton formula', *Journal of Economic Behavior and Organizations*, **77** (2), 97–106.

Hausman, D. (1992), *The Inexact and Separate Science of Economics*, Cambridge: Cambridge University Press.

Heath, C., M. S. Svensson, J. Hindmarsh, P. Luff and D. vom Lehn (2002), 'Configuring awareness', *Computer Supported Cooperative Work*, **11** (3), 317–347.

Heifetz, A. (2008), 'Epistemic game theory: Incomplete information', in S. Durlauf and L. Blume (eds), *The New Palgrave Dictionary of Economics*, Basingstoke: Palgrave Macmillan.

Heifetz, A., M. Meier and B. C. Schipper (2006), 'Interactive unawareness', *Journal of Economic Theory*, **130** (1), 78–94.

Henriksen, L. F. (2013), 'Economic models as devices of policy change: Policy paradigms, paradigm shift, and performativity', *Regulation & Governance*, **7** (4), 481–495.

Hirschman, D. and E. Popp Berman (2014), 'Do economists make policies? On the political effects of economics', *Socio-Economic Review*, **12** (4), 779–811.

Holzer, B. and Y. Millo (2005), 'From risks to second-order dangers in financial markets: unintended consequences of risk management systems', *New Political Economy*, **10** (2), 223–245.

Hörning, K. (2001), *Experten des Alltags: Die Wiederentdeckung des praktischen Wissens*, Weilerswist: Velbrück.

Howlett, P. and M. Morgan (eds) (2011), *How Well Do Facts Travel? The Dissemination of Reliable Knowledge*, Cambridge: Cambridge University Press.

Hutter, M. and D. Stark (2015), 'Pragmatist perspectives on valuation: An introduction', in A. B. Antal, M. Hutter and D. Stark (eds), *Moments of Valuation: Exploring Sites of Dissonance*, Oxford: Oxford University Press, 5–21.

Imam, S., R. Barker and C. Clubb (2008), 'The use of valuation models by UK investment analysts', *European Accounting Review*, **17** (3), 503–535.

Iser, W. (1993), *The Fictive and the Imaginary: Charting Literary Anthropology*, Baltimore: Johns Hopkins University Press.

Jasanoff, S. (1990), *The Fifth Branch: Science Advisors as Policymakers*, Cambridge, MA: Harvard University Press.

Jasanoff, S. (1991), 'Acceptable evidence in pluralistic society', in D. Mayo and D. Hollander (eds), *Acceptable Evidence: Science and Values in Risk Management*, Oxford: Oxford University Press, 29–47.

Jasanoff, S. (2005), *Designs on Nature: Science and Democracy in Europe and the United States*, Princeton, NJ: Princeton University Press.

Jovanovic, F. (2012), 'Finance in modern economic thought', in K. Knorr Cetina and A. Preda (eds), *The Oxford Handbook of the Sociology of Finance*, Oxford: Oxford University Press, 546–566.

Kahneman, D., H. Markowitz, R. Merton, M. Scholes, B. Sharpe and P. Bernstein (2005), 'Most Nobel minds', *CFA Magazine*, November–December, 36–43.

Kalthoff, H. (2005), 'Practices of calculation: Economic representations and risk management', *Theory, Culture & Society*, **22** (2), 69–97.

Kalthoff, H. (2011), 'Un/doing calculation: on knowledge practices of risk management', *Distinktion: Journal of Social Theory*, **12** (1), 3–21.

Karpik, L. (2010), *Valuing the Unique: The Economics of Singularities*, Princeton, NJ: Princeton University Press.

Kay, J. (2011), *Obliquity: Why Our Goals Are Best Achieved Indirectly*, London: Profile.

Keller, E. F. (2002), *Making Sense of Life: Explaining Biological Development with Models, Metaphors, and Machines*, Cambridge, MA: Harvard University Press.

Keynes, J. (1936), *The General Theory of Employment, Interest and Money*, reprinted in E. Johnson and D. Moggridge (eds) (1973), *The Collected Writings of John Maynard Keynes*, vol. 7, London: Macmillan.

Keynes, J. (1937), *The General Theory and After: Part II, Defence and Development*, reprinted in E. Johnson and D. Moggridge (eds) (1973), *Collected Writings of John Maynard Keynes*, vol. 14, London: Macmillan.

Knight, F. H. (1921), *Risk, Uncertainty and Profit*, Mineola, NY: Dover.

Knorr Cetina, K. (1997), 'Sociality with objects: Social relations in post-social knowledge societies', *Theory, Culture and Society*, **14** (4), 1–30.

Knorr Cetina, K. (1999), *Epistemic Cultures: How the Sciences Make Knowledge*, Cambridge, MA: Harvard University Press.

Knorr Cetina, K. (2009), 'The synthetic situation: Interactionism for a global world', *Symbolic Interaction*, **32** (1), 61–87.

Knorr Cetina, K. (2015), 'What is a financial market? Global markets as weird institutional forms', in P. Aspers and N. Dodd (eds), *Re-Imagining Economic Sociology*, Oxford: Oxford University Press, 103–124.

Knorr Cetina, K. and U. Brügger (2002), 'Global microstructures: The virtual societies of financial markets', *American Journal of Sociology*, **107** (4), 905–950.

Knorr Cetina, K. and A. Preda (2001), 'The epistemization of economic transactions', *Current Sociology*, **49** (4), 27–44.

Knuuttila, T. (2005), 'Models, representation, and mediation', *Philosophy of Science*, **72** (5), 1260–1271.

Knuuttila, T. (2009), 'Isolating representations versus credible constructions? Economic modelling in theory and practice', *Erkenntnis*, **70** (1), 59–80.

Knuuttila, T. (2011), 'Modeling and representing: An artefactual approach', *Studies in History and Philosophy of Science*, **42** (2), 262–271.

Knuuttila, T. and M. Merz (2009), 'Understanding by modeling: An objectual approach', in H. W. de Regt, S. Leonelli and K. Eigner (eds), *Scientific Understanding: Philosophical Perspectives*, Pittsburgh: University of Pittsburgh Press, 146–168.

Koen, B. V. (2003), *Discussion of the Method*, New York: Oxford University Press.

Kornberger, M., L. Justesen, A. Koed Madsen and J. Mouritsen (eds) (2015), *Making Things Valuable*, Oxford: Oxford University Press.

Krämer, S. (2014), 'Connecting performance and performativity: Does it work?', in L. Cull and A. Lagaay (eds), *Encounters in Performance Philosophy*, Basingstoke: Palgrave Macmillan, 223–237.

Kruglanski, A. W., A. Raviv, D. Bar-Tal, A. Raviv, K. Sharvit, S. Ellis, R. Bar, A. Pierro and L. Mannetti (2005), 'Says who? Epistemic authority effects in social judgement', *Advances in Experimental Social Psychology*, **37**, 345–392.

Landström, C. and S. J. Whatmore (2014), 'Virtually expert: Modes of environmental computer simulation modeling', *Science in Context*, **27** (4), 579–603.

Lane, S. N., C. Landström and S. J. Whatmore (2011), 'Imagining flood futures: Risk assessment and management in practice', *Philosophical Transactions of the Royal Society A*, **369** (1942), 1784–1806.

Lapierre, B. (2015), 'To quant or not to quant?', *Peak Capital Management Report*, **6** (8), 4.

Larsen, G. (2012), 'Discounted cash flow methods for equity valuation', in F. Fabozzi (ed.), *Encyclopaedia of Financial Models*, vol. 2, Hoboken, NJ: John Wiley & Sons, 15–31.

Lépinay, V. A. (2011), *Codes of Finance: Engineering Derivatives in a Global Bank*, Princeton: Princeton University Press.

Lévi-Strauss, C. (1966), *The Savage Mind*, Chicago: University of Chicago Press.

Li, J. (2009)', Information structures with unawareness', *Journal of Economic Theory*, **144** (3), 977–993.

Lindblom, C. E. (1959), 'The science of "muddling through"', *Public Administration Review*, **19** (2), 79–88.

LiPuma, E. (2017), 'The social dimensions of Black-Scholes', paper presented at the conference "Chains of Value: How Intermediaries Evaluate Financial Instruments", University of Edinburgh, 4–5 May.

Lockwood, E. (2015), 'Predicting the unpredictable: Value-at-risk, performativity, and the politics of financial uncertainty', *Review of International Political Economy*, **22** (4), 719–756.

Lucas, R. (1972), 'Expectations and the neutrality of money', *Journal of Economic Theory*, **4** (2), 103–124.

Luhmann, N. (1992), *Beobachtungen der Moderne*, Opladen: Westdeutscher Verlag.

MacKenzie, D. (2001), 'Physics and finance: S-terms and modern finance as a topic for science studies', *Science, Technology and Human Values*, **26** (2), 115–144.

MacKenzie, D. (2003), 'An equation and its worlds: Bricolage, exemplars, disunity and performativity in financial economics', *Social Studies of Science*, **33** (6), 831–868.

MacKenzie, D. (2006), *An Engine, Not a Camera: How Financial Models Shape Markets*, Cambridge, MA: MIT Press.

MacKenzie, D. (2007), 'Is economics performative? Option theory and the construction of derivatives markets', in D. MacKenzie, F. Muniesa and L. Siu (eds), *Do Economists Make Markets? On the Performativity of Economics*, Princeton, NJ: Princeton University Press, 54–86.

MacKenzie, D. (2009), *Material Markets: How Economic Agents are Constructed*, Oxford: Oxford University Press.

MacKenzie, D. (2011), 'The credit crisis as a problem in the sociology of knowledge', *American Journal of Sociology*, **116** (6), 1778–1841.

MacKenzie, D. and T. Spears (2014a), '"The formula that killed Wall Street"? The Gaussian copula and modelling practices in investment banking', *Social Studies of Science*, **44** (3), 393–417.

MacKenzie, D. and T. Spears (2014b), '"A device for being able to book P&L": The organizational embedding of the Gaussian copula', *Social Studies of Science*, **44** (3), 418–440.

MacKenzie, D. and Y. Millo (2003), 'Constructing a market, performing theory: The historical sociology of a financial derivatives exchange', *American Journal of Sociology*, **109** (1), 107–145.

MacKenzie, D., F. Muniesa and L. Siu (eds) (2007), *Do Economists Make Markets? On the Performativity of Economics*, Princeton, NJ: Princeton University Press.

Mäki, U. (1992), 'On the method of isolation in economics', in C. Dilworth (ed.), *Idealization IV: Intelligibility in Science*, New York: Rodopi, 319–354.

Mäki, U. (2009), 'MISSing the world: Models as isolations and credible surrogate systems', *Erkenntnis*, **70** (1), 29–43.

Mansnerus, E. (2015), *Modelling in Public Health Research: How Mathematical Techniques Keep Us Healthy*, Basingstoke: Palgrave Macmillan.

Mars, F. (1998), *Wir sind alle Seher*, PhD dissertation, University of Bielefeld.

McCloskey, D. and A. Klamer (1995), 'One quarter of GDP is persuasion', *American Economic Review*, **85** (2), 191–195.

McFall, L. (2011), 'A "good, average man": Calculation and the limits of statistics in enrolling insurance customers', *Sociological Review*, **59** (4), 662–684.

McGoey, L. (2012), 'Strategic unknowns: Towards a sociology of ignorance', *Economy and Society*, **41** (1), 1–16.

McMullin, E. (1985), 'Galilean idealization', *Studies in History and Philosophy of Science*, **16** (3), 247–273.

Mennicken, A. and E. Sjögren (2015), 'Valuation and calculation at the margins', *Valuation Studies*, **3** (1), 1–7.

Mikes, A. (2009), 'Risk management and calculative cultures', *Management Accounting Research*, **20** (1), 18–40.

Mikes, A. (2011), 'From counting risk to making risk count: Boundary-work in risk management', Working Paper 11-069, Harvard Business School, accessed 10 June 2017 at www.hbs.edu/research/pdf/11-069.pdf.

Millo, Y. and D. MacKenzie (2009), 'The usefulness of inaccurate models: Towards an understanding of the emergence of financial risk management', *Accounting, Organizations and Society*, **34** (5), 638–653.

Milne, F. (1995), *Finance Theory and Asset Pricing*, Oxford: Oxford University Press.

Mitchell, S. (2009), *Unsimple Truths: Science, Complexity, and Policy*, Chicago: University of Chicago Press.

Möllering, G. (2001), 'The nature of trust: From Georg Simmel to a theory of expectation, interpretation and suspension', *Sociology*, **35** (2), 403–420.

Morgan, M. S. (2002), 'Models, stories and the economic world', in U. Mäki (ed.), *Fact and Fiction in Economics: Models Realism and Social Construction*, Cambridge: Cambridge University Press, 178–201.

Morgan, M. S. (2005), 'Experiments versus models: New phenomena, interference, and surprise', *Journal of Economic Methodology*, **12** (2), 317–329.

Morgan, M. S. (2012), *The World in the Model: How Economists Work and Think*, Cambridge: Cambridge University Press.

Morgan, M. S. and T. Knuuttila (2012), 'Models and modelling in economics', in U. Mäki (ed.), *Philosophy of Economics: Handbook of the Philosophy of Science*, Amsterdam: Elsevier Science, 49–87.

Morgan, M. S. and M. Morrison (eds) (1999), *Models as Mediators: Perspectives on Natural and Social Science*, Cambridge: Cambridge University Press.

Morgenstern, O. (1928), *Wirtschaftsprognose: Eine Untersuchung ihrer Voraussetzungen und Möglichkeiten*, Vienna: Julius Springer.

Morris, S. (1995), 'The common prior assumption in economic theory', *Economics and Philosophy*, **11** (2), 227–253.

Morris, S. and H. Shin (2003), 'Global games: Theory and applications', in M. Dewatripont, L. Hansen and S. Turnovsky (eds), *Advances in Economics and Econometrics* (Proceedings of the Eighth World Congress of the Econometric Society), Cambridge: Cambridge University Press, 56–114.

Mouritsen, J. and K. Kreiner (2016), 'Accounting, decisions and promises', *Accounting, Organizations and Society*, **49** (1), 21–31.

Muniesa, F. (2007), 'Market technologies and the pragmatics of prices', *Economy and Society*, **36** (3), 377–395.

Muniesa, F. (2014), *The Provoked Economy: Economic Reality and the Performative Turn*, London: Routledge.

Muniesa, F. and M. Callon (2007), 'Economic experiments and the construction of markets', in D. MacKenzie, F. Muniesa and L. Siu (eds), *Do Economists Make Markets? On the Performativity of Economics*, Princeton, NJ: Princeton University Press, 163–189.

Muniesa, F. and M. Lenglet (2013), 'Responsible innovation in finance: Directions and implications', in R. Owen, J. Bessant and M. Heintz (eds), *Responsible Innovation: Managing the Responsible Emergence of Science and Innovation in Society*, Chichester, UK: John Wiley & Sons.

Muth, J. F. (1961), 'Rational expectations and the theory of price movements', *Econometrica*, **29** (3), 315–335.

Neth, H. and G. Gigerenzer (2015), 'Heuristics: Tools for an uncertain world', in R. Scott and S. Kosslyn (eds), *Emerging Trends in the Social and Behavioral Sciences: An Interdisciplinary, Searchable, and Linkable Resource*, New York: Wiley Online Library, 1–18.

Nocera, J. (2009), 'Risk mismanagement', *New York Times Magazine*, 2 January, accessed 10 June 2017 at www.nytimes.com/2009/01/04/magazine/04risk-t.html.

Nowak, L. (1980), *The Structure of Idealization: Towards a Systematic Interpretation of the Marxian Idea of Science*, Dordrecht: Reidel.

Nowak, L. (1989), 'On the (idealizational) structure of economic theories', *Erkenntnis*, **30** (1), 225–246.

Oakeshott, M. (1962), *Rationalism in Politics, and Other Essays*, London: Methuen.

Ortmann, G. (2003), *Regel und Ausnahme: Paradoxien sozialer Ordnung*, Frankfurt/Main: Suhrkamp.

Ortmann, G. (2004), *Als Ob: Fiktionen und Organisationen*, Wiesbaden: VS.

Patterson, S. (2010), *The Quants: How a New Breed of Math Whizzes Conquered Wall Street and Nearly Destroyed It*, New York: Crown Business.

Penét, P. (2015), 'Rating reports as figuring documents: How CRAs build scenarios of the future', in M. Kornberger, L. Justesen, A. K. Madsen and J. Mouritsen (eds), *Making Things Valuable*, Oxford: Oxford University Press, 62–88.

Petersen, A. C. (2008), 'The practice of climate simulation and its social and political context', *Netherlands Journal of Geoscience*, **87** (3), 219–229.

Phelps, E. S. (2007), 'Foreword', in Frydman, R. and M. D. Goldberg, *Imperfect Knowledge Economics: Exchange Rates and Risk*, Princeton, NJ: Princeton University Press, xiii–xx.

Pickering, A. (1995), *The Mangle of Practice: Time, Agency, and Science*, Chicago: University of Chicago Press.

Piore, M. (1995), *Beyond Individualism*, Cambridge, MA: Harvard University Press.

Piore, M. (2006), 'Qualitative research: Does it fit in economics?', *European Management Review*, **3** (1), 17–23.

Porter, T. M. (1995), *Trust in Numbers: The Pursuit of Objectivity in Science and Public Life*, Princeton, NJ: Princeton University Press.

Posner, K. (2010), *Stalking the Black Swan: Research and Decision Making in a World of Extreme Volatility*, New York: Columbia University Press.

Power, M. (2003), 'The invention of operational risk', London School of Economics and Political Science, ESCR Centre for the Analysis of Risk and Regulation, Discussion Paper no. 16.

Power, M. (2007), *Organized Uncertainty: Designing a World of Risk Management*, Oxford: Oxford University Press.

Power, M. (2016), 'Riskwork: The organizational life of risk management', in M. Power (ed.), *Riskwork: Essays on the Organizational Life of Risk Management*, Oxford: Oxford University Press, 1–25.

Preda, A. (2009), *Information, Knowledge, and Economic Life: An Introduction to the Sociology of Markets*, Oxford: Oxford University Press.

Proctor, R. (2008), 'Agnotology: A missing term to describe the cultural production of ignorance (and its study)', in R. Proctor and L. Schiebinger (eds) (2008), *Agnotology: The Making and Unmaking of Ignorance*, Palo Alto, CA: Stanford University Press, 1–33.

Proctor, R. and L. Schiebinger (eds) (2008), *Agnotology: The Making and Unmaking of Ignorance*, Palo Alto, CA: Stanford University Press.

Rappaport, A. and M. J. Mauboussin (2001), *Expectations Investing: Reading Stock Prices for Better Returns*, Boston, MA: Harvard Business School Press.

Reckwitz, A. (2002), 'Toward a theory of social practices: A development in culturalist theorizing', *European Journal of Social Theory*, **5** (2), 245–265.

Reichmann, W. (2010), 'Epistemic participation: Economic forecasts and the new relationship between scientific subjects and objects', paper presented at the 105th Annual Meeting of the American Sociological Association, in Atlanta (USA), 14–17 August.

Reilly, F. K. and K. C. Brown (1997), *Investment Analysis and Portfolio Management*, Fort Worth, TX: Dryden.

Reiss, J. (2012), 'The explanation paradox', *Journal of Economic Methodology*, **19** (1), 43–62.

Rheinberger, H.-J. (1997), *Toward a History of Epistemic Things: Synthesizing Proteins in the Test Tube*, Stanford: Stanford University Press.

Roffe, J. (2015), *Abstract Market Theory*, Basingstoke: Palgrave Macmillan.

Rona-Tas, A. and S. Hiss (2011), 'Forecasting as valuation: The role of ratings and predictions in the subprime mortgage crisis in the United States', in J. Beckert and P. Aspers (eds), *The Worth of Goods: Valuation and Pricing in the Economy*, Oxford: Oxford University Press, 223–246.

Salmon, F. (2009), 'Recipe for disaster: The formula that killed Wall Street', accessed 10 June 2017 at www.wired.com/techbiz/it/magazine/17-03/wp_quant?currentPage=all.

Savage L. J. (1954), *The Foundations of Statistics*, New York: John Wiley & Sons.

Schatzki, T. R. (1996), *Social Practices: A Wittgensteinian Approach to Human Activity and the Social*, Cambridge: Cambridge University Press.

Schatzki, T. R., K. Knorr Cetina and E. von Savigny (eds) (2001), *The Practice Turn in Contemporary Theory*, London: Routledge.

Searle, J. (2001), 'Social ontology and the philosophy of society', in E. Lagerspetz, H. Ikäheimo and J. Kotkavirta (eds), *On the Nature of Social and Institutional Reality*, Jyväskylä: SoPhi, 15–38.

Shackle, G. L. S. (1949), *Expectations in Economics*, Cambridge: Cambridge University Press.

Shackley, S. (1998), 'Introduction to special section on the use of models in appraisal and policy-making', *Impact Assessment and Project Appraisal*, **16** (2), 81–89.

Shackley, S. (2001), 'Epistemic lifestyles in climate change modeling', in C. A. Miller and P. N. Edwards (eds), *Changing the Atmosphere: Expert Knowledge and Environmental Governance*, Cambridge, MA: MIT Press, 107–133.

Shackley, S., J. Risbey, P. Stone and B. Wynne (1999), 'Adjusting to policy expectations in climate change modeling: An interdisciplinary study of flux adjustments in coupled atmosphere-ocean general circulation models', *Climatic Change*, **43** (2), 413–454.

Shen, L. (2017), 'Robots are replacing humans at all these Wall Street firms', accessed 5 July 2017 at http://fortune.com/2017/03/30/blackrock-robots-layoffs-artificial-intelligence-ai-hedge-fund/.

Shiller, R. (2015), 'Financial singularity: Is it a mirage?', *The Guardian*, 16 July, accessed 19 June 2017 at www.theguardian.com/business/2015/jul/16/financial-singularity-is-it-a-mirage.

Simmel, G. (1908 [1955]), *Soziologie: Untersuchung über die Formen der Vergesellschaftung*, in K. Wolff (ed.), *The Sociology of Georg Simmel*, New York: Free Press.

Skidelsky, R. (2009), *Keynes: The Return of the Master*, London: Penguin.

Smith, C. W. (2011), 'Coping with contingencies in equity option markets: The "rationality" of pricing', in J. Beckert and P. Aspers (eds), *The Worth of Goods: Valuation and Pricing in the Economy*, Oxford: Oxford University Press, 272–294.

Smithson, M. (1989), *Ignorance and Uncertainty: Emerging Paradigms*, Dordrecht: Springer.

Soros, G. (1998), *The crisis of Global Capitalism: Open Society Endangered*, New York: Public Affairs.

Soros, G. (2013), 'Fallibility, reflexivity, and the human uncertainty principle', *Journal of Economic Methodology*, **20** (4), 309–329.

Spears, T. C. (2014), *Engineering Value, Engineering Risk: What Derivatives Quants Know and What Their Models Do*, PhD dissertation, University of Edinburgh.

Stark, D. (2009), *The Sense of Dissonance: Accounts of Worth in Economic Life*, Princeton, NJ: Princeton University Press.

Stark, D. (2011), 'What's valuable?', in J. Beckert and P. Aspers (eds), *The Worth of Goods: Valuation and Pricing in the Economy*, Oxford: Oxford University Press, 319–338.

Suárez, M. (2004), 'An inferential conception of scientific representation', *Philosophy of Science (Symposia)*, **71**, 767–779.

Suárez, M. (2010), 'Fictions, inference and realism', in J. Woods (ed.), *Fictions and Models: New Essays*, Munich: Philosophia, 225–245.

Sugden, R. (2000), 'Credible worlds: the status of theoretical models in economics', *Journal of Economic Methodology*, **7** (1), 1–31.

Svetlova, E. (2010), 'Plausibility check of consensus: Expectation building in financial markets', *Journal of Financial and Economic Practice*, **10** (1), 101–113.

Svetlova, E. (2012a), 'On the performative power of financial models', *Economy and Society*, **41** (3), 418–434.

Svetlova, E. (2012b), 'Talking about the crisis: Performance of forecasting in financial markets', *Culture and Organization*, **18** (2), 155–169.

Svetlova, E. (2013), 'De-idealization by commentary: The case of financial valuation models', in *Synthese: An International Journal for Epistemology, Methodology and Philosophy of Science*, **190** (2), 321–337.

Svetlova, E. (2016), 'Value without valuation? An example of the cocos market' (online first), *Critical Perspectives on Accounting*, special issue on Critical Finance.

Svetlova, E. and V. Dirksen (2014), 'Models at work: Models in decision-making', *Science in Context*, **27** (4), 561–577.

Svetlova, E. and M. Fiedler (2011), 'Understanding crisis: On the meaning of uncertainty and probability', in O. D. Asenjo and C. Marcuzzo (eds), *The Recession of 2008: Competing Explanations*, Cheltenham, UK and Northampton, MA, USA: Edward Elgar Publishing, 42–62.

Svetlova, E. and H. van Elst (2013), 'How is non-knowledge represented in economic theory?', in B. Priddat and A. Kaballak (eds), *Ungewissheit als Herausforderung für die ökonomische Theorie: Nichtwissen, Ambivalenz und Entscheidung*, Marburg: Metropolis, 41–72.

Svetlova, E. and H. van Elst (2015), 'Decision-theoretic approaches to non-knowledge in economics', in M. Gross and L. McGoey (eds), *Routledge International Handbook of Ignorance Studies*, London: Routledge, 349–360.

Taleb, N. (2007), *The Black Swan: The Impact of the Highly Improbable*, New York: Random House.

Taleb, N. (2010), 'Why did the crisis of 2008 happen?', accessed 3 July 2017 at www.fooledbyrandomness.com/crisis.pdf.

Tayler, P. (1998), 'The business of modelling: Some anecdotes on modelling in business and story-telling', *Impact Assessment and Project Appraisal*, **16** (2), 133–138.

Tett, G. and A. Gangahar (2007), 'System error: Why computer models proved unequal to market turmoil', *Financial Times*, 15 August, 7.

Tett, G. and P. Thal Larsen (2005), 'Market faith goes out the window as the "model monkeys" lose track of reality', *Financial Times*, 20 May, accessed 9 June 2017 at www.ft.com/cms/s/0/9fed15be-c8cd-11d9-87c9-00000e2511c8.html?ft_site=falcon&desktop=true#axzz4jVqlURrq.

Toon, A. (2012), *Models as Make-Believe: Imagination, Fiction, and Scientific Representation*, Basingstoke: Palgrave Macmillan.

Triana, P. (2007), 'Derivatives tool that renders math irrelevant', *Financial Times*, 15 January, 6.

Triana, P. (2008), 'Whither Black-Scholes?', *Forbes Magazine*, 8 April, accessed 14 June 2017 at www. forbes.com/2008/04/07/black-scholes-options-oped-cx_ptp_0408black.html.

Triana, P. (2009), *Lecturing Birds on Flying: Can Mathematical Theories Destroy the Financial Markets?* New York: John Wiley & Sons.

Triana, P. (2011), *The Number That Killed Us: A Story of Modern Banking, Flawed Mathematics, and a Big Financial Crisis*, New York: John Wiley & Sons.

Tuckett, D. (2011), *Minding the Markets: An Emotional Finance View of Financial Instability*, New York: Palgrave Macmillan.

Tuckett, D. (2012), 'Financial markets are markets in stories: Some possible advantages of using interviews to supplement existing economic data sources', *Journal of Economic Dynamics and Control*, **36** (8), 1077–1087.

Turner, S. (1994), *The Social Theory of Practice: Tradition, Tacit Knowledge, and Presuppositions*, Chicago: University of Chicago Press.

van Daalen, C. E., L. Dresen and M. A. Janssen (2002), 'The roles of computer models in the environmental policy life cycle', *Environmental Science & Policy*, **5** (3), 221–231.

van den Bogaard, A. (1999), 'Past measurement and future prediction', in M. S. Morgan and M. Morrison (eds), *Models as Mediators: Perspectives on Natural and Social Science*, Cambridge: Cambridge University Press, 282–325.

van Egmond, S. and R. Zeiss (2010), 'Modeling for policy: Science-based models as performative boundary objects for Dutch policy making', *Science Studies*, **23** (1), 58–78.

van Fraassen, B. C. (1980), *The Scientific Image*, Oxford: Clarendon.

von Foerster, H. (2003), *Understanding Understanding: Essays on Cybernetics and Cognition*, New York: Springer.

von Foerster, H. (2008), *KibernEthik*, Berlin: Merve.

Walton, K. (1990), *Mimesis as Make Believe: On the Foundations of the Representational Arts*, Cambridge, MA: Harvard University Press.

Wansleben, L. (2012), 'Financial analysts', in K. Knorr Cetina and A. Preda (eds), *The Oxford Handbook of the Sociology of Finance*, Oxford: Oxford University Press, 250–271.

Wansleben, L. (2013), *Cultures of Expertise in Global Currency Markets*, London: Routledge.

Wansleben, L. (2014), 'Consistent forecasting vs. anchoring of market stories: Two cultures of modeling and model use in a bank', in *Science in Context*, **27** (4), 605–630.

Weber, M. (1948), 'Science as a vocation', in H. Gerth (ed.), *Max Weber: Essays in Sociology*, London: Routledge, 129–156.

Weick, K. (1995), *Sensemaking in Organisations*, Thousand Oaks, CA: Sage.

Weick, K. (2001), *Making Sense of the Organization*, Malden, MA: Blackwell.

Weick, K. and K. Sutcliffe (2001), *Managing the Unexpected: Assuring High Performance in an Age of Complexity*, San Francisco: Jossey-Bass.

Wenzel, H. (2001), *Die Abenteuer der Kommunikation: Echtzeitmedien und der Handlungsraum der Hochmoderne*, Weilerwist: Vellbrück.

Wigglesworth, R. (2017a), 'Final call for the research analyst?', *Financial*

Times, 7 February, accessed 5 July 2017 at www.ft.com/content/85ee225a-ec4e-11e6-930f-061b01e23655?mhq5j=e2.

Wigglesworth, R. (2017b), 'Goldman Sachs' lessons from the "quant quake"', *Financial Times*, 9 March, 9.

Wittgenstein, L. (1958), *Philosophical Investigations*, Oxford: Blackwell.

Woermann, M. (2013), *On the (Im)Possibility of Business Ethics: Critical Complexity, Deconstruction, and Implications for Understanding the Ethics of Business*, Amsterdam: Springer.

Zadeh, L. (1973), 'Outline of a new approach to the analysis of complex systems and decision processes', *IEEE Transactions on Systems, Man, and Cybernetics*, **3** (1), 28–44.

Zaloom, C. (2003), 'Ambiguous numbers', *American Ethnologist*, **30** (2), 258–272.

Zaloom, C. (2009), 'How to read the future: The yield curve, affect, and financial prediction', *Public Culture*, **21** (2), 245–268.

Žižek, S. (1993), *Tarrying with the Negative: Kant, Hegel and the Critique of Ideology*, London: Verso.

Žižek, S. (2001), *On Belief*, London: Verso.

Zuckerman, E. (2012), 'Market efficiency: A sociological perspective', in K. Knorr Cetina and A. Preda (eds), *The Oxford Handbook of the Sociology of Finance*, Oxford: Oxford University Press, 223–249.

Index

Colander, D. 58
Coleman, L. 119
collateralized debt obligations (CDOs)
   2, 109, 122
communication devices, models as
   119–22
"communism of models" 149
consensus, plausibility check of 89–92
consumptive regime of valuation 44
contingent convertible bonds
   (COCOS) 42–4, 153
   selling 43
   valuation 43–4
Coombs, N. 116
counter-performativity 64–5, 129, 141
"credible worlds" 50, 53, 55–6
credit rating agencies 6, 110, 112–14,
   127, 128
Croft, J. 111
cultures of model use 4, 7, 37–8, 49,
   147, 152, 154–5

DCF model *see* discounted cash flow
   (DCF) model
de Certeau, M. 102
decision-making, financial 45
   as "acting sensibly" 26–30, 50
   as action-like 3, 29, 32, 38, 39,
       49–51, 66, 69, 86, 107, 126, 145,
       148
   calculation and qualculation 30–33
   credit rating agencies 112–14
   cultures of model use 66–7
   discounted cash flow model 20–23
   diversity of models 108–10
   financial regulators, consequences
       for 114–16
   implied modelling 88–93
   as "incision" and "acting sensibly"
       26–30
   judgment and 30–33
   "at large" 38–40, 45, 154
   nature of 15–17
   performative concept 102–105
   qualitative overlay *see* qualitative
       overlay
   quantamental investing 70–74
   radical uncertainty 3
   risk cultures 110–12
   theory and economics 147–51

decision-selling, models in 45, 117–19
   communication devices 119–22
   failure of models as failure of
       performance 129–31
   persuasion routines 123–4
   theatricality 124–7
   useful fictions 126, 127–9
   see also decision-making, financial
de-idealization 53–5, 153
Derman, E. 2, 22, 120
Derrida, J. 27, 51
Deutsche Bank 43
discounted cash flow (DCF) model 75,
   76–81, 128
   application in wealth department
       77–83
   fair value of assets 21–2
   judgment and 82–3, 85
   for portfolio managers 76–81
   problems with 20–23
discount rate 21
diversity of model cultures 108–10, 147
dividend discount model (DDM) 95
doing calculations 37, 38, 69, 143

earnings per share (EPS) growth 90
econometric forecasting models 75
economic forecasting 132–3
   backstage and front-stage 138–40
   role of surprises 137–8
   staging the "soft landing" in
       February 2008 133–5
   uncertainties and lack of knowledge
       135–7
economic models
   credible worlds 55
   de-idealization 54–5
   idealization 53–4
effecting calculation 30–33
efficient market hypothesis (EMH) 64,
   66, 120
endogenous events 17
epistemic cultures 8, 51, 145, 146
epistemic practices 48, 60
error maximization problem 98
Esposito, E. 18, 19, 91, 107
ethics, finance and responsibility
   154–6
European Securities and Markets
   Authorities (ESMA) 127